THE THEORY OF EVERYTHING ELSE

DAN SCHREIBER
THE THEORY OF EVERYTHING ELSE
* A VOYAGE INTO THE WORLD OF THE WEIRD *

WILLIAM MORROW

An Imprint of HarperCollins*Publishers*

HarperCollins books may be purchased for educational, business, or sales promotional use. For information, please email the Special Markets Department at SPsales@harpercollins.com.

Originally published in the United Kingdom in 2022 by Mudlark.

FIRST WILLIAM MORROW HARDCOVER PUBLISHED 2023.

Illustrations copyright © 2022 by Sam Minton

Library of Congress Cataloging-in-Publication Data has been applied for.

ISBN 978-0-06-325919-5

23 24 25 26 27 LBC 5 4 3 2 1

For Fenella, Wilf, Ted, and Kit
My four favourite weirdos

What if a chicken is an egg's way
of making more eggs?

Anonymous

CONTENTS

CONTENTS

CONTENTS

CONTENTS

Foreword
THE ROUGH CORNER

There is a concept practised by Zen gardeners called "the Rough Corner." The idea being that somewhere, in every beautifully tended garden, there should remain a patch of land left completely untouched, growing wild and chaotic so as to remind the gardener of how the universe intended it to look.

I believe we should all be cultivating a healthy Rough Corner in our minds. A small nook at the back of the brain that ensures we never fail to get goosebumps when we're told a mad-as-hell idea, no matter how batshit it may be. It's important to keep this Rough Corner ragged and free to grow as nature intended, because great things have been achieved by those who believe in weird ideas . . .

Disclaimer
A WARNING

The author of this work does not accept responsibility for any overgrown Rough Corners the reader might end up cultivating as a result of reading this book.

All the theories in this book want you to believe in them. Don't even think of it. Read up on them, yes; discuss them with your friends, definitely; sit back and let the ideas alter your universe for just a few seconds, absolutely; but for God's sake, don't believe in a single one of them.

However, I know it's not up to me what you'll make of all these theories, no matter how much I warn you against them. Any idea you connect with that helps make sense of your place in this universe can develop into an unstoppable force.

To some extent all of these theories are alive; at least that's certainly the impression they give. They've been translated into multiple languages and are at this very moment being discussed at breakfast tables and dinner parties around the world. They crop up in innumerable school classrooms, are debated by the finest minds in the world's leading universities and have become the all-consuming obsession of amateur sleuths. They have their own websites, social media accounts and Netflix specials. One has even done so well that it has its very own soundtrack, written and performed by Stevie Wonder.

They're all incredibly successful at being talked about and will do their absolute best to make you think that they're true. But please remember, this isn't a book of facts; it's a book of "facts." None of the theories in this book are true.* They're just ideas, speculations, beliefs, and claims, begging to be accepted as truths. So, should you walk away at the end of this book believing that the only reason we became the dominant species on this planet is because predators found us too smelly to eat; or that the living descendants of Christ are a family of garlic farmers living in Japan; or that office plants should be employed as police detectives—well, that's on you.

* Not yet, anyway.

Introduction
HELLO FROM THE ODDER SIDE

In 1956 archaeologist George Michanowsky was plodding his way through a remote region of the Bolivian bush when he stumbled upon a group of locals partaking in a festival of dance, drink, and general debauchery.* After making some enquiries, Michanowsky learnt that this was an annual event, and that every year, for thousands of years now, whole communities from hundreds of miles away would gather together to celebrate.

"Celebrate what?" asked the archaeologist.

"Can't remember," replied the Bolivians. Somewhere along the line, they'd all forgotten why they were actually doing this.

However, not ones to let a minor administrative error like that get in their way, they continued to meet up once a year

---

* Orgies.

1

to make sure to commemorate . . . whatever it was they were supposed to be commemorating.

*   *   *

I first spotted this anthropological puzzle a few years back while flipping through a 1973 edition of *Time* magazine as I browsed a secondhand bookshop in London. It's a story I've thought a lot about since. Though it may sound trivial, for me the mystery of the dancing Bolivians perfectly illustrates something that's at the very heart of this book: which is that no matter where you look in this world, you can guarantee that something bizarre, improbable, and unexplained is going on. And, more importantly, no matter how small that mystery may seem, there's most likely someone (or something) out there dedicating their time to solving it.

Right now, as you read these words, there are scientists in Silicon Valley who are spending their days trying to work out if the universe is actually just a giant video game; there are ornithologists in Australia who are attempting to prove their theory that there's a species of bird singing pop songs from the 1920s in the wild; and in Poland there is a ghost hunter who continues to warn us of his belief that ghosts have become so annoyed by the recent rise of scepticism about their existence, that they're threatening to go on strike. "If you're going to have *that* attitude, we're not going to bother haunting you anymore" appears to be the message.

Everyone, it seems, has a theory they're trying to prove—be it about something as big as the meaning of life, or as small as trying to work out why Australians speak the way they do.* There's just so much we don't know. Why are we here? Do ghosts exist? Are we being visited by extraterrestrials? Are plants sentient? And why when you're in the shower does the shower curtain always billow in towards you?†

We don't know the answers to any of these questions, but in this book I'll be introducing you to some people who think they've more or less figured them out. Along the way you'll learn the word for "thank you" in plant language from a leading botanist; you'll be invited by conservationists to help save an endangered species from being shampooed out of existence; and you'll discover why you should probably try to avoid winning a Nobel Prize in the Sciences. Most importantly, though, you'll learn that pretty much everyone in the world harbours their own little bit of batshit.‡

---

* No one is quite sure how the Australian accent developed. One theory has it that, due to Australia's vast fly population, Aussies were forced to talk with their teeth gritted, otherwise they'd end up with a mouth full of the insects.

† As it stands there are four competing theories, the most recent of which comes from scientist David Schmidt of the University of Massachusetts, who ran a simulation and had his computer spend two weeks crunching 1.5 trillion calculations in an attempt to prove his theory. As of this writing, no theory has been accepted as conclusive and the hunt for a grand unified theory of shower curtains continues. Interestingly, there is a theory that we have our best ideas while in the shower. So, it may be possible that the solution will come to someone mid-wash as the curtain slowly creeps in towards them.

‡ In this book, I will be using the term batshit a lot. It is used affectionately. Just like how my dad calls me "dickhead," it is said with love. To be clear, all my favourite people are a little bit batshit.

3

Even the most unexpected people turn out to have odd beliefs. For example, take Nicholas Witchell, the current BBC Royal Correspondent, and a man who has covered virtually every major royal news story since 1998—who would have thought this serious, plummy journalist would be a former Loch Ness Monster hunter?

But it turns out that for six months in 1972, a 19-year-old Witchell lived on the banks of Loch Ness, in a self-built wooden hut, staring at the water every day with a pair of binoculars and a long-lensed camera.

Nessie has been a big part of Witchell's life. It's in fact thanks to Nessie that Witchell pursued a career in journalism at all. After his six-month stint looking for the monster, he was supposed to be heading to Leeds to study law, but when

Nicholas Witchell, BBC Royal Correspondent and former Nessie hunter.

an opportunity to pen a book on Nessie arose, it forced him to reconsider. Two years later, Witchell published his book, *The Loch Ness Story*, which today is still considered one of the finest books of its genre.

I can understand how Witchell might have been lured into spending six months staring into its waters, having visited the loch myself a few years ago. When you start looking at it, you can't help but search for Nessie. It was honestly hard to tear my eyes away from the water for fear that the second I did, it might be the moment the beast surfaced.

"Yeah. The first decade's the hardest with that," veteran Nessie hunter Steve Feltham told me over a Zoom call recently. "But you get used to it after about ten years." Feltham, who has been living on the banks of the loch looking for the monster from his Nessie hunting mobile home for the last 31 years, holds the Guinness World Record for "Longest continuous vigil seeking the Loch Ness monster."

WHAT'S YOUR BIT OF BATSHIT?

So before we begin, let me ask you an important question: what's your bit of batshit? Do you believe in ghosts? Think you can sense when someone is staring at you from behind? Superstitious? Feel that coincidences have meaning? Have you spotted a UFO?

Perhaps you're not aware of what your exact bit of batshit is. Throughout the writing of this book I've found that most people were unable to immediately identify what their weird beliefs are, largely because to them they're not weird beliefs but part of their everyday reality. But don't worry, you'll realise what it is once you think about it long enough.

Or maybe you know exactly what your strange belief is but are just too afraid to say it out loud. I appreciate that too—people can be pretty unforgiving towards people who say things like, "I believe in the Mongolian death worm!"* It can affect your work life, your relationships, everything.

In the course of writing this book I've met three people who believe they've discovered the meaning of life; had one friend ask me in total sincerity to break character and confirm that I was an actor in his own version of *The Truman Show*; drank a beer with someone who claimed to be half-reptilian; and listened intently as another recounted waking up early one morning to find the Virgin Mary standing at the end of their bed. That last person was my wife, Fenella.

Fenella is a bit of a weirdness magnet, and will feature periodically throughout this book. Unlike me—who spends countless hours rummaging through hidden bookshops, tracking down lost documentaries, and attending odd shows and conferences—the weirdnesses just seem to come directly to Fenella. For some inexplicable reason people reveal a whole host of random odd things about their life within moments of meeting her.

Just recently we had a plumber over to fix a leak in the bathroom. After saying a quick hello I wandered off to make him a cup of tea, leaving Fenella to show him where the

---

* A mythical animal that is said to attack humans by shooting acid out of its mouth and lightning bolts out of its anus.

problem was. A few minutes later she joined me in the kitchen.

"What an interesting guy," she said. "He was just telling me that when he was a baby in Kazakhstan, he was sitting in a field when an eagle swooped down from the sky, grabbed him by the shoulders, and flew off with him."

Most would assume this story to be the ramblings of a mad plumber with an overactive imagination. But as it happens, I had met a "Children stolen by eagles" expert a few years back, and so instead of quickly ushering him out of my house, I got him to down tools so I could note down his story.

"Fortunately," he told me, "as the bird was flapping away and struggling to gain height, my mother was able to chase after us and beat the eagle with a big stick until it dropped me back down."

Fenella was eight months pregnant with our second child when she saw the Virgin Mary at the end of our bed. To be fair, it was March 2020 and the country had just gone into its first national lockdown. Earlier that evening, before the divine visit, we'd sat goggle-eyed on the sofa and watched the TV as an uncharacteristically stern Prime Minister told us that it was now dangerous to leave the house, and that pregnant women were particularly at risk. Fenella was terrified.

Mary appeared not long after this. At first Fenella was scared, and thought she had come to take our unborn child. However, after extensive googling, she learnt that Mary was actually there to tell her that everything was going to be OK. I wasn't awake to see her, but to this day, Fenella insists it happened.

We inherit a lot of our weirdness from our family, that's for sure. Fenella comes from a religious family, and her visit from the Virgin Mary was greeted with excitement by many of them. I too have not escaped this conditioning from my own parents, and I now realise they are absolutely the reason for my interest in the wilder shores. It all really began for me at the age of 13, when, following a childhood in Hong Kong, my hairdressing parents shut down their salon and relocated our family to a sleepy town in the Northern Beaches of Sydney, Australia, called Avalon. Avalon is named after the mythical resting place of King Arthur and, when I first arrived, rocked a very New Age feel.

I knew we had arrived somewhere *different* when, not long after we moved in, our friends, Mike and Rebecca, sold up and moved 60 miles inland because Rebecca had had a dream that Avalon's coast was going to be hit by a tsunami sometime soon. Two decades later, it is yet to hit.

Another time, years later, my parents got a call from our neighbour Sharon, who asked if they could pop over to help out with a tech problem she was having: she needed to unfriend someone on Facebook but didn't know how. When my parents arrived, Sharon explained that she'd recently learnt through a spiritual healer that this so-called "friend" of hers had actually killed her in a previous life in Ancient Egypt. "I don't want to be friends on Facebook with someone in this life who killed me in a previous one," she told them.

Just like Fenella, my parents have a gift for attracting weirdness, and I would often experience wonderful nights listening as dinner guests would drunkenly wax lyrical about esoteric matters—everything from ghosts to UFOs—before slipping me copies of books by authors like ancient alien theorist Erich von Däniken as they stumbled out the door.

While this fascinating life in Avalon was instrumental in feeding my "Rough Corner" perhaps my real leap into the world of batshit began when I started at my new high school.

THE MISEDUCATION OF DAN SCHREIBER

I was educated at a school founded by a descendant of Atlantis. I didn't know this fact until I started researching this book, and it was news to my parents too.

Glenaeon Rudolf Steiner School is located down the backroad of a tiny suburb seven miles north of the Sydney

Rudolf Steiner, philosopher and Atlantian.

Harbour Bridge. Built into the surrounding four and a half acres of bushland, it had the feeling of a mythical getaway. Imagine if *The Celestine Prophecy* had set up its own Hogwarts and made *The Secret* author Rhonda Byrne headmistress.

The establishment was the first Steiner institution in Australia, based on the teachings of Rudolf Steiner, an Austrian philosopher, architect, and hippy-like character who set out to create a school that didn't believe in competition; where classes would be taught in eccentrically built rooms that excluded any right angles in their design; and where students could be guided to flourish not as academics but as creatives. At least that appeared to be the official position. What they didn't mention was that Steiner was also a world-leading occultist, mystic, holistic doctor, clairvoyant, and Atlantian.

Steiner was not a good guy, a fact I learnt from a podcast called *Behind the Bastards*. He held horrible ideas about racial superiority and was also the creator of anthroposophical medicine, which proposes that your illnesses may have been influenced by your past life, and that in some cases—tough luck—no prescription can be given, as it's just your karmic destiny playing out. Today at anthroposophical hospitals in Austria, cancer patients are treated with mistletoe and patients with Covid-19 are reportedly given homeopathic pellets said to contain the dust of shooting stars.

For me, though, Steiner was a world away from my more academic primary school in Hong Kong and I loved every second of it. I can't speak for how it is today, but 20 years ago, the oddity of it was immediate and unavoidable. When I

first arrived, my homeroom teacher was away being treated for cancer. His treatment didn't involve chemo or any other Western medicines; instead he'd decided to meditate his way back to health, which he successfully managed with guidance from a bunch of monks. And it worked. He was back at school halfway through my first term, and as a result of his experience we'd start the day by doing 15 minutes of group meditation, followed by 10 minutes of the songs of The Beatles and Simon & Garfunkel.

The curriculum itself was very similar to other schools, though the teachers were perhaps a bit eccentric in their marking. I was genuinely once given top marks in History for a presentation I decided to give on how the secret passages below the Great Pyramids of Giza were said to contain ancient crystal computers from the lost city of Atlantis. (I now understand why I did so well.)

After graduating from Steiner, I decided to move to the UK to try and pursue a life in comedy. It was at this point that I shed my beliefs in all things conspiracy theories, and fell madly in love with the world of science (where the theories and speculations were often far more wild and exciting than those of the pseudoscientific world) building a career that was more focused on facts rather than "facts." However, though I'd like to say that these recent years have changed me and that I've become a font of scientific knowledge and renounced my early miseducation, the truth is I've never stopped loving the fringes and the many people who embody it.

PERSISTENCE, PERSISTENCE, PERSISTENCE

This is a book about those people who ask big questions and investigate them, no matter how much ridicule is piled upon them. And they're not few in number—they're everywhere. Just look around you. We're a multitude of realities. Every day, as you go about your life, you'll be walking among people who think very differently to you. Next time you look up at the sky at night and see the moon, just remember that some see it as a natural satellite of the Earth, while for others it's completely artificial, built by aliens. Some believe we landed humans on it, others that Stanley Kubrick filmed a hoax landing in a Hollywood studio. Some believe it influences the tides, others that it influences humans to grow fur and howl. Occasionally, one of these off-piste thinkers will be proved right, and their lifelong persistence to show that things are not quite as they seem will win out.

And that's what it's about: persistence. Persistence in getting to the bottom of a matter—regardless of how long it takes, and even if it only reveals a mundane truth—is paramount. Take the Parkes Observatory radio telescope in Australia, a hugely important dish. It was the telescope that enabled the world to receive TV signals from Neil Armstrong as he stood on the moon, and it's currently one of the few telescopes being used as part of Operation Breakthrough Listen, the most comprehensive search for alien communications to date. But it's also where, behind the scenes, astronomers had been persistently trying to crack a long-unsolved mystery.

Their problem was this: for 17 years the Parkes dish had been picking up strange interference, absolutely befuddling the scientists trying to work out why. Over the years multiple theories were thrown up. In 2011 a scientific paper was published speculating that the cause could be lightning strikes or solar bursts, but further investigation discounted both of these.

In the end, their near-two-decade lesson in why persistence pays off ended when the in-house astronomers finally discovered the culprit: the microwave oven in the observatory kitchen. Seventeen years of speculation, and the puzzling signals turned out to be the cleaning staff heating up their ready-made lasagnas. Mystery solved.

This wasn't the only mystery in which an Australian observatory played a role. While discovering a pulsar in a far-off constellation, astronomers at Molonglo Observatory noticed a curious wisp of gas. It looked very much like the debris left by a star after it exploded. If it had been a star, at only 1,500 light years away it would have been the closest-ever supernova explosion to our planet and would have lit up the sky for months, day and night—a hundred times brighter than Venus and brighter, possibly, than the moon. (One wild theory has it that its influence may even have been greater—perhaps showering Earth with enough dangerous radiation to cause significant mutations to our planet's lifeforms.) So why then, asked the astronomers, were there no historical records of it?

Only four other supernovas had been recorded at this point, including one witnessed in China, which, thanks to the astronomers of the time, we know occurred in the year 1054. Scientists wanted to date the supernova detected by Molonglo, but without any historical records they had no way of doing so—it could have occurred at any time between 15,000 and 6,000 years ago. And so in 1972 the journal *Archaeology* published an unusual request from three NASA astronomers, asking archaeologists for their help in identifying the age of this celestial gas cloud. There must have been, they suggested, some primitive witness who felt compelled to mark this event by scrawling a record of it on a rock or carving it on a wall. If they could find that artist's rendition, they could date the supernova.

This request was eventually spotted by a member of the Explorers Club in New York: the eccentric, controversial veteran archaeologist George Michanowsky. Casting his memory back years, he remembered an interesting carving on a large, flat rock he'd seen on one of his many adventures. The carving consisted of six circles, five of which, Michanowsky noticed, matched the brightest stars in the night sky. However, the final and largest of the circles carved in the rock was nowhere to be seen.

This curious rock belonged to an unusual group of Bolivian Indians, who, for reasons unknown to them, kept getting together once a year to do some dancing. Michanowsky asked them whether this rock was intrinsically connected to the dancing. Yes, they said. So did they at least know what the carvings on the rock meant? Nope. No idea. They'd forgotten that too.

Undeterred, Michanowsky continued to investigate. His research led him to study the Mesopotamian records, and learn to read cuneiform. It was while reading one particular cuneiform tablet that Michanowsky discovered a reference to a giant star in a part of the sky that we know doesn't have any stars to match its description. The coordinates, noted Michanowsky, corresponded to the exact spot where the supernova was said to have been. With that, Michanowsky developed his hypothesis. According to him, in the millennia that followed the supernova, the impact of this incredible event could be detected in cultures all around the world. He believed that when the ancient Sumerians witnessed this celestial wonder, they started developing astronomy, mathematics and writing, and the keeping of record books. The supernova, and the mind-expanding wonder it inspired, speculated Michanowsky, might just have been the catalyst that led to the birth of civilisation.

So, why were these Bolivian locals dancing? After 18 years of pondering, Michanowsky believed he finally had his answer. They were commemorating what was quite possibly the single most important event in human history, a moment that turned our brains on to the awesomeness of the universe and expanded human consciousness in the process. "Next to the sun," Michanowsky said, "it may have been the most important star in the history of mankind." What those Bolivian locals had forgotten, was that they were dancing to celebrate a moment never to be forgotten. At least, that was his theory . . .

PART I

THE IMPORTANCE OF BEING A LITTLE BIT BATSHIT

People are strange—and that's no bad thing. Genius and madness often go hand in hand. Thomas Edison, for all his brilliance, believed that changing into pyjamas at night messed with your body's chemistry and gave you insomnia, so he always slept in his work clothes.* P. L. Travers, author of the *Mary Poppins* series, claimed that once, while out on a country walk, she'd discovered a giant footprint made by an enormous alien using our planet as a stepping stone, later writing: "The shape was unmistakable, as though somebody of great size, coming from Uranus, perhaps, had landed on Earth for a moment, taken a step or two upon it and set off again, leaving his mark."

The last book that *Dracula* author Bram Stoker wrote included a chapter pushing his theory that Queen Elizabeth I was secretly a man. The first expedition Edmund Hillary went on after scaling Mount Everest was in search of the Yeti (a mythical creature that is believed to exist by both Jane

* To test out this theory, I asked 20 insomniacs to give it a go for a couple of nights. The overwhelming response was that (1) it does not work and (2) Thomas Edison clearly never slept in an underwired bra.

Goodall and David Attenborough, among others). Guglielmo Marconi, the pioneering inventor of radio, believed sounds never died, but just got softer, and spent the last years of his life dreaming up a device to track down Christ's Sermon on the Mount. The list goes on. In this section we'll take a look at some of the people who have made it to the top of their industries, from the greatest sports stars to the most successful musicians, and discover that no matter where you look, you're always going to bump into a little bit of batshit . . .

CHAPTER 1
THE WEIRDO WHO SAVED THE WORLD
THE THEORY OF THE UN-PROVABLE

It was late one Friday night in 1985 when Kary Mullis decided to use the outhouse of his Californian countryside cabin before retiring to bed. Grabbing a torch, he made his way downhill towards the toilet, which stood just 50 feet away. As Mullis neared it, he suddenly became aware of a bizarre glow emanating from under a nearby fir tree. Focusing his flashlight in its direction, Mullis discovered the source. It was a glowing raccoon. "Good evening, doctor," said the raccoon. "Hello . . ." replied Mullis.

★   ★   ★

Though you probably don't recognise the name, Kary Mullis has played an important role in your life over the last few years. It's thanks to him that millions of people didn't die during the recent coronavirus pandemic. The man who found himself in conversation with an English-speaking phosphorescent raccoon was also the 1993 co-recipient of the Nobel

The 1993 Nobel Prize–winning inventor of PCR, Kary Mullis.

Prize in Chemistry for his invention of the polymerase chain reaction. That's right, folks: Mullis is the reason we have the humble PCR test.

Prior to the Covid-19 outbreak, I'd never heard of PCR, and if the survey I conducted online is anything to go by, I reckon 70 per cent of you reading this hadn't either. I don't quite know how this happened. The *New York Times* has described its invention as being so significant it basically divided biochemistry into two epochs: before PCR and after PCR. Before PCR, DNA was incredibly hard to study. It's famously tiny, and that was the big problem. PCR fixed this by making billions of copies of very specific samples of DNA, meaning that doctors could expand the area that needed studying to a much larger size. Now the technique is used everywhere, from criminal forensics, where it revolutionised the accuracy of fingerprinting,* all the way to archaeology, where it helped to identify King Richard III's bones when they were found in a Leicester car park in 2011 by a screenwriter using "psychic intuition." Then, when the world came to a standstill in 2020 and scientists around the world desperately tried to develop a vaccine to stop the rampaging virus, PCR became the most important tool we had to curb its spread.

The idea for PCR came to Mullis in 1983 in a sudden burst of inspiration while he was driving up California's Highway 128 on his way to his Mendocino cabin.

"I didn't sleep that night," Mullis later recounted in his Nobel Prize acceptance lecture. Arriving at his cabin that evening, he got to work immediately: "I started drawing little diagrams on every horizontal surface that would take pen, pencil, or crayon, until dawn when, with the aid of a bottle of good Anderson Valley Cabernet, I settled into a perplexed semi-consciousness."

Mullis knew he had hit on something great, even telling his girlfriend at the time that he would be awarded the Nobel Prize for it one day. But when he pitched the idea to his colleagues at Cetus, the biotechnology company he was working for at the time, no one appeared interested.

---

* A 2019 report by the US National Registry of Exonerations showed the use of PCR had exonerated 494 wrongfully convicted people (and in a third of those cases it also successfully uncovered the actual perpetrator).

THE SCIENTIST WHO CRIED BATSHIT

This was probably largely Mullis's fault. He was the scientist who cried batshit. There were so many mad ideas coming out of his mind that the idea for PCR effectively got lost in a sea of rant. This was a man who, over the years, claimed that humans should be able to turn on a lightbulb with the power of the mind; who believed in ghosts;* who said astrology was an essential science and should be taught in every school classroom; and who once claimed his life was saved by a woman when she mentally travelled across the "astral plane" from hundreds of miles away to resuscitate him while he lay dying, alone on his bedroom floor, following an accidental overdose of laughing gas.

There is a tendency to fall in love with rogue scientists like Kary Mullis. They come across as exciting rule-breakers, whose antics more fit the mould of gonzo journalists like Hunter S. Thompson than that of a traditional scientist. Mullis can come across as very endearing on paper. The sad truth is that he was dangerous. His public opinions, particularly his denial that HIV causes AIDS, were so influential that it has been argued he indirectly caused hundreds of thousands of deaths after his opinions were adopted as fact by dictators in developing countries. A bitter yin to the yang of all the lives he saved.

* In his official Nobel Prize biography, Mullis wrote that his grandfather visited him in a "non-substantial form" as his spirit was leaving the physical realm. Mullis believes he did this so he could spend a couple of days in San Francisco with Mullis before disappearing altogether.

He was extremely problematic and unpredictable—following his Nobel Prize win, his public appearances would see him denouncing the idea that humans had any impact on climate change; then there was the womanising, the drug-taking (he was a huge advocate and frequent user of LSD), and the questionable practices—like including random irrelevant images of naked women in his slide shows when lecturing on scientific topics. He was such a liability, in fact, that when he was brought on board by former NFL star O. J. Simpson's defence team to testify about DNA samples during the infamous murder trial, Simpson's team ended up dropping him because they realised Mullis would make their client look bad.

This might account for why the term "PCR" has become recognised in households globally, but the name Kary Mullis hasn't. He was too controversial to promote. That was fine with him, though; he knew that fame was fickle. He had experienced the ups and downs of "celebrity" life the day his Nobel Prize was announced. As he wrote in his autobiography, *Dancing Naked in the Mind Field*, "In the morning, you were plastered all over the front pages of newspapers, and by night-time, you are being crapped on by around a theoretical 328,716 caged birds."*

---

* This is derived from a calculation devised by bird expert Jamie Yorck, who reckoned that one sixty-seventh of people on Earth owned a bird, and that each of these owners would replace the newspaper at the bottom of the cage every day. Mullis based his number on a world population in 1993 of 5.5 billion, a newspaper 25 pages thick, and the fact his face would take up one-tenth of the front page.

THE ART OF CASHING IN

Mullis was never adequately paid for his invention of PCR, receiving only a bonus of $10,000 from his employers, Cetus, who a few years later would go on to sell it for $300 million. Bitter about the pitiful money he received from them, Mullis attempted to capitalise on his discovery by other means—most notably by starting his own line of jewellery in a business called StarGene. Using his invention of PCR, the plan was to take a lock of a dead celebrity's hair, amplify the genes, and preserve bits of the DNA in artificial gemstones—which would then be sold as a range of earrings, rings, necklaces, watches, dog tags and so on, to the general public.

According to the *Los Angeles Times* the company got off to a good start when Mullis managed to purchase the rights to extract DNA from the hair of Elvis Presley, George Washington and Marilyn Monroe. This was thanks to Mullis's excellent hair-dealer—a man called John Reznikoff, owner of possibly the world's largest collection of historical hair. Reznikoff's library of moulted strands includes Beethoven, Napoleon Bonaparte, John Wilkes Booth, and the man he assassinated, President Abraham Lincoln (taken from his deathbed, this item is notable as it has attached to it a little bit of Lincoln's brain matter).* Mullis also made sure to quash any worries that he might be in the business of cloning whole bodies, by assuring the estates and descendants of the

---

* Another interesting strand of hair in Reznikoff's collection reportedly came from Hitler's mistress and eventual wife, Eva Braun. When analysed, it showed her to have had Jewish ancestry.

deceased that the amount of DNA being used was so minuscule that it absolutely could not be used to resurrect the dead celebrity in question.

The project sadly never took off, however, as producing the jewellery itself proved to be too hard and costly, so instead Mullis altered the idea to become trading cards laced with DNA. Each of these would feature a drawing of a famous person's face, and a bump in the card would contain within it a tiny bit of that person's DNA. On the reverse, instead of their sports stats, you'd see a sequence of letters spelling out the nucleotides in the DNA contained in the card. This project never materialised either.

THE BIG UNSOLVED MYSTERY

Kary Mullis might just be the perfect example of someone who was both brilliant and also a little bit batshit; a superb scientist, sure, but one who refused to conform to the ideas held by the scientific community, from which he was ostracised as a result. There are many similar characters to him out there. (Read on, and you'll be introduced to a bunch of them). They doggedly refuse to give up on their ideas, no matter what ridicule may have been poured on them.

Mullis had two things he couldn't let go of. The idea of PCR, which, despite the rolling eyes of his colleagues, he pursued and solved. Then there was the other thing, which he would spend much of the rest of his life trying to resolve—that talking raccoon. What the hell had happened to him that night in 1985? He couldn't remember anything

about the hours following the incident. Time seemed to have just . . . skipped forward. There he was, walking to the outhouse in the pitch black, when suddenly the next thing he knows it's around 6 a.m. and he finds himself walking along a different road uphill from his house. How on earth had he got there?

At first Mullis had no memory. He thought he must have passed out, but there were no signs on his clothes of his having slept on the damp ground. Then it came back to him. As he later wrote in his autobiography, "I remembered the little bastard and his courteous greeting. I remembered his little shifty black eyes. I remembered the way my flashlight had looked on his already glowing face."

It wasn't until years later, while browsing the shelves of a bookshop, that Mullis realised what might have happened to him that night. Finding himself drawn to a book with a cover depicting the oval head of an alien on it, Mullis started to wonder if maybe he had been abducted by extraterrestrials. The book he had picked up was Whitley Strieber's *Communion*.

Strieber has been described as one of the world's most famous abductees. *Communion*, in which he recalls his encounters with an ET, was a monstrous hit, reaching No. 1 in the *New York Times* bestseller list and selling over 10 million copies worldwide. Just like Mullis, Strieber's encounter took place in 1985, only instead of a glowing raccoon, Strieber had spoken to an alien owl.

Mullis bought the book and headed home. Later, as he lay on his bed reading it, he received a phone call from his daughter Louise. She began raving about an amazing book, telling her father that he had to read it immediately. It was called *Communion* by Whitley Strieber. What an extraordinary coincidence, thought Mullis.

When Mullis pressed his daughter on why she was reading it, she explained that not long ago, while staying at his Mendocino cabin with her fiancé, she decided to head to the outhouse before retiring to bed. The next thing she knew, three hours had passed and she was walking along a different road (the same road Mullis found himself on), with no idea how she got there. Her fiancé, who had been frantically searching for her the whole time, couldn't work out where she had gone.

Mullis found it hard to believe what he was hearing. He had never told his daughter about his own experience. "Did you happen to see any talking raccoons?" he asked her. She hadn't.*

*　　*　　*

Kary Mullis died suddenly in August 2019, only just missing out on witnessing how his invention would become so important to a world shut down by a rampaging global disease.

He also never met the talking alien raccoon again. He'd have loved to have written up an academic paper about the whole encounter, but due to the irreproducible nature of the event, he was never able to: "I can't make glowing raccoons appear. I can't buy them from a scientific supply house to study," he wrote. But he never stopped believing that something inexplicable had happened to him that night. "It's what science calls anecdotal," he wrote, "because it only happened in a way that you can't reproduce. But it happened."

---

* Mullis wouldn't be the only person ever to see the furry creature. According to UFOlogist Bill Chalker, Mullis's friend reported seeing the glowing raccoon, and at the very same spot Mullis had. It happened the night that Mullis was throwing a celebration party at his cabin for his Nobel Prize victory. His friend, unaware of Mullis's own story, saw the raccoon as he was heading to the john, but quickly fled the moment he saw it, before bumping into a "glowing man" on the way back up.

CHAPTER 2
THE SCIENTIST WHO BLEW UP EVERYTHING
THE THEORY OF MAD SCIENTISTS

Winning the Nobel Prize is a huge milestone in any scientist's life, promising global recognition, a large sum of cash and, if the recipient happens to work for the University of California, Berkeley, access to some sweet Nobel Laureate car parking spaces.

The Prizes were created in 1901, following an instruction left in the will of their founder, Dr. Alfred Nobel (so the story goes). This was prompted after he read an obituary that mistakenly named him, instead of his brother, as the deceased. As the co-inventor of dynamite, the piece described him as someone "who became rich by finding ways to kill more people faster than ever before." Horrified by this, Nobel decided he wanted to rectify his legacy. Since then, the prizes have become the benchmark of academic excellence.

However, in recent years something worrying has been observed—a "disease" has been spreading through the community of those laureates with Nobel Prizes to their name. It is known as Nobelitis.

Nobelitis, or the Nobel Disease, is a condition whereby the recipient of the prize suddenly feels they're an expert on things they know next to nothing about. Sufferers of extreme Nobelitis become suddenly emboldened to speak up about the mad ideas they'd previously kept secret for their entire careers. Kary Mullis, as we've seen, had it bad.*

The growing list of scientists (31, and counting) who have been hit by the Nobel Disease include:

---

* Nobelitis-spotters have observed the condition to mainly affect winners of the science prize, though an honourable mention must go to Jean-Paul Sartre, who was offered (but rejected) the 1964 Nobel Prize in Literature. Following a bad trip on mescaline, Sartre believed for many years that he was being followed around by a group of lobsters.

Linus Pauling, winner of the 1954 Nobel Prize in Chemistry (as well as the Nobel Peace Prize in 1962). After the award he became a major proponent of eugenics and believed that people with genetic defects should be given a mark on their head so that people knew not to procreate with them.

William Shockley, co-winner of the 1956 Nobel Prize in Physics, for co-inventing the transistor. After winning the award, Shockley also revealed his support for eugenics and proposed that anyone with an IQ below 100 be paid to undergo voluntary sterilisation. He also donated his semen to the controversial Nobel Prize sperm bank, officially known as the Repository for Germinal Choice, which was designed to exclusively stock the sperm of Nobel laureates (but which later expanded to include other so-called geniuses). This sperm bank for geniuses—founded in 1979 by an optometrist called Robert Graham, who started it because he believed that human beings were turning into idiots—ran for 19 years, and produced 218 children. Only three laureates were known to have actually donated sperm (Shockley being one of them, and the only one to reveal his identity), although, following a huge backlash from the public, they all pulled out and had their samples removed from the bank before any of it was used. Curiously, for something with such objectionable aims, the sperm bank for geniuses did have a positive lasting effect on the sperm banks of today; Graham's method of identifying donors and sharing their information with the recipient was adopted and many sperm banks started to promote the donors themselves, which led to a more transparent system.

Brian Josephson, winner of the 1973 Nobel Prize in Physics for his discoveries in quantum physics. After being given the award he became isolated from the scientific community for claiming water has memory and that humans can communicate through telepathy.

Luc Montagnier, winner of the 2008 Nobel Prize in Physiology or Medicine for his discovery of identifying the HIV virus. After the award Montagnier became a fervent anti-vaxxer. He also once advised Pope John Paul II to cure his Parkinson's disease by swallowing fermented papaya capsules.

*   *   *

Included on the list is Austrian physicist Wolfgang Pauli, who won the prize for his discovery of the Exclusion Principle, also known as the Pauli Principle. Pauli was a pioneer of quantum physics, venerated by fellow Austrian Albert Einstein, and someone whom the community feared thanks to his unforgiving eagle eye for scientific detail, earning him the moniker the "conscience of science."* He was also interested in the mysteries of life—in particular, he had an obsession with the number 137.

---

* Pauli was also highly principled. Despite being Austrian, he held an open anti-Nazi stance and refused to extend his arm in the *Sieg Heil* salute. Unfortunately for him, following an incident at a party in which he fell off a boat and broke his arm, Pauli would spend months in a full arm cast, which was required to be positioned permanently at a 45-degree angle to the horizontal.

Wolfgang Pauli, sufferer of Nobelitis.

Known as the fine-structure constant, 137 (or rather 1/137) is a number that keeps popping up in science.* According to science writer Michael Brooks, "This immutable number determines how stars burn, how chemistry happens and even whether atoms exist at all." Another Nobel Prize–winning physicist, Richard Feynman, was fascinated by it too, even speculating that the periodic table would end at number 137 (there are currently 118 elements). It's of such importance that one professor at the University of Nottingham has suggested that should we ever make contact with aliens, we should greet them with the number 137 to show them we're of a higher intelligence. "It's one of the *greatest* damn myster-

---

* The number is also represented as 0.007297351 or as the Greek letter α (alpha).

ies of physics," wrote Feynman. "*A magic number* that comes to us with no understanding by man." It's *the* number that many physicists believe might hold the key to cracking the theory of everything and explaining the universe.*

Pauli would spend his life exploring this number. But an equally intriguing mystery that came to consume him was that every time he went near any electrical equipment, his mere presence would cause it to break. Fellow scientists who noted this phenomenon even went as far as to give it a name—the "Pauli Effect."

Coined by physicist George Gamow,† the theory had it that "theoretical physicists cannot handle experimental equipment; it breaks whenever they touch it. Pauli was such a good theoretical physicist that something usually broke in the lab whenever he merely stepped across the threshold."‡ The term was tongue-

---

* Which, incidentally, many scientists estimate to be 13.7 billion years old.

† A hugely influential scientist himself. In 1948 George Gamow co-authored one of the most important astrophysics papers ever published, on the Big Bang. His PhD student was Ralph Alpher and they wrote it together. Gamow had a physicist colleague, Hans Bethe, who had nothing to do with the paper, but Gamow couldn't resist adding his name to the authors' list to make it the "Alpher, Bethe, Gamow" paper. He even asked another colleague to change his name to Delta so he could add him on. Alpher was furious, and never forgave Gamow for what's now known as the "αβγ paper."

‡ I searched the biographies of other Nobel Laureates to see if any suffered the Pauli Effect. The only other example I could find was John Bardeen, who, along with sperm-bank-man William Shockley, won the 1956 Nobel Prize in Physics for co-inventing the transistor (the device that allows us to switch electricity on and off). Sixteen years after winning his first Nobel Prize, Bardeen was awarded a second Nobel Prize in Physics.

in-cheek, effectively a jab at theoretical physicists who had no experimental experience. But Pauli wasn't so sure it was a joke.

Once, when Pauli was visiting the town of Princeton to do some research, it was noted that a particle accelerator at the nearby Princeton University spontaneously combusted, resulting in a fire that burnt for more than six hours. And when a measuring device at the University of Göttingen randomly broke, James Franck, who was performing the experiment, jokingly enquired if Pauli was in town. He wasn't. Franck later wrote to Pauli to tell him about the incident, only to receive a letter back from Pauli explaining that actually, on the day of the explosion, he had caught a train to Copenhagen to visit the physicist Niels Bohr and that, while on the journey, Pauli had to change trains in Göttingen, which meant he was in town on the day the machine broke.

As more and more examples of the "Pauli Effect" continued to pile in, many scientists reportedly started getting nervous about his presence around their incredibly expensive equipment—Nobel Prize–winning physicist Otto Stern even banned Pauli from his lab as a result.

Others saw it as funny—one group of scientists concocted a stunt to hoax Pauli into believing he was the causer of chaos by rigging a chandelier to fall from the ceiling as soon as he walked into the room. However, when he arrived, the mechanism built to drop the chandelier got stuck, and the prank failed—further proving his effect.

He almost missed the drinks party celebrating the announcement, however, when the invention that won him his *first* Nobel Prize malfunctioned on his garage door, leaving him without a car to get him to the party.

While the term was a joke to many within the scientific community, Pauli certainly wasn't laughing, as he genuinely believed something telekinetic was going on. Whenever objects blew up around him, Pauli would claim to have felt an energy building up within him before the object broke.

At this point the events were occurring so frequently that Pauli started actively looking for meaning behind them. For example, when he attended the opening of the C. G. Jung Institute in Zurich, for no reason anyone could figure out a Chinese vase fell from a shelf and smashed on the floor, spilling water all over the ground. Many joked it was Pauli, but Pauli couldn't help but notice that in order to attend the institute's opening he had abandoned the research he was doing on the sixteenth-century physician Robert Fludd. Could the flood of water from the vase and Fludd the scientist be in some way linked, he wondered? Pauli was a patient and friend of Jung, and they had spent many hours interpreting Pauli's dreams. Their interest in the subject would even lead the two to write a book together in 1955 called *The Interpretation of Nature and the Psyche.*

Despite all his investigations, however, Wolfgang Pauli never got to discover why electrical equipment kept breaking around him, nor did he ever get to the bottom of the magical number that might solve the theory of everything. Both would remain a mystery to him till his dying day, which sadly came prematurely at just the age of 58, when he died after a short illness at the Rotkreuz hospital in Zurich, in room number 137.

CHAPTER 3
THE IMPROBABLE TALE OF TU YOUYOU
THE THEORY OF ANCIENT CHINESE MEDICINE

Of all the names that appear on the list of Nobel Prize winners in the sciences, the one that truly sticks out is Tu Youyou's. For starters, it's unique. Tu Youyou is surely the only person you'll have heard of to be named after the sound an animal makes. Her first name, Youyou, was inspired by a line from her father's favourite poem, which he found in an old collection called the *Chinese Book of Odes*. The line reads: "呦呦鹿鸣, 食野之蒿" ("Deer bleat 'youyou' while they're eating the wild [qing]hao.") The word he picked out from the sentence and bestowed on his baby daughter was Youyou ("呦呦.")

Tu's name also sticks out for another reason. Not only was she the first native Chinese scientist ever to win a Nobel Prize in Physiology or Medicine, she also did it practising a discipline that's considered to be pseudoscience—Chinese herbal medicine—and doing so without a doctorate, or even a medical degree.

Tu Youyou, who in 2015 won the Nobel Prize in Physiology or Medicine for discovering a cure for malaria in a 1,600-year-old traditional Chinese medical book called Emergency Prescriptions to Keep Up One's Sleeve.

It's natural for us to believe that we're somehow better and smarter than those who lived in the civilisations of the past, and that the knowledge of old offers nothing to us these days. We tend to mock the past rather than actively engage with it, and we mock even more those who still choose to live their lives according to apparently bygone ideas. While we understand that these ideas are what got society to where it is today, we feel that we're living in a more developed and advanced era.

And so while many academics thank those from the past for all that they have done, they also believe that these proto-sciences (such as alchemy and Chinese herbal medicine) should be retired and no longer practised.

I'd have agreed too, were it not for the tale of Tu Youyou.

Born in the city of Ningbo in 1930, Tu first became interested in studying medicine when, aged 16, she contracted tuberculosis and was hospitalised for two years. Wanting to discover a cure for such diseases, she applied to medical college as a pharmacologist. After graduating, she began to work at the Academy of Traditional Chinese Medicine. She was trained in medicinal plant classification, and specialised in both extracting their active ingredients as well as determining their chemical make-up. At the same time she began training in modern Western approaches, which was a risky move. The 1950s and 1960s were not a good time to be a scientist in China—as a researcher Tu Youyou would have been classified as a member of the "Nine Black Categories" under dictator Mao Zedong's regime, which saw intellectuals as dangerous. Many were killed, or taken from their families and placed in "reformative" work or re-training programmes. When the Communist Party finally came for Tu, though, it wasn't to stop her work. It was to engage her in a clandestine operation.

PROJECT 523

In 1967 Chairman Mao created a secret task force known as "Project 523," the aim of which was to try to find a new treatment for malaria. Chinese forces in North Vietnam were being ravaged by the disease, and the drug that had been used for so many years, chloroquine, was no longer working as the parasites had become resistant to it. In 1969 Tu was made head of the task force, thanks to her training in both modern pharmaceutical sciences and traditional medicines. At the time of her arrival, there were 50 secret laboratories set up all over China dedicated to coming up with an effective treatment for the disease.*

Tu started her investigations at a time when some 240,000 compounds had already been screened, with none proving to be in any way effective. How was she to stand any chance of finding one that worked? Deciding on a different approach, Tu looked somewhere unorthodox: in the medical journals of ancient China. Perhaps, she thought, the cure for malaria could be sitting there in some ancient herbal remedy book from the Han, Zhou, or Qing dynasties. Over the next two years Tu travelled around China, meeting up with practitioners, tracking down and reading ancient medical manuscripts, and collecting all of her findings in a notebook she called "A Collection of Single Practical Prescriptions for Anti-Malaria." The book quickly filled up.

---

* Malaria is one of mankind's oldest foes. Ancient Greek and Chinese accounts of distinctive periodic malaria fevers date as far back as 1000 BCE. According to the Greek historian Herodotus, the workers building the great pyramids in Egypt were given garlic in an effort to ward off the disease. In fact, Malaria is even older than the human race—traces of it have been found in 30-million-year-old mosquitoes trapped in amber, *Jurassic Park* style. Humans have been fighting malaria for 10,000 years. It is found on every continent on Earth except Antarctica, and it is estimated that it has killed around an astonishing 5 per cent of all humans who have ever lived.

Her quest to find a cure would eventually see her making 380 herbal extracts from over 200 herbs she had found in over 2,000 traditional recipes.

Remarkably, Tu's efforts paid off when she discovered the details of a remedy to combat "intermittent fevers" in a 1,600-year-old recipe book titled *Emergency Prescriptions to Keep Up One's Sleeve*. The directions given were to soak a single bunch of the plant qinghao, also known as sweet wormwood (*Artemisia annua*), in hot water and then drink the juice.

Tu and her team set about trying to extract the active in-gredient from the qinghao and at the start the plant gave them some success, but the results were inconsistent. Slowly Tu and her team had to discover the finer details of why it was only sometimes working. They noticed, for example, that it was specifically the leaves that were efficacious, not the stems, but it wasn't *all* the leaves, only certain ones, produced at a specific time of year just before the plant flowered. But even then, the remedy remained somewhat hit and miss. Frustrated, Tu went back to the ancient medical books for more advice, and it was while reading another recipe written in the 340 CE text that she found her answer: the water in which the leaves were steeped should be cold, not boiling, it said—so simple a difference, yet a game-changer that would save millions of lives.

Tu and her team experimented with using lukewarm ether to extract the compound and discovered, when testing the treatment on monkeys and mice, that it gave a 100 per cent cure rate. Now all she needed to do was test it on humans to see if it would work for them too. In order for the cure to undergo human trials, she needed proof that it wasn't itself a harmful medicine to take. However, as there was no existing structure for clinical trials in China, she was unable to get permission to conduct this vital stage of her research. And so, like many badass scientists before her, she and two colleagues tested it out on themselves. When it proved to have no side effects, the medicine was finally rolled out.*

Due to the secretive nature of the project, it would take over four decades before Tu Youyou would receive any credit for her extraordinary discovery. This came in 2015, when she was finally recognised for her incredible achievement and awarded the Nobel Prize. It's a remarkable story, one that shouldn't really have happened. Scientists globally were searching for the cure, yet it was somehow found by someone who didn't have proper scientific training, and who was looking for it in what would be deemed the *wrong* place. Her story serves as a humbling lesson in collaborating with the past, and a reminder to listen to the voices of the ancients and not always brush them off as primitive or irrelevant.

---

* One curious thing about the malaria vaccine is that we effectively have been hiding it from the parasite. The vaccines concocted to fight malaria are as ingenious as the disease is lethal. The type of vaccine prescribed varies depending on the stage of the malaria the patient is suffering from— but the problem is stopping the parasite from adapting to the vaccine-triggered antibodies that neutralise it, and mutating to render our current cure useless. To solve this problem, the current vaccine cure administered is actually a package of several different drugs, which, simply put, comprises the vaccine and several "decoys," so that the parasite struggles to identify its attacker.

呦呦鹿鸣，食野之蒿

For Tu, however, there was something else. Many people believe they are put on this planet for a purpose, to achieve something particular, something they were always destined to do. It was something that Tu now found herself considering as well.

In the poem that Tu's father took her name from, the bleating deer is chewing on a single plant. Of all the tens of thousands of different species that plant could have been, it just so happens that the one the deer is seen to be eating is the exact same plant that Tu would go on to discover to be the cure for malaria: the qinghao. "How this links my whole life with qinghao," said Tu, "will probably remain an interesting coincidence forever."★

★ One more thing: the drug that Tu discovered was named "artemisinin" by Western scientists, the root of the word coming from the Greek goddess Artemis, who is always depicted accompanied by just one animal—a deer.

CHAPTER 4
THE EXORCISM OF RINGO STARR
THE THEORY OF THE DEVIL IN MUSIC

When Ringo Starr was inducted into the 2015 Rock and Roll Hall of Fame in recognition of his contribution to the history of popular rock, Paul McCartney delivered a speech as part of the ceremony and a video featuring some of the world's greatest living drummers, including Dave Grohl (Nirvana), Questlove (The Roots), Chad Smith (Red Hot Chili Peppers), and Stewart Copeland (The Police) was played. All of them praised the former Beatle for his genius and unique drumming style, describing him as iconic, badass, and one of the greatest drummers of all time. In his speech, McCartney recalled the first time The Beatles auditioned Ringo, and remembered him "standing there and looking at John and then looking at George, and the look on our faces was like, *fucking . . . What is this?* And that was the moment, that was the beginning, really, of The Beatles."

When Ringo took to the stage to give his acceptance speech, many people were thanked for their role in his journey. From band members to managers and fellow musicians. However, there was one very notable name missing from his list. There was no mention of the woman who was truly responsible for Ringo's whole drumming style—his grandmother, Annie Bower, aka the voodoo queen of Liverpool.

THE VOODOO QUEEN OF LIVERPOOL

It is a little-known fact that the reason Ringo Starr is such a unique drummer is because as a young boy his grandmother performed multiple exorcisms on him. I discovered this in a book by Beatles expert Mark Lewisohn, whose seminal biography of the band *Tune In* is probably the most detailed account of The Beatles ever published.* Curiously, though, there are scant details in the book about what these exorcisms actually consisted of, but what we do know is that they took place when Ringo's granny discovered that her grandson was left-handed and therefore decided he'd been possessed by the devil (or possibly witches, says Lewisohn). The exorcisms were designed to knock out the devil and turn Ringo into a right-handed boy. According to Ringo, Annie Bower, the "voodoo queen of Liverpool," was a twentieth-century witch, known in Merseyside for making remedies and potions, as well as for expelling Satan from her neighbours and friends.

As a child Ringo was often ill. When he was six he con-

---

* The expanded edition is the one to go for. It's incredibly exhaustive, running to 1,728 pages, and ends just as The Beatles release their first songs. Volume 2 is expected sometime this decade.

tracted peritonitis following a burst appendix, which resulted in his falling into a coma for a number of days (his mother was told by doctors on three occasions that he wouldn't survive the night) and having to spend six months recovering in a hospital bed. He was nearing his release day from hospital when an accident saw him fall out of bed, which ripped open his stitches, extending his stay by another six months. Some years later Ringo was back in hospital, aged 13, with tuberculosis; fortunately, streptomycin had just been discovered and he was able to recover in a sanatorium.

It was during this second stay in recovery that Ringo discovered the drums after a teacher came by with some maracas, tambourines, and other percussive instruments. It was instant love, and Ringo refused to play any other instruments on the teacher's subsequent visits.

After he left hospital for the second time, Ringo moved in

with his voodoo granny who kept an eye on her grandson's left-handedness. "My grandmother thought that was not a good sign and so she turned me right-handed," Ringo would tell talk-show host Conan O'Brien years later.*

It was at this time that Ringo got his first drum set, which, now that he was right-handed, was a right-handed kit. Over time, however, and once he'd left his grandmother's home, Ringo slowly started favouring his left hand again, and would lead with it. But he didn't rearrange his kit to suit a left-handed player, presumably because he had felt comfortable with how his feet worked the hi-hat and bass drum, which meant he effectively was playing backwards. This resulted in a unique style that many drummers refer to as the "Ringo swing" (Paul McCartney's touring drummer Abe Laboriel Jr. describes it as a "sloppy swampy, falling down the stairs kind of sound.") His unique way of playing has even become a byword for a whole style of drumming. "Give me Ringo" a drummer might be asked when in the recording studio. It's a style that marked The Beatles out from other groups of their time. It's what gave The Beatles their *beat*, and it's all thanks to an exorcist in Merseyside.

Ringo isn't the only Beatle to have had an encounter of the biblical kind.

---

* Left-handedness being associated with the devil goes back hundreds of years, and schools would try to cure their pupils of the "sin" by forcing them to write with their right hand, something that Ringo still does to this day.

THE MESSIAH WHO CAME TO TEA

On February 9, 1967, Paul McCartney was at his home in London when he got a knock on the door from a man claiming to be Jesus Christ.

"Well, you better come in then," Paul told the man, reasoning that while it probably wasn't Christ, he couldn't actually be certain it wasn't, and so he thought it best to let him enter. "I'm not going to be the one to turn *him* away," McCartney later said.

According to McCartney's account, he and Jesus had a cup of tea and chatted for a while, before McCartney explained that he had to get to a Beatles recording session. Would Jesus like to join them?

And so it was that Jesus went along to the studio and watched as the Fab Four recorded their latest track, "Fixing a Hole," for their upcoming *Sgt. Pepper's Lonely Hearts Club Band* album.

After that there's no other mention of what happened to the Messiah.*

* This was actually the second time Paul had met someone claiming to be Jesus. According to their good friend Tony Bramwell, a few years back, Paul, the rest of The Beatles, and their management team were called into the office to hear an announcement from John Lennon, who the previous evening, along with his wife Cynthia and school friend Pete Shotten, had dropped LSD and had now developed a Messiah complex. He asked Tony to immediately arrange the meeting, as he thought the others should know. "I have something very important to tell you all," John said. "I am Jesus Christ. I have come back again. This is my thing." "Right. Meeting adjourned," said Ringo. "Let's go get some lunch." At the lunch a fan approached John and told him he loved his music. "Actually, I'm Jesus

★   ★   ★

Just like the exorcism of Ringo Starr, McCartney's afternoon with the Messiah has rarely popped up in interviews. Which surprises me. For a man whose life has been so thoroughly analysed, in countless documentaries, articles, and books, how is it that no one has bothered to ask what Paul and Jesus discussed? Did he ask any deep questions of the man claiming to be the Messiah? Has he ever had any other similar mystical encounters?*

Paul McCartney is arguably the most successful musician of all time. His output of songs with The Beatles, Wings, and as a solo artist, have meant his songs have spent a collective 30-plus years in the music charts, and he has had more No. 1 hits to his name than anyone else in history. He is often portrayed as a cosy family man who, when he's not talking about his music, likes to go on about vegetarianism and peace. But look closer at his interviews and you'll discover bubbling away underneath it all is a wonderful amount of batshit. There's the time he claimed to have discovered the meaning of life while high on pot ("There are seven levels," he wrote on a scrap of paper. Unfortunately he has no memory of what it means.); he claims to have

Christ," John told the man. "Well," the man replied, "I still loved your last record."

* Personally, to me, it makes sense that if the Messiah returned, it would be to witness The Beatles at the height of their fame while in the middle of recording what's commonly held to be the greatest album of all time. The whole thing stinks of honeytrapping the Lord back to Earth.

channelled songs in his sleep (like "Yesterday") as if gifted to him from some unknown source; and he's rumoured to hold a secret interest in conspiracy theories—most notably the JFK assassination. According to conspiracy theorist Mark Lane, McCartney asked to write the soundtrack for the first major documentary on the subject, but was talked out of it by the conspiracy theorists themselves, who said it would ruin his reputation.

Most interesting to me, however, is McCartney's claims to have made contact with the other side. He has often alluded to a belief in the afterlife. According to McCartney, when the three remaining Beatles got back into the studio to record a new track in 1994, not only was the spirit of John Lennon literally with them for the recording, but he made contact with them using a method that once saw The Beatles being accused of satanism, and projecting evil thoughts into the minds of the young via their records.

And McCartney has the evidence to prove it.

BACKMASKING

The Beatles were one of the first bands to use a technique known as "backmasking." Backmasking is when a spoken message is deliberately flipped backwards in a song, so that the listener has to the play the song itself backwards to make sense of the gibberish. The band credited with first doing this were the Eligibles, who in 1959 released a song called "Car Trouble," which, when played backwards, revealed the nonsense garble to be "And you can get my daughter back by 10:30, you bum!" and "Now, lookit here, cats, stop running these records backwards."

The idea of backmasking really took off around the world, however, thanks to The Beatles and their use of the technique on the songs "Rain" and "Revolution 9."

By the late 1970s backmasking went from being a fun little Easter egg for fans to being thought of as a sinister plot to brainwash the world's young. Fundamentalist Christians claimed that satanic messages were appearing in records and then slipping into the unconscious mind, like some subliminal devilish advertising, and converting healthy, wholesome children into worshippers of the Dark Lord. Rumours even started emerging that musicians were working directly with the Church of Satan, or even in direct cahoots with the Devil himself.

This wasn't entirely without precedent, as the backwards playing of records had previously been used for occult purposes. Aleister Crowley, the so-called "wickedest man on Earth," who popped up in the collage of notables on the *Sgt. Pepper* cover, suggested in his 1913 book *Magick* that as part of occult training one should "listen to phonograph records, reversed, and let him accustom himself to these that they appear natural and appreciable as a whole."

THE DEVIL AND MUSICIANS THROUGH THE AGES

Music has always had a close relationship with satanism. From blues guitarist Robert Johnson, who supposedly sold his soul to the Devil at the crossroads, to the members of Led Zeppelin who were said to have invoked evil spirits while performing occult rituals. And while these days the idea that a musician might be in cahoots with a demon is seen as good PR fodder for a new album release, audiences of the past used to take it far more literally, which became a nuisance to some musicians.

In 1828 an annoyed Italian violinist called Niccolò Paganini found himself publicly publishing a letter that was written to him by his mother, just so he could prove to the public that his parents were both human and quash rumours that he was the son of Satan.

Born in Genoa in 1782, Paganini took up the violin as a seven-year-old boy and by 15 was going on solo tours. His skills were immense—he could play 12 notes a second and reach three octaves with the span of one hand. He was also cocky—when he performed his 1st Concerto, instead of playing the piece in the key of D as advertised, he announced he'd play it in E flat, a very difficult key for violinists to play in. Many believed his virtuosity lay beyond the accepted range of human ability and that he must have been the son of—or at the very least had done an excellent deal with—the Devil.

As he grew in fame, rumours spread claiming that he'd been witnessed in the company of the Devil on stage when he played. There were darker rumours too, including that he had murdered a woman and was using her intestines for his violin strings. Many said if you listened carefully when he played you could hear her screams, as her soul remained trapped inside the strings.

The violin is historically the Devil's instrument and Paganini wasn't the only musician to be connected to Satan through it. The Violin Sonata in G Minor, a piece for solo violin by Italian composer Giuseppe Tartini, runs at roughly 15 minutes, noted both for being very technical and for having been "co-written" with Satan.

"One night, in the year 1713," wrote Tartini, "I dreamed I had made a pact with the devil for my soul."

BACKMASKING PART 2

The theory of satanic messaging in records built up so much steam that by 1983 the state government of California introduced a bill for it to be outlawed, arguing that it "can manipulate our behaviour without our knowledge or consent and turn us into disciples of the Antichrist." Had the bill passed, any album released there containing backmasking would have had to declare so, otherwise it was an invasion of privacy. The suggested wording read: "Warning: This record contains backward masking which may be perceptible at a subliminal level when the record is played forward." (It was a bizarre period for putting warning labels on albums, including one that stated "Explicit Lyrics," which was placed on the Frank Zappa album *Jazz from Hell*, despite it being entirely instrumental.)

In Arkansas, where a similar bill went through, it was mandated that all records should carry a label on them. This bill, however, was never enforced as it was brought back to the state senate by another Bill—Governor Bill Clinton—and defeated.*

Of course, there has never been any evidence that subliminal messages played backwards on a record can influence the minds of the young. Though according to one notable author, a Beatles record did speak a message that ended up saving a life.

LET ME TAKE YOU DOWN . . . TO A&E

Science-fiction author Philip K. Dick had a lot to thank The Beatles for. According to Dick, they saved his son's life by diagnosing his medical condition through their song "Strawberry Fields Forever."

Dick was a prolific author who, in his relatively brief lifetime would pen 44 novels and 121 short stories, many of which we've seen adapted for both the big and small screen— *Minority Report, Bladerunner* (originally published as *Do Androids Dream of Electric Sheep?*) and *The Man in the High Castle.*

In 1974 Dick started claiming to have received numer-

---

* Interestingly, the reason "Parental Guidance: Explicit Lyrics" labels exist at all is largely down to Clinton's vice president Al Gore, whose wife Tipper petitioned for them to be mandatory. The story goes that Tipper and her young daughter heard Prince singing about masturbation in his song "Darling Nikki."

ous alien messages, which were being beamed into his brain. Dick would obsess over these messages for the rest of his life, trying to work out who sent them and where in the universe they were sent from (a posthumous wad of 8,000 pages containing hypotheses about what it all meant would eventually be published under the title *The Exegesis*).

The very first time Dick received these messages he said a "pink light" entered his brain. Once, while he was listening to The Beatles' "Strawberry Fields Forever," a message told him that his son was dying. Writing in *The Exegesis*:

> *I get up. I open my eyes because the lyrics speak of "going through life with eyes closed." I look toward the window. Light blinds me; my head suddenly aches. My eyes close & I see that strange strawberry ice cream pink. At the same instant knowledge is transferred to me. I go into the bedroom where Tessa is changing Chrissy & I recite what has been conveyed to me: that he has an undetected birth defect & must be taken to the doctor at once & scheduled for surgery.*

Remarkably, not only did the doctors not turn him away but Dick was right. His son Christopher had an undiagnosed hernia, and had it not been quickly treated it would have killed him. Dick wrote, "God talked to me through a Beatles tune."

FREE AS A BIRD

Perhaps the most interesting example of hidden messages in a Beatles song was to be experienced by The Beatles themselves. Fourteen years after Lennon's death, the three remaining Beatles, Paul McCartney, George Harrison, and Ringo Starr, got back into the studio to transform two unreleased demos made by John Lennon from his solo career into Beatles' tracks. The songs chosen were "Free as a Bird" and "Real Love."

Now, before you read this next bit, can I ask you to put the book down and go quickly to listen to "Free as a Bird"? You'll find it online somewhere: YouTube, Spotify, wherever you go for your music, it should be there. Make sure to listen to the song in its entirety, right to the end. Once you're done, come back and continue.

When the three remaining Beatles got together in 1994 to record the track, Paul suggested they get past the awkward feeling of John not being there by imagining that he had already laid down the track, and then gone off on holiday, leaving the other three to fill in the other bits. However, as the recording went on, Paul started to sense that perhaps John was in the recording studio after all.

Little things kept alerting him to his presence. When the group were outside taking a photo by a tree, a peacock suddenly entered the frame. McCartney wondered to the others that it might be John. As the band were wrapping up on production of "Free as a Bird," it was suggested that what they should do is add some ukulele music at the end. They also decided to have a bit of fun by sticking some backmasking onto the track.

Asking the production team to locate a sample of John Lennon speaking from one of the demos, the message they ended up using was a snippet of Lennon saying, "Turned out nice again." This turned out to be a perfect line to put over the ukelele as it was the catchphrase of musician and ukulele player George Formby. And so they flipped the audio around as a little surprise for the keen fans, and laid the backmask on the track.

What happened next is what convinced McCartney that John Lennon was in fact with them for the recording. When the band went in the studio to hear the mastering of the song, someone noticed something astonishing: it was the back-masked audio. As they listened to the moment Lennon's voice came over the ukelele, it didn't produce a garbled sentence as expected. Instead, what everyone heard was the voice of John Lennon, through a backward record, saying the words "Made by John Lennon."

"It's impossible," said Paul. And how could it be anything but? What are the chances that a completely randomly chosen bit of audio, played backwards, would form a coherent set of words, let alone result in the person saying their own name?* For Paul it was the sign he had been looking for. He knew John was there, and now through the technique of backmasking, which Lennon helped popularise, the dead

---

* A friend of mine, the comedy writer and über Beatles nut Jason Hazeley, has isolated the vocal even further, and discovered you can actually make out Lennon saying, "It's a hit, made by John Lennon."

Beatle had let his presence be known. McCartney never really knew whether Jesus was with him in the studio all those years ago, but he could be sure that his old mate John was that day.

"I swear to God, he definitely says it!" said McCartney. "We could not in a million years have known what that phrase would be backwards. It's impossible. So there is real magic going on."

CHAPTER 5
ROSEMARY BROWN AND THE LOUNGEROOM OF DEAD COMPOSERS
THE THEORY OF CLAIRVOYANCE

As I write these words I'm listening to a classical album on Spotify called *A Musical Séance* compiled by a former dinner-lady from London called Rosemary Brown. The album was released in 1970 by the record label Philips, whose other output around this time includes David Bowie's *Space Oddity* LP and many of Elton John's US singles.

The album contains a collection of classical pieces by a number of different composers, including eight works by Liszt, three by Chopin, and one each by Beethoven, Schubert, Brahms, Debussy, Grieg, and Schumann. What makes this album special is that each of the pieces is unique, in that none of them appear in any other catalogues of published works by these composers. This is because all of the composers wrote these pieces long after they had died. Brown was a medium, and it was through her that they imparted their tunes, from the other side.

The album is really nice, by the way, although you do

Rosemary Brown.

wonder whether some of the composers were taking a bit too much inspiration from the music of the 1960s. Grieg was definitely watching too much *Spider-Man* on the TV when he composed "Shepherd Piping," as the music bears a strong resemblance to Spidey's theme tune at the beginning, and Schumann has clearly got Frank Sinatra's latest hit stuck in his head, the opening few bars of his piece being a flat-out rip-off of "My Way."

Track 10 of the album is perhaps the most intriguing, as out of nowhere you get a six-minute-long commentary track in which Brown takes you through the songs and explains how she collaborated with the musicians on them.

"Chopin isn't at all like I thought he would be," she says. "He's not melancholy at all . . . he makes jokes and he is light-hearted. Schubert is lovely too. He communicates smoothly and quietly. He alters music just after he's given it. He'll edit. All the other composers seem to have them all prepared. But he is writing it as he goes."

Brown was just seven years old when she first had an encounter with a dead composer. The year was 1923, and she was in her parents' bedroom at her home in Balham, southwest London, when a man with a flowing cassock appeared before her and explained that he'd one day make her famous. Ten years later, she saw a drawing of the composer Franz Liszt (1811–1886) and immediately recognised him as that strange visitor from all those years ago. It wasn't until three decades on from that moment, though, that Liszt would finally return to Brown "in person" and begin to fulfil his promise of making her famous. He did this by starting to dictate original tunes to her.

In total, Liszt gave Brown over 200 pieces of music, guiding her hands across the keyboard like automatic writing. He also spoke to her in excellent English, "which he has practised a great deal since leaving our world," according to Brown.

While most people who contact spirits from the other side are barely given the time of day, Brown was to become a curious exception. After making her debut on BBC TV in 1969, she quickly became a star, and what followed was a career that saw the former dinner-lady playing eminent venues such as London's Queen Elizabeth Hall and the Town Hall in New York. She appeared on Johnny Carson's talk show (America's biggest programme at the time) where she revealed, among other things, that there's no sex in heaven; she wrote and published three memoirs; and even recorded and released the above-mentioned LP, which was performed by Peter Katin, a musician notable for his interpretations of Chopin's real piano music. She became infamous among other classical musicians, too, many of whom were happy to record the piano works she was "receiving."

Back at home, when she wasn't sitting at the keyboard taking dictation, Brown and the composers would often hang out and chat. Liszt in particular was basically viewed as one of the family. According to Brown, they'd talk about current pop music, watch TV, and Liszt would even help out with the kids' homework. (Thomas, her son, once yelled out, "Mummy, what's one square plus two square plus three square plus four square . . . ?" and before he could finish the question, she had already been passed on the answer: "Liszt says it's 385." Thomas would report the next day that the answer was correct.) Liszt would join Brown on her grocery shopping trips too, and was particularly helpful one time with picking out bananas. He was also helpful with keeping her out of danger. "Be careful today. You are going to have three fires in the house," he told her, and she did. After a while, Liszt became so comfortable "living" in the 1960s, he even lost his Victorian clothing and started dressing in the fashion of the day.

As she went on, Brown started meeting with other spirits outside of the classical music world. She began writing poetry dictated to her by Emily Brontë, William Blake, and Samuel Taylor Coleridge, among others. She transcribed two new plays by George Bernard Shaw, one of which, *Caesar's Revenge*, was performed at the 1978 Edinburgh Fringe. And she even took up art classes after she started having conversations with Turner and Van Gogh.

As well as helping the dead composers realise their new compositions, Brown also liked to pass on advice to living ones. When Richard Rodney Bennett (a leading British classical composer, who also wrote the *Four Weddings and a Funeral* movie score) was having trouble with a Debussy composition, Brown, in communication with the dead Frenchman, advised that more pedal was needed, and certain chords should be more staccato. Bennett followed the advice and it solved the problem.

The composer was amazed. So much so that he's quoted on the back of one of her memoirs as saying, "I've no doubt she's psychic . . . A lot of people can improvise but you couldn't fake music like this without years of training. I couldn't have faked some of the Beethoven myself."

Brown died aged 85 in 2001, having stopped being visited by the spirits when she became ill. I think I'd like to have known her, as she wasn't really doing this for the money. Just a humble dinner-lady, whose life became a fascinating journey thanks to a bunch of dead guys in wigs. Much loved and respected by many of the classical musicians of her day, Brown's journey was perhaps best summed up by respected composer Sir Donald Tovey, who provided a blurb for her album *A Musical Séance*:

There are always those who scoff at that which they cannot or will not understand, and the threat of these Philistines may induce hesitation in some people to place before the world new or unusual ideas and experiences . . . Those who are most likely to block progress in your world are the inveterate sceptics who fondly assume that their immovable intellectualism denotes an ingenious and infallible judgement.

Tovey wrote these words 30 years after his death, as relayed to Brown from the beyond.

★　　★　　★

There's a long history of famous celebrities creating art from beyond the grave. One particularly interesting publication was said to have been written by Mark Twain, seven years after he died.

JAP HERRON: A NOVEL WRITTEN FROM THE OUIJA BOARD

Dictated from the other side by: the spirit of Mark Twain
Received on this side by: Emily Grant Hutchings and the
　　medium Lola Hays

It could have been the greatest copyright trial ever.

In 1918, Harper & Brothers (H&B), who published the original works of Mark Twain during his lifetime, found themselves in the odd position of having to sue the publishing house Mitchell Kennerley, for a new book they'd released, which claimed to be an original work by Twain, written from beyond the grave. The book was called *Jap Herron*, the story of a boy called Jasper, aka Jap, from a river village in Missouri sometime after the Civil War and Twain was said to have dictated it from the other side via the ouija board to Mrs. Emily

Title page of the novel Jap Herron.

Grant Hutchings and her collaborator Lola V. Hays, whose hands manned the ouija board.

Hutchings probably got the idea to contact the spirit of Twain and ask him to write the book after seeing the success of one of her friends, Pearl Curran, whom Hutchings had introduced to ouija boards. Curran subsequently made contact with the spirit of a British woman from the 1700s called Patience Worth and would go on to publish many books said to be penned by Worth, including seven novels, as well as poems, plays, and short stories. In June 1917, Worth, via Curran, published *The Sorry Tale*, a novel running to 644 pages that told the story of the last days of Jesus.

The Sorry Tale was released to critical acclaim, unlike *Jap Herron*.* Roland Greene Usher, dean of history at Washington University, said it was "the greatest story of Christ penned since the Gospels were finished." And it received positive re-

---

* The *New York Times* wrote, "If this is the best that 'Mark Twain' can do by reaching across the barrier, the army of admirers that his works have won for him will all hope that he will hereafter respect that boundary."

views from the *New York Globe*, *Columbus Dispatch*, and *The National*, who between them were amazed at the author's accuracy on everything from the sights and smells of the locations to the descriptions of Roman palaces and ancient marketplaces. The *New York Tribune* even called it "a work approximating absolute genius."

How exactly Pearl Curran was able to so accurately describe the streets of ancient Jerusalem having never been there remains a curious mystery to many.

Hutchings originally approached Twain's publisher H&B to publish *Jap Herron*, but after they refused, she went elsewhere. Ouija boards were in vogue at the time, so when the book was published in 1918 it sold many copies—presumably to a mixture of believers and curious readers. When Twain's daughter Clara Clemens spotted the book on the market she and Twain's publishers immediately took Hutchings to court.

The preparations for the court case threw up many interesting scenarios, the most exciting of which being the possibility that the spirit of Mark Twain himself might have to be called to the stand, although it was thought highly unlikely that testimony by ouija would be accepted by the court. If this had happened, however, it would have been a game-changing moment on every level. Imagine the ghost of Mark Twain successfully testifying to a jury, who, let's remember, were living in a time when spiritualism was hugely popular, and many believed it possible to communicate with the dead. What would that mean for the law of the land? And what, moreover, would it do to the world of publishing?

Fortunately for the spirit of Mark Twain, the case never made it to court, because had it done so he might have been royally screwed. *Jap Herron* was released using his pen-name "Mark Twain," the rights to which the author, real name Samuel Clemens, had signed over to H&B before he died. Which meant, had a jury sided with the spirit of Mark Twain, acknowledging his after-life existence, the publishers could then potentially have had to sue the ghost of Samuel Clemens for breach of contract. Another exciting near first in legal history.*

A NEW COMEDY

Dictated from the other side by: William Shakespeare
Received on this side by: Victor Hugo and his son

There's one play of William Shakespeare's that, so far as I can tell, has never been performed in the English language. He wrote it some 200 years after his death, with the help of a three-legged table and the author Victor Hugo.

The year was 1853, and a 51-year-old Victor Hugo had only a few years before fled France with his family following

---

* This wasn't the only time a ouija board featured in a court of law. One British murder case went to retrial a month after the accused was found guilty of committing double murder, when it was discovered that four of the jurors had got drunk in a hotel room and consulted a bootleg ouija board to find out if he was guilty. Using materials in the hotel they were staying in, they crafted a makeshift talking board with pieces of paper and a wine glass. They then asked a spirit, who identified himself as a man named Harry Fuller, if the accused had done it. "Yes" was spelt out by Fuller. You might think that this sort of thing would have been quite common in the heyday of spiritualism, but it happened in 1994.

Author Victor Hugo, who only completed Les Misérables
because a three-legged table told him to.

the issuing of a warrant for his arrest by Napoleon III. Hugo
was exiled largely thanks to a pamphlet he had written titled
Napoléon le Petit, which criticised the emperor. Initially he
fled to Belgium, but he was soon exiled from there too and so
he made his way to the island of Jersey, where he'd com-
mence the weirdest two years of his life.

After arriving in Jersey, Hugo made it his mission to see
that *Napoléon le Petit* was distributed far and wide in France,
and for a while he effectively ran a smuggling ring. He did
this by printing the tract on extra-thin paper (known as onion
paper) and having it smuggled into the country in everything
from sardine tins and hay bales to underwear and hollow
walking sticks. He even had copies hidden in busts of
Napoleon III himself. As Graham Robb reports in his biog-

raphy of Hugo, friends would arrive on the island with baggy trousers and would leave hoarding many copies.

One night on the island a woman named Delphine de Girardin arrived at the Hugo house bearing a three-legged table that she had found in a toy shop. She brought it along to introduce Hugo and his family to the world of seances. The method she showed them was known as table turning, the idea being that the three-legged table would tap the floor every time it was communicating a letter: one tap meant A and 26 taps meant Z.

Though he was sceptical at first, Hugo quickly became a convert and over the next two years would speak to, among others: Abel, Alexander the Great, Aristophanes, Aristotle, Lord Byron, Dante, Galileo, Jesus Christ, Joan of Arc, Moses, Mozart, Plato, Shakespeare, Socrates, Voltaire, Sir Walter

Scott, and a resident of the planet Jupiter called Tyatafia. He also spoke to spirits claiming to be Civilisation, Death, the Finger of Death, Happiness, Inspiration, a comet, the Ocean, the concept of Russia, and the Sea Wind.

He learnt much about life from these spirits (including the supposed fact that reincarnation was real and that Cleopatra had been reincarnated as a worm); he helped them to draw pictures (like the time he channelled the spirit of a comet in outer space, and helped it to draw a picture of itself); he watched as songs were composed in his presence by the greats (Mozart composed music through the table by having one of its legs positioned on a piano keyboard); and Shakespeare dictated a whole comedy to Hugo, working closely on small changes to each line (dictated in French, as Shakespeare had come belatedly to realise in death that it was the superior language).* So far as I can tell, we are yet to see an English language performance of this original Shakespeare/Hugo collaboration.†

Eventually, Hugo was exiled from Jersey, and that is the last we hear of the table.

I wish we knew where that table was, because we have a lot to thank it for. It was one night while Hugo was using the

---

* One book argues that it was Hugo's son who took the dictation as Hugo decided it too much to collaborate with Shakespeare.

† An extract from the Hugo/Shakespeare collaboration: ACT ONE. A starry sky. Serene night. The stars are twinkling. Their twinkling murmurs mysterious words. Suddenly, two of the stars begin to expand in a strange manner and become enormous, as if the audience's opera glasses had been changed into magic telescopes.

table to talk to a spirit claiming to be the concept of Civilisation, that he started expressing frustrations about the writing of his latest novel, which he was considering abandoning. But Civilisation urged him to press on, and Hugo agreed. It's arguable that without that conversation, Hugo would never have finished writing what would eventually go on to be considered his masterpiece: a book called *Les Misérables*.

A SEQUEL TO *THE PILGRIM'S PROGRESS*

Dictated from the other side by: the spirit of John Bunyan
Received on this side by: Alfred Deakin, Australia's second
    prime minister

The Pilgrim's Progress, written by John Bunyan, is often regarded as one of the most important works in theological literature. First published in 1678, it has never been out of print. The pressure to release a worthy sequel must have been great. You can understand why he took 200 years to mull it over. In 1876 Alfred Deakin, who would go on to become arguably the greatest Liberal prime minister Australia has ever known, channelled the spirit of John Bunyan, author of *The Pilgrim's Progress*, and together they spent 49 sessions writing a sequel to the book. When it was published just a year later, the timing couldn't have been better, as it managed to tie in with the bicentenary of the original work.

Deakin entered the world of the occult at a very young age. Showing a great talent for communicating with the spirit world, he'd eventually run schools where he taught the art, as well as invited experts in the field to come and give lectures. I would have loved to have seen them. On one notable occasion the spiritualist Thomas Walker came not to lecture in his own voice, but rather he acted as a vessel for a guest lecturer from the beyond—a sixteenth-century monk called Giordano Bruno, who was burned at the stake for, among other things, claiming that the Virgin Mary was no virgin.

As a talented paranormal investigator, Deakin also travelled across Australia appraising the claims made by the many mediums who fought to be seen as genuine by studying their methods. One lady, Mrs. Paton, received the seal of approval from Deakin when she successfully manifested a wet rock and some seaweed during various seances. He also conducted countless seances at his own home. It was during one of these that Deakin was informed he was going to make a great leader, and so he entered the world of politics.

In his final years Deakin would come to regret the John Bunyan book, and though he couldn't bring himself to destroy his personal copies, he did make sure to scratch away the name of the publisher and anything else that would help identify the origins of the book. It has been suggested that the real reason he didn't destroy them, however, is because he actually quite liked the book. Writing some 20 years after its publication, he said he was surprised to find it was still a great read.

BEYOND DELICIOUS: THE GHOST WHISPERER'S COOKBOOK: MORE THAN 100 RECIPES FROM THE DEARLY DEPARTED

Dictated from the other side by: the spirits of a hundred
dead people

Received on this side by: Mary Ann Winkowski

Beyond Delicious: The Ghost Whisperer's Cookbook: More than 100 Recipes from the Dearly Departed, written by Mary Ann Winkowski, is a groundbreaking book that mixes ghost-hunting with gastronomy—each chapter concludes with a ghost recommending a dish. For example, the recipe for "Mrs. White's Clear Consommé" came from an incident when Winkowski was called in to help a woman called Ruth Johnson, who complained about a poltergeist in her house after she noticed that the lights in the kitchen were blowing out and the radio kept going weird.

One night Johnson saw a shadow outside her bedroom in the hall. Having lived there for 25 years, she knew some new energy must have entered the house, so she contacted Winkowski. When Winkowski arrived at the house it didn't take long to work out what the problem was: it was a pissed-off ghost called Mrs. White. When Winkowski enquired why she was there, Mrs. White explained, "She's using my pot wrong."

A while back, Johnson had been browsing in a second-hand store when she spotted a pot that looked perfect to make her apple sauce in. What she didn't know was that the pot was haunted, and when she brought the pot home she brought Mrs. White along with it. "Ask her," continued

Mrs. White, "isn't her apple sauce always burning?" It turned out that this was absolutely true. Mrs. White explained that the pot was made for consommé, not fruit, and she was furious to see it misused in this way. Hence the haunting.

Johnson became rather excited by this revelation, as she had always wanted to make a soup broth—and asked if the ghost of Mrs. White would be up for handing over the recipe? A compromise was reached with the assurance that she'd call it consommé and not broth, and would always clean the pot. And so the recipe was handed over, and reprinted in *Beyond Delicious*.

It turns out Winkowski is a big deal in the world of ghost-hunting. Her method for getting ghosts to move on is by creating a "white light." The "white light," explains Winkowski, is a portal that allows ghosts to travel from this realm into the spiritual one. According to an interview she did with Reuters, the white light appears at funerals:

Everybody attends their funeral to check out who is there, what they are wearing, and most people at the cemetery will talk into the white light and cross over . . . but you have free will and if you don't want to go into that white light then you don't have to. Suicides, people who were murdered, teenagers, and people with young children often choose not to. But that white light will go 24 to 72 hours after the funeral. If you don't go into it, then it disappears and you are stuck. These are the spirits I see and talk to and in the end they cause problems.

If a ghost changes their mind, they can get access to the white light again by attending someone else's funeral. Or they can visit Winkowski, who can generate a white light herself.

Winkowski has written numerous other books, and was also the inspiration for a TV drama, *Ghost Whisperer*, starring Jennifer Love Hewitt. In each episode Love Hewitt's character, who is based on Winkowski, travels to a new house to help deal with a ghost. This is something Winkowski did for Love Hewitt in the real world too.

When Love Hewitt met Winkowski for the first time at Love Hewitt's house, she asked Winkowski if there were any ghosts present. Yes, said Winkowski, there are two. After having a discussion with the first one, Winkowski was able to identify it as the ghost of the ex-wife of Lon Chaney Jr. (an actor who appeared in many horror movies in the 1940s).

The second ghost was more sinister. It turned out that he was an obsessive fan of Love Hewitt's when he was alive, but hadn't got round to stalking her until after he died. Now, he told Winkowski, he was able to watch her all day long, including every time she took a shower. Winkowski told him off for doing so, and sent the "stalker-ghost" into a white light, forcing his exit from the house.

When Winkowski and Love Hewitt met again the next day, the latter explained that she had called some old friends to enquire about the man, and one of them recognised the description and said that when his house was cleaned up after his death, there was a wall in the house entirely covered in photos of Love Hewitt.

THE FINAL CHAPTERS OF *THE MYSTERY OF EDWIN DROOD*

Dictated from the other side by: the spirit of Charles
 Dickens

Dictated from the other side to: T. P. James

At the time of his death, on June 9, 1870, Charles Dickens was still working on his fifteenth novel, *The Mystery of Edwin Drood*. As was tradition at the time, Dickens was publishing the book in instalments as he wrote it, but had only produced half the story when he died, leaving behind no notes or any ideas to solve the novel's main mystery, which was the disappearance and probable murder of its main character.

However, just over three years after Dickens' death, the solution to the story was finally published thanks to the work of spiritualist T. P. James, who channelled Dickens to finish it. The book includes the original unfinished novel by the author, but where the original book ends, the new writing takes over and completes the story.

Titled *Part Second of the Mystery of Edwin Drood. By the Spirit Pen of Charles Dickens, through a medium*, the book also included a preface by Dickens (again, penned from the other side).

James writes at the end of his preface that he and Dickens have already completed work on the first chapter of their next novel, titled *The Life and Adventures of Bockley Wickleheap*. Sadly, this book never materialised.

Many in the spiritual world were sceptical that James had contacted Dickens to write this book, including Arthur Conan Doyle, who claimed to have proof that James was not telling the truth, having personally asked the spirit of Dickens himself at a seance. The spirit of Dickens told Doyle that he hadn't. However, the spirit of Dickens suggested that James wasn't making it all up, and that he had channelled another spirit who had pranked him by posing as Dickens.

CHAPTER 6
OH, THE PLACES YOU'LL GO . . . NEXT
THE THEORY OF LAST WORDS

On July 13, 1930, over 10,000 people crammed into London's Royal Albert Hall in anticipation of seeing the great Sir Arthur Conan Doyle deliver a message. It wasn't the first time Doyle had been engaged in one form or another at the venue—in 1901 he had been there as a judge for the world's first-ever bodybuilding contest, then in 1919 he had appeared again for the Spiritualists' National Union. This time, though, was a bit special, and many were sceptical that he'd show up. It was his memorial after all. Sir Arthur Conan Doyle had died six days earlier.

Doyle's funeral itself had already taken place two days before, although it wasn't so much a funeral as a celebratory garden party. Doyle passed away in his garden, clutching a flower and looking into his wife's eyes. His last words were, "you are wonderful." The Doyle family didn't really get too upset by the concept of death, because they all believed the spirit carried on regardless. Doyle's son's belief in the afterlife

was so great that he said his father might as well have moved to Australia. And so they held the funeral in the grounds of their home at Windlesham, with everyone dressed in everyday clothes.

On the day of his Albert Hall memorial, facing the vast crowd in attendance was a line of seats on the stage. All were filled but one. On it sat a placard inscribed with the words "Sir Arthur Conan Doyle." Sitting next to this empty chair was Doyle's wife, as well as an assortment of other family members. Finally, there was clairvoyant extraordinaire Mrs. Estelle Roberts and the chairman of the Spiritual Society, the suitably named George Craze.

Doyle was a big player in the world of spiritualism. When Agatha Christie went missing, the chief constable of Surrey approached him for help. Rather than employing the deductive skills that saw him solving numerous real-life crimes,

Doyle instead decided to procure one of Christie's gloves, which he presented to Horace Leaf and asked him to help in the hunt. Leaf practised psychometry, the art of eliciting information from physical objects. Leaf, who was given the glove, without a name, said that Agatha was quite safe and that they'd all hear from her on Wednesday. This surprisingly turned out to be correct. She had checked into a hydropathic hotel in Harrogate and was spending her evenings dancing to a band called The Happy Hydro Boys.

As the memorial at the Albert Hall began, George Craze took to the stage to announce:

> This evening we are going to make a very daring experiment with the courage implanted in us by our late leader. We have with us a spirit sensitive who is going to try and give impressions from this platform. One reason why we hesitate to do it in such a colossal meeting as this is that it's a terrific strain on the sensitive. In an assembly of ten thousand people a tremendous force is centred upon the medium. Tonight, Mrs. Roberts will try to describe some particular friends, but it will be the first time this has been attempted in such a tremendous gathering. You can help with your vibrations as you sing the next hymn, "Open My Eyes."

A contemporary review, published in *Time* magazine, stated: "Mrs. Estelle Roberts, clairvoyant, took the stage. She declared five spirits were 'pushing' her. She cried out their messages. Persons in the audience confirmed their validity."

As Mrs. Roberts continued to contact members of the audience's dead friends and relatives, the crowd grew restless. Many started to leave the venue, while others jeered and heckled. Sensing the crowd turning against her, she focused her attention towards the chair left empty for the great author. "He is here," she yelled, while starting to make movements that gave the impression that someone was approaching, "he is wearing evening clothes." Mrs. Roberts then leant her head to one side, to indicate she was listening to an important message. Audience members reported that they saw her head jerk back with the message she had been given, and then watched as she dashed over to Doyle's widow to deliver the news. "Sir Arthur told me that one of you went into the hut this morning. Is that correct?" she asked. Yes, confirmed the shocked Lady Doyle. "The message is this," continued Mrs. Roberts. " 'Tell Mary . . .' " And that is all we know, for at this precise moment—and for some inexplicable reason—the organist of the Royal Albert Hall began to play, drowning out any chance of hearing what followed.

What did Mrs. Roberts say that night? We don't know. But whatever it was, Lady Doyle would later claim:

I am perfectly convinced . . . that the message is from my husband. I am as sure of the fact that he has been here with us as I am sure that I am speaking to you. It is a happy message, one that is cheering and encouraging. It is precious and sacred. You will understand that it was secret to me.

WHAT HAPPENS TO US WHEN WE DIE?

No one knows what happens to us when we leave this planet. It's terrifying to think we cease to exist entirely. That is why I take comfort in stories like Conan Doyle's supposed post-death adventure. I personally don't believe that there is anything beyond this life (a belief I hope to shake off before I die). But I do hear some stories that make me wonder.

Sam Kinison, America's original 80s rock 'n' roll stand-up comedian, was high. He usually was. It was his thing—at least for the majority of his life. He could write jokes while high, he could navigate business meetings while high, he could even drive cars while high—which is exactly what he was doing on the night of April 10, 1992, as he made his way to a small town in Nevada where he was booked to perform stand-up to a sold-out crowd, presumably while high. Unfortunately, not everyone was as good as Sam under the influence, and en route a truck driven by a drunken 17-year-old veered into Kinison's lane and smashed head-on into his car.

Watching the collision from behind was Kinison's brother Bill and his support act, Carl LaBove, who were tailing him in a van. They immediately pulled over and rushed to Sam, whom they found lying between the front seats. His head had been cut up from smashing into the windscreen, but other than that there were no obvious injuries. What they couldn't see was the internal damage he had suffered, including a dislocated cervical spine and some torn blood vessels in his abdominal cavity. Sam's wife, travelling in the front seat next to him, was unconscious, but she had remained in her seat and would later make a full recovery at the local hospital.

Carl pulled Sam from the car and laid him down in his arms. "I don't want to die yet," said Sam, over and over, looking up at him. "I don't want to die." "You're not dying," replied Carl, but Sam wasn't listening. It quickly dawned on Carl that Sam wasn't talking to him. He was talking to someone else, someone not there, who appeared to be just over Carl's shoulder. "I don't want to die," continued Sam. Finally, he paused, as if listening to an explanation, then he asked, "But why?" Another pause followed. Whatever reply came to that question must have given Sam comfort, as Carl saw his face turn into a smile and, finally, with a tone of excitement in his voice, he said, "OK . . . OK . . . OK . . ." then died, right there, in Carl's arms.

WHO WAS SAM TALKING TO?

I'm fascinated by last words. Not the classic ones you read about where someone says something poignant or quick-witted, but rather the kind that suggest something more mystical, giving a glimpse and an insight into another realm.*

---

* Though I must admit I do have a soft spot for Roald Dahl's parting words. As he lay in his hospital bed, surrounded by family, Dahl looked around the room and said, "It's just that I will miss you all so much." Then he passed away. At least that's how it was supposed to happen. Unfortunately, as the family sat silently waiting for him to die, the nurse decided to make his passing a little easier with a hit of morphine, pricking him with a needle; Dahl suddenly regained consciousness, yelled "Oww, fuck!" then died.

When John Lennon's Auntie Mimi died, it was reported that her last words came after she looked into the distance and said, "Hello, John." What did she see?

One suggestion is that what both Kinison and Auntie Mimi were seeing was what has been described as a phenomenon known as the "third man." The third man is the idea that in moments of great trauma, a spirit, an entity, a *presence* of some sort will arrive to provide comfort. The term was coined by T. S. Eliot, from a line in his poem *The Waste Land*.

Eliot wrote the line, misremembering the number "four" as "three," after reading about Ernest Shackleton's experience as detailed in his 1919 diary, published as *South*, in which the explorer wrote: "During that long and racking march of thirty-six hours over the unnamed mountains and glaciers of South Georgia, it seemed to me often that we were four, not three."

According to psychologist Peter Suedfeld, the phenomenon tends to usually occur to "mentally healthy people," so it cannot be classified as a psychotic episode, and believes it might be an adaptive response of the brain. The experience tends to occur in explorers—everyone from astronauts to divers—but seems to be most prevalent in mountaineers, who believe in the presence of these visiting entities and actively engage with them. In 1933, the British explorer and climber Frank Smythe was so convinced on the upper slopes of Mount Everest that he had been joined by someone else that when he pulled out some Kendal mint cake from his pocket for a quick bite to eat, he snapped it in half to offer a piece to the other person.

One mountaineer who has written widely about the experience is Peter Hillary, son of Sir Edmund, who is an accomplished explorer himself having scaled Everest and reached both Poles. Hillary saw these extra entities on his expedition to the Antarctic, later writing, "Oh, yes. They're still out there. I see them come and go . . . And I still don't know what to do." On one trip, Hillary claims that in a moment of total isolation, his mother, who had died in a plane crash in 1975, appeared beside him. She joined him numerous times on that trip, as did some other old faces— including two explorer friends who were dead. "It was like she'd come out there to keep me company. It was like she was really there. Right there. In a way that was almost scary. Yet it seemed natural as anything to walk along talking to her."

Hillary didn't think it was genuinely his mother, but at the same time he did believe she was there, if only via a projection of the mind. The phenomenon is discussed in great detail in the book *The Third Man Factor* by Canadian author John Geiger, who claims that it's not just experienced by explorers but has been reported by many other people, such as those rushing out of the Twin Towers on 9/11. Geiger points out that it's a sort of positive hallucination that actively gives us support. It's as if our brain has worked out that in times of extreme peril we need someone beside us, so we very literally conjure up an imaginary friend to help us survive, or rather comfortingly, see us through to the end.

★   ★   ★

The surgeon, Joseph Henry Green.

I do hope I get a visit from a friendly ghost as I breathe my final breath, even if it is only one manifested by my brain. I wonder who I'll see? For now though, here are my last words on last words. I believe I have found the greatest last words, or rather, last word, ever spoken. It was uttered on December 13, 1863, by the surgeon Joseph Henry Green. I believe Green achieved something wholly original with his last word. He became the first person in history to pronounce themselves dead.

As he lay dying in his bed, Green placed his fingers on his wrist, monitoring his slowing pulse. As the last throb came and went, Green said "Stopped," and then promptly died.

CHAPTER 7
NOVAK DJOKOVIC AND THE POWER OF ALIEN PYRAMID ENERGY
THE THEORY OF SUPERNATURAL DOPING

You probably haven't ever heard of the small city of Visoko in Bosnia. I certainly hadn't until I started writing this book. For a long time it was a place that rarely popped up in international news. And even when it did, it usually only concerned one local resident, Adnan Nević, who became notable for being recognised by the United Nations as Earth's official sixth-billionth human.* Otherwise, it never really made much of a dent in global news coverage. Fortunes changed for the city in 2020, however, when the then world No. 1–ranked tennis player, Novak Djokovic, started making pilgrimages there so he could charge up on the cosmic energy being emitted by the local ancient pyramids built by an advanced lost

---

* Two days after Adnan was born, Kofi Annan, the UN's then Secretary-General, was there personally to hold him aloft for the cameras. In a 2011 article Adnan said that his title was a bit of a hindrance and that he had not heard anything from the UN since. Fortunately, he has found someone to share his grievances with, having friended the "fifth-billionth human" on Facebook. Feeling similarly abandoned by the UN, the two of them have been known to bitch about the UN to each other in private messages.

Champion tennis player Novak Djokovic collecting mystical energy from a 12,000-year-old Bosnian pyramid.

civilisation. "There is truly a miraculous energy here," Djokovic told reporters. "If there is a paradise on Earth, then it's here."

The pyramids were first recognised as ancient artefacts by Bosnian-American businessman Semir Osmanagić when he dropped in on Visoko in 2005. He couldn't help noticing the peculiarly shaped hill standing over the city—it looked suspiciously "pyramid-y" to him and he wondered whether it might be artificial. When he checked the hill's orientation against a compass, he concluded that the hill was perfectly aligned to the cardinal points, each flank facing north, south, east, and west. Surely that couldn't be a coincidence, he thought.

A year later he published his book *Bosnian Valley of the Pyramids*, in which he put forward his belief that these grass-covered hills were in fact the oldest man-made structures on Earth, dating them to 12,000 years ago.* This wasn't his first book to make bold claims. As well as being a successful businessman manufacturing steel parts in Houston, Osmanagić had a side career as a modern-day pseudo-archaeological author. In his 2005 book *The World of the Maya* he claimed that Mayan hieroglyphics indicate that their ancestors weren't from the planet Earth, but came from the Pleiades, a cluster of stars 444 light years away. The Pleadians are a speculated species of alien that conspiracy theorists believe periodically visit our planet. They're said to be humanoid in looks, with a lifespan of a thousand years. According to Osmanagić, when they arrived here they created an advanced civilisation in Atlantis.†

★   ★   ★

I should mention that despite now being called the "Bosnian Pyramids," and being located in the "Valley of the Pyramids," archaeologists and geologists from all over the world would very much like you to know that they're absolutely not that.

---

* Or possibly 29,000 years ago. Or 35,000. Osmanagić keeps changing the numbers. Regardless, any of these times in the past would have been a curious period in which to build pyramids, as most of Europe was going through an ice age and was under ice. Although an advanced ancient civilisation with superior technology could, arguably, overcome that little problem.

† In another book—simply titled *History*—Osmanagić claimed that Hitler escaped Germany and moved to an underground base in Antarctica.

The unusual geology of these hills is a very natural phenomenon known as "flatirons," which is when land forms in a triangular-sloping shape due to erosion-resistant layers of rock lying on top of softer strata. Similar hills are found all over the world.

Fortunately for Osmanagić, many high-ranking officials have ignored the science, including two Bosnian presidents, one of whom, Sulejman Tihić, said of it: "One does not need to be a big expert to see that those are the remains of three pyramids." The city's council itself even got on board by investing €250,000 into tourism off the back of the interest in the "pyramids."

Since coming up with his initial hypothesis, Osmanagić, often referred to by locals as the "Pharaoh," has led numer-

Semir Osmanagić and the Bosnian Pyramids.

ous archaeological digs on the site, discovering along the way: a total of five pyramids; evidence of artificial walls built by an ancient civilisation; a cosmic Wi-Fi system that can send messages across the galaxy in an instant; and miles of underground passages previously thought to have been built for mining. Nearly 20 years on, however, he's yet to find any evidence that satisfies the more conventional archaeologists who question his claims regarding the hill's origins.

Academic dismissal doesn't appear to bother Osmanagić, nor does it seem to worry the thousands of visitors who have been flocking to his great "find" since 2005. The phenomenon of the Bosnian "pyramids" has boosted the tourism of the city to such an extent that it's now building multi-storey hotel complexes to accommodate the thousands of people who flock there every day.* Local businesses jumped on board too, with restaurants serving food on pyramid-shaped plates and street vendors selling everything from pyramid-themed T-shirts to pyramidal piggy banks for a while.

Then, in 2020, the pyramids received their greatest boost yet when one of the greatest tennis players of all time, Novak Djokovic, started visiting the town and meditating inside the tunnel complex near the pyramids.

---

* Around 300,000 tourists were said to have visited the pyramids by 2007.

DINNER WITH DJOKOVIC

Positive energy is very important to Djokovic, and something he directs to many areas of his life. Indeed, in his rollercoaster of a book *Serve to Win: The 14-Day Gluten-free Plan for Physical and Mental Excellence*, he shares these many beliefs with the reader, including the fact that he believes that conversation is very influential on the food we eat. According to Djokovic, any negative conversation around broccoli, for example, might result in it being stripped of its nutrients as well as its taste. As a result, Djokovic won't allow any negative energy to get near his dinner table—this means a ban on texting and emailing, and watching television. In his book Djokovic explains: "I believe that if you are eating with some kind of fear or worry or anger, the taste of the food and the energy you get from it won't be as powerful . . . What you give is what you get." And although positive chat is allowed, there isn't much of that either, as Djokovic basically spends much of the meal involved in mental dialogue with his food. After each bite, he places the fork back down on the table and becomes entirely focused on the chewing. He wants to instruct the food where it needs to go so it can help in the healing of any wounds he may have acquired during recent tennis matches. "As I chew, the process of digestion is already starting. The enzymes in my saliva mix with the food, so that when it hits my stomach it's a fully formed piece of 'information.'"

Djokovic's belief that food and drink respond to our conversations comes from when he witnessed some food and drinks transformed from being in a "toxic" state to becoming

edible and drinkable again, simply by someone beaming happy thoughts at them. In an online chat with the wellness guru Chervin Jafarieh, Djokovic explained that "scientists have proven that molecules in the water react to our emotions, to what is being said."

Though he doesn't specify exactly which experiment demonstrated this, what Djokovic might possibly be referring to is a researcher, who isn't named, showing how water would react if you subjected each glass to positive and negative emotions. In the experiment, each glass contained water from the same source. The researcher projected nothing but anger, fear, and hostility to the first glass, while to the other he projected only love and happiness. After a few days, the glass experiencing all of the negative energy turned slightly green, with Djokovic describing it as looking as if algae had started growing in it. The other glass, which received all the positive comments, remained crystal clear.

"Sounds crazy, right? I know," wrote Djokovic in *Serve to Win*. "But to me, that test is proof that every single thing in the world shares the same kind of energy—people, animals, the elements, everything."

Djokovic's interest in experimenting with alternative ways of consuming his food properly began when he was contacted by Dr. Igor Četojević, after Djokovic's game collapsed at the 2010 Australian Open. When Četojević heard that asthma was being given as the reason for the collapse, he decided to get in contact with the tennis star, as he believed it was something more.

Četojević was convinced the tennis player had an undiagnosed gluten intolerance, and decided to diagnose him using a method employed by natural healers called "kinesiological arm testing," which requires patients to hold their arm straight out in front of them while a second person attempts to push it down. The exercise is then repeated, only this time the kinesiologist introduces another element to see how it affects the resistance of the outstretched arm. In Djokovic's case, a slice of bread was held against the tennis champ's stomach. When Četojević depressed Djokovic's arm, Djokovic was noticeably weaker than when there was no bread present. Djokovic accepted this as definitive proof of serious gluten intolerance.*

---

* This test had a huge influence on Djokovic's thinking, so much so that it has become his party trick. If you want to give it a go, you just need to replace the slice of bread with a mobile phone. According to Djokovic, the radiation from the phone will influence the power of the human body and weaken the arm being held out in front. He closes this party piece by

One of the odd consequences of the 2020 pandemic is that it has forced some people's previously private beliefs into the open. In the case of Djokovic, the world watched as he had a stand-off with the Australian authorities over whether or not he'd be allowed to compete in the Australian Open owing to the fact that he was unvaccinated.

Many have put his unorthodox interests and behaviour down to his extraordinarily traumatic childhood in war-torn Serbia. It's been suggested his alternative views are precisely what he needs in order to help him escape the trauma of his early years. "Two and a half months, every single day and night, bombs coming into the city. We saw planes flying over our heads, and literally rockets and bombs landing half a mile away," he told CNN.

These were the conditions under which the future champion trained. Every day, as the bombs came raining down, Djokovic would be outside, training for up to five hours every day. His coach, former tennis pro Jelena Genčić, who had previously coached tennis champion Monica Seles, took on Djokovic aged six, and would select each day's location for tennis practice by getting him to travel to wherever the most recent bombing raid had occurred, assuming it to now be safe, as NATO planes probably wouldn't hit the same place again so soon. When he wasn't in bombed-out swimming pools, he'd be up in the Serbian mountains, hitting balls while surrounded by wolves. "I spent a lot of time with

saying that, for obvious reasons, you should think twice about keeping your phone in your trouser pocket.

wolves," writes Djokovic. "This is wolf energy. I'm not kidding."

Once you start looking at Djokovic in this context, you start to notice there is no end to his interesting views. There's his choice of coaching staff: for a while his team included the "guru" Pepe Imaz, a former tennis player turned coach, who runs a tennis school with a philosophy of preaching "love and peace," as well as introducing meditation and "very long hugs" into the routines of players. There's also Djokovic's belief in telepathy and telekinesis, which sits alongside the aforementioned interest in kinesiology, Bosnian pyramids, and *not* talking rudely around his food.

Djokovic is flatout batshit, but he's possibly going to end his tennis career as the greatest player to ever play the game. And he isn't unique in holding odd beliefs. The history of tennis is littered with players who have made it to the top despite their wild ideas. Like the 1950 US Open champion Tappy Larsen, who used to get mid-match coaching tips from an invisible eagle sitting on his shoulder; or Serena Williams, who will only wear one pair of socks throughout an entire tennis tournament; or Rafael Nadal, who won't stand on any of the lines on the court between points. Odd beliefs have been practised in the background of sports for centuries. They're just usually hidden away from us. Though sometimes, very occasionally, we're accidentally given a glimpse of them . . .

THE PSYCHIC WORLD OF THE LOS ANGELES DODGERS

In 2010 it was revealed that for five years, the Los Angeles Dodgers baseball team were paying a Russian scientist to beam positive thoughts to the team players from 3,000 miles away during their games. Vladimir Shpunt, part physicist, healer, and psychic, was secretly hired by the team's owners and put on the payroll between 2005 and 2010.

Shpunt first discovered he could transmit powerful energy through his hands and thoughts back in the 1970s, when living in Russia.

Shpunt calculated that his hands were capable of transmitting 10–15 per cent more energy than an average person's, and so he decided to make a career of it and started treating patients.

In 1998 Shpunt immigrated to the United States, where he would eventually be introduced to Jamie and Frank McCourt, a married couple who were joint owners of the LA Dodgers. The McCourts apparently became aware of Shpunt and his healing powers after Jamie began to suffer from an eye infection that was threatening to send her blind. Taking him on as her healer, Jamie McCourt was treated both in person and from a distance (Shpunt beaming the healing at her through the air) and eventually her eye improved and she retained her vision. Impressed by his powers, the McCourts wondered if he might be able to help use his powers to boost the team's abilities. They decided to give it a go.

Shpunt only ever attended one baseball game the entire time he was employed, preferring instead to beam his positive energy from his home in Boston while watching the players on TV. He'd spend four hours a day focusing his positive thoughts on the team, often with his eyes closed as if meditating. His promise was not that he could make them win, but that he could increase each player's ability, albeit by only up to a maximum of 15 per cent.*

In 2008, when the team made it to the play-offs for the first time in five years, emails went around praising Shpunt, acknowledging the power of his "V Energy." Shpunt's involvement with the team was never publicised, and the only reason we ever found out about it is thanks to a nasty divorce. When Jamie and Frank McCourt dissolved their marriage, as part of the court proceedings all of their financial records concerning the team were released. These showed Shpunt to be the recipient of hundreds of thousands of dollars. The couple had kept Shpunt's role in the team so secret that even top-level Dodgers staff remained unaware of the arrangement.

Shpunt no longer works for the Dodgers, but has hinted that he's taken on individual professional clients. Who these

---

* Interestingly, this wasn't the first time that the Dodgers were involved with these sort of bizarre mind games. In 1964 counter-culture guru and San Francisco Giants fan Michael Murphy tried to put a voodoo curse on the Dodgers during a home game. As reported in the book *The Men on Magic Carpets*, Murphy talked 200 spectators in the crowd into helping him curse the Dodgers by using their hands to form the shape of the devil's horns. He was sure the curse would succeed, having spent years practising—even claiming to have once successfully forced a pitcher to keel over using his mental powers. Whether the curse was effective or not it's impossible to know, but the Giants won that day.

players are remains to be seen, but the next time you watch any sporting match, do make sure to keep an eye out for any player suddenly giving it an extra 10–15 per cent—they may be juiced up on V Energy.

LEICESTER CITY'S ODDS

The Los Angeles Dodgers aren't unique in their attempts to use mental energy to boost their players' powers. The English football team Leicester City also once utilised the power of the mind.

When Leicester City FC kicked off the 2015/16 football season, the chances of them winning the Premier League were so low that both Ladbrokes and William Hill betting agencies offered 5,000–1 odds on the team. This would end up costing both betting agencies £5 million.

It was an extraordinary season, and while many praised the team's captain, Jamie Vardy, and the coaching staff for all the success, others have wondered if their unprecedented Premier League victory was in fact down to the efforts and influence of a bunch of praying monks. Much like the LA Dodgers, Leicester City's owner, the Thai billionaire Vichai Srivaddhanaprabha, decided to engage outside energies to help boost his team to victory. Whenever there was an important match, Srivaddhanaprabha would fly a set of Buddhist monks into Leicester so they could bless the team's stadium goalposts, changing rooms, and pitch.

The monks would meet the players and bless them before the matches. According to an interview with the *Mirror* given by Vardy, "They dip the sticks in the holy water and then lash us on our legs and feet. It's not too hard, it's just that you're literally having a shower, there's that much water going everywhere. It's all over your gear you've just hung up."

The monks would then spend the match in deep meditation in a room specifically designed for them in the stadium, gauging how the game was going from the noises being made by the fans.

It was the most remarkable season in modern football when, despite the odds, Leicester won the Premier League. Did the monks somehow play a part in it? Can the very act of beaming thoughts at a game affect the outcome?*

THE MENTAL POWER OF SPORTS FANS

One curious thing many sports fans have reported on is their own personal worry that they can affect the outcome of a match, simply by the way they watch it.

One friend, who's entirely secular and has no truck with the paranormal, told me that he was going to watch all of England's football matches at the 2020 Euros in his house because the team looked to be making their way to the tournament's final. Having watched all the early Euro matches in his house, he was worried that if he moved locations, it would jinx England's chances. When I pointed out that this was su-

---

* Sadly, we won't get to see the continued experiments of Vichai Srivaddhanaprabha. In 2018, after watching a night match at Leicester's home stadium, the helicopter he left in crashed soon after taking off. There were no survivors.

perstitious, he quickly switched tack and said that actually the real reason he was staying at home was because it was safer than going to a pub during a pandemic. This was true, of course. But I think my friend was a bit unnerved to discover that despite all his rationalism, somewhere within him he held the belief that his actions were going to affect the outcome of the game.

Someone who certainly believed he had an influence on games was the great American crooner Bing Crosby. When Crosby's team* the Pittsburgh Pirates made it to Game 7 in baseball's 1960 World Series against the New York Yankees, Crosby became so worried he'd jinx their chances of winning the championships if he watched the game that he flew out of the country to Paris, just so it would be impossible to accidentally catch a glimpse of it on TV. The game went on to be known as "the greatest game ever played," with the Pirates securing the win. Crosby is yet to receive credit for it.

Superstition may have stopped Crosby from watching the match live, but the world of baseball owes a debt of gratitude to his odd belief. As was accepted practice at the time, the tapes of the games were recorded over and for 50 years after it was played, "the greatest game ever" could only be re-lived through the few surviving short videos and audio clips, as well as photographs. Then, in 2010, it was reported that a pristine copy of the full match had been discovered. It was sitting in Crosby's old wine cellar. Though he refused to watch the match live, Crosby did plan on watching it at a

---

* Literally—he was a co-owner.

later date, and so while he sat in a hotel room halfway across the world desperately avoiding it, he arranged for a film crew to be installed in his house while he was gone, to film the game directly off the television using kinescope. Superstition saved "the greatest game ever played."

IT'S ALL IN THE HEAD

"Getting into the head" of an opponent is vital in many major sports—Premier League football, US baseball—anything that has a competitive edge. And tennis is perhaps the most psychological sport of all. Mind games are effectively going on in the background continuously, although you may not notice it. The number of times a tennis player bounces a ball before a serve, for instance, or the deliberate loudness of a "grunt" as a player hits the ball—it's all done to get inside the opponent's head and provide an additional edge.

One player who really got inside the head of a rival was Andre Agassi, who made his opponent Boris Becker believe that he was using the powers of telepathy to read his mind and win the matches. Or at least he seemed to be.

It was all to do with Becker's serve. It was impenetrable, unlike anything Agassi—the greatest returner of serve in the game at the time—had ever seen. He just couldn't work out how to reach it. For three straight matches Becker's unreadable serve wiped the floor with the American. Growing ever more frustrated, Agassi eventually collected videotapes of Becker and began watching his serve over and over again. Undoubtedly, every other coach and player in the game was doing the exact same thing: looking for any patterns, for any giveaway. And then Agassi noticed something, a literal game-changer. He tested his theory on the court and it worked. He had cracked Becker's serve and before long it was Becker who was now stumped. Agassi appeared to know where the serve was going to go before he even hit the ball. How? It was as if Agassi had extrasensory powers.

It wasn't until years later, after both men had retired from the sport, that Agassi would tell Becker how he'd done it. He wasn't reading Becker's mind at all; he was reading his tongue. As Agassi sat at home watching those videos of Becker serving, he noticed that just before the ball was released, Becker would slightly pop his tongue out of his mouth. If his tongue stayed straight, it meant the ball was

Boris Becker, about to send a ball to the corner of the service box.

going down the middle; and if it slid to the left, then the serve would be to the corner of the service box.

Once he discovered this, Agassi's biggest challenge was to avoid Becker spotting what he was doing. "I had to resist the temptation of reading his serve for the majority of the match and choose the moment when I was gonna use that information on a given point to execute a shot that would allow me to break the match open," he told a sport channel. Agassi, with his new superpower, went on to win 10 of their next 11 matches. Becker nearly fell off his chair when Agassi told him this, because for years it had completely stumped him. As he'd told his wife at the time, "It's like he reads my mind."

SHOULD PYRAMID ENERGY BE CLASSIFIED AS A DOPING OFFENCE IN SPORT?

Both Boris Becker and Andre Agassi have at different times served as Novak Djokovic's coach, and no doubt were both glued to the TV on the July 10, 2022, as Djokovic secured his twenty-first grand slam title, defeating Australia's Nick Kyrgios in the Wimbledon men's singles final.

Just a few days after his win, Djokovic left London and hopped on a plane bound for Bosnia so he could once again return to the city of Visoko and recharge his batteries on cosmic energy. Only this time, the trip was to be even more special. Fifteen months previously, Djokovic and Semir Osmanagić had hatched a plan to create a space that would allow for Djokovic, and other local tennis players, to truly take advantage of the pyramid's super-strength giving powers, by building two tennis courts near to the base of the great giant pyramids. Now players would be able to maximize on the mystical energies being emitted from the "ancient structures."

I can't wait to see what these grounds produce. Will we soon see the game of tennis being dominated by a new superior breed of super-strength mutant tennis player, juiced up on cosmic pyramid-power?

"The first step has been taken," Djokovic told reporters. "This is only the beginning."

CHAPTER 8
THE SOFT ROCK
THE THEORY OF IMPOSSIBILITIES

Many years ago a friend of mine called Eric was at a festival in Europe when one evening, after getting particularly drunk, he separated from his group of campers and disappeared off on his own, not to be seen again until the next morning. On his return to the camp he explained to his friends that he'd made an incredible discovery.

According to his account, after hours of wandering around, Eric found himself a nice tree to fall asleep under. It was there, as he looked around for a makeshift pillow to rest his head, that he spotted it.

"It was a soft rock," he told his friends.

"A what?" they replied.

"Yeah, man, it was the softest rock ever. It made the perfect pillow."

No one believed him, but all day long Eric kept insisting that he wasn't crazy: he had discovered a soft rock.

Many of us have a "soft rock," something that we insist

happened to us but cannot prove—something unbelievable, something utterly impossible, yet something that seemed so real at the time that it has become a truth to us. As we've seen so far in this book, for Fenella it was the Virgin Mary appearing at the end of her bed; for Kary Mullis it was his glowing raccoon; for Tu Youyou, the sense of destiny; for Wolfgang Pauli, his inexplicable ability to destroy equipment without touching it; and for Paul McCartney, it was the return of his best friend. Perhaps you have one too?

Many of us have experienced something impossible that absolutely happened to us. Something that doesn't fit into our belief system, is out of whack with the rest of our worldview, but something nonetheless that we can't deny. If you don't have a soft rock yourself, you most certainly will have friends that do.

My friend, the author David Bramwell, has a soft rock. In 1976, when David was eight years old, living in the town of Doncaster, his family took a day trip to Ladybower reservoir in Derbyshire. "The reservoir was built between 1935 and 1943. And to build it two villages had to be drowned. So these villages were abandoned in 1943," David told me. Everything was reduced to rubble, all except for Derwent church. "They kept the church steeple, I don't know why. It might have been out of superstition or respect, but the steeple remains, while everything else was sort of bulldozed." As a result whenever there was a drought and the water levels of the reservoir fell sufficiently low the church steeple would re-emerge through the water, and locals would travel to see it. Which is what the Bramwell family was doing on this day.

What a stunning and strange thing to see—a church right in the middle of a huge body of water.

> *I remember the heat, I remember where we parked, I remember walking over the dam, and I can see in my mind's eye right now, that church poking out of the water.*

The sight of this church steeple left a huge impact on Bramwell. Over the years he became obsessed with it, when his band Oddfellows Casino released its fourth album, it was there on the cover. He had art commissioned for his house of it. "It's been my screensaver for many years. I am properly obsessed over this experience because I was sort of haunted by it as a kid."

The church steeple.

Around 15 years ago, Bramwell found himself in a bookshop and discovered a little booklet called *Silent Valley* by Valerie Hallam, a local writer from Derbyshire who lived near Ladybower reservoir. Wanting to read more on the story, he bought the book. "I'd always been curious as to why I couldn't find any colour photographs of the drowned church from 1976 on the internet. Then I read in Valerie's book that the authorities blew the church up in 1947."

Which means there was no church steeple in 1976. "The four of us, me, my sister, Mum and Dad, we all remember seeing the church," insists Bramwell. "If you google [it], the *Yorkshire Post* newspaper, which ran a feature about it a few years ago, shows a picture and it says 'the church steeple, as seen in 1976 by many people.' I've talked about this at festivals, and I've had people come up to me with sort of pained expressions saying 'I saw that too. Are you telling me I didn't see that and the church wasn't there?' So we had a mass hallucination? I don't know what we experienced."

Bramwell continues to question what he experienced that day. "I have a very, very strong visual memory of it. All the senses really, the smells, that heat, the weirdness of it, you know I was eight years old, my sister was 12, we all remember it. We all remember it."

★   ★   ★

Rationalists hate soft rocks. And you can see why—they're evidence-less; they often defy the laws of physics and they're usually the coolest story at the dinner party. I understand their pain: "Trust me, it happened" is great for social events, but it can get dangerous when it's affecting other people's lives.

As another day at the festival wound down and Eric was still excitedly waxing on about his discovery, the group, tired of his fantastical pillow, asked him to show them the rock. And so, tracing back his footsteps from the night before, Eric led his gang to the spot where he'd slept under a tree.

"There," he said, pointing at it. "There's the soft rock."

They all stared in amazement, not because it was a new type of rock, but because they were astonished that Eric hadn't noticed he'd been sleeping all night with his head on a cow pat. Having roasted all day in the blazing Portuguese sun, the pile of dung had hardened, creating a stiff outer shell that yielded to the weight of his head, cradling it like a memory-foam mattress.

"I guess I should have realised at the time," Eric recently reflected. "I mean, I woke up with flies buzzing round my head."

Had Eric not gone back to see what it actually was, he'd no doubt still be talking about the soft rock to this day. I suppose I'm telling you this because while I love impossible stories (this book is full of them), it's important that we also recognise that maybe the impossible *didn't* happen. It doesn't mean that "impossible" things can't happen. It's a weird universe, so they must do. But think again about your soft rock: was it a one-off event lost to time? Or is it something you can re-visit? Is it something that really happened? Or is it, as Eric discovered, just a pile of bullshit?

PART II

THE UNIVERSITY OF REJECTED SCIENCES

Today I'm reading a book about incredible coincidences by an author called Dr. Surprise.* The book is called *Synchronicity*, which is a word that was coined by the Swiss psychiatrist and psychologist Carl Jung to describe "circumstances that appear meaningfully related, yet lack a causal connection." The book argues that coincidences aren't always just a coincidence. Something else is going on. It might almost be as if the universe were winking at you.

I spotted the book while wandering around my favourite London bookshop. Hidden in a backstreet around Leicester Square is a shop that many would rather didn't exist, for inside are thousands of ideas that they'd rather you didn't think about. Watkins Books is London's oldest esoteric bookshop, and a quick look in its windows will help you get your bearings on what awaits you inside. In one I can see books on elves, vampires, and Bigfoot. There's also a book by a druid,

* Dr. Kirby Surprise insists this is his real name. I must admit, of all the things in this book, this is the thing I find hardest to believe. But he insists it's true.

as well as others by a variety of ghosthunters, a UFOlogist and, oddly, the singer Tina Turner.

Dotted around these books are crystals, incense sticks, Tibetan prayer bowls, and a "Synchronicity Oracle" created by the shop's owner, American entrepreneur Etan Ilfeld. In a second window there are no books, but two chairs and a table, where an astrologer named Demian reads Tarot cards for clients; members of the public can subtly snoop on his readings as they walk by. Should you decide to head inside, you'll discover the upper floor to be one of the greatest New Age shops around, but I recommend heading down to the basement first. There you'll see shelves packed with works by the full range of batshit thinkers: everyone from the modern "prophet" Edgar Cayce and the counterculture guru Robert Anton Wilson to the ancient aliens theorist Erich von Däniken, as well as a ton of works by Rudolf Steiner. Much to Fenella's dismay, our bookshelf at home now houses many of these books. Including titles like *Atlantis and the Kingdom of the Neanderthals*, *Homo Serpians*, and *For Nobody's Eyes Only*.

Watkins Books is where all the unaccepted ideas live. Originally set up in 1897 by the occultist John M. Watkins, it has ever since been the go-to place for those who see things differently. "It was referred to at some point as the 'University of Rejected Sciences,'" Etan Ilfeld told me. "It used to have a lot of weird catalogues. John Watkins was a friend of the occultist Madame Blavatsky* and was the bookseller for the Theological Society." When John Watkins died, his son

---

* Madame Blavatsky (1831–91) was an occultist and mystic.

Geoffrey took over the business from his father.* An eccentric bookseller, Geoffrey would often advise customers to *not* buy certain books when he thought them too ignorant to own a copy. And when he found that he needed to stock up on new popular books, he'd often place them on the bottom shelves, or behind the counter, just so he could make it more difficult for customers to get to them. The shop became a meeting ground for those who wanted to think differently. Where, according to the philosopher Alan Watts, "One would expect at any moment to come across a Mahatma or a high Lama visiting England on a secret mission to feel out potential initiates for the Great White Lodge, and who might arrange for you to be whisked off to an unknown sanctuary in Bhutan."

The Rejected Sciences, as one might call this entire field of fringe beliefs, is an aspect of human knowledge that I find fascinating. How is it that so many of us come to experience similar things, yet according to science these experiences mean nothing? Destiny. Luck. Premonition. Cosmic energy. So many millions around the world swear by them, yet there's virtually no proof—by the standards of modern science—that any of them are real. Here are some of the questions people are dedicating their lives to trying to answer . . .

---

* According to Ilfeld, Geoffrey Watkins was possibly hired by Winston Churchill during the Second World War as his personal astrologer. Churchill didn't himself believe in astrology, but many high-ranking Nazis did, and supposedly made many of their strategic decisions based on the conjunction of the planets and stars. Churchill therefore used Watkins to help him understand how and why the Nazis might be making their moves.

CHAPTER 9
ARE AUTHORS STEALING THEIR IDEAS FROM THE FUTURE?
THE THEORY OF PREMONITIONS

"What are you reading?"

It's 9 p.m., Fenella and I are sitting upright in bed, books in our hands, while our two boys Wilf and Ted lie between us snoring.

"It's called *Primal Skin*, by Leona Benkt Rhys," I reply. "It's apparently the first ever Neanderthal–human erotica novel. It's . . ."

"You're reading porn in bed?"

"No, of course not. Well, technically yes, but . . ."

"You're reading porn. In our bed. Next to our sons . . . Again."

Look, I'm a researcher. Part of my job is reading source material for the subjects I'm looking into. That can mean anything from peer-reviewed scientific papers all the way through to, in this case, very niche erotica. And when I do that research, I don't discriminate against where I read the stuff. And that was no different from when I was "caught" in bed reading *Taken by the T-Rex* and then later *Bigfoot's Bitch*.*

"Hun, this book is honestly amazing. It was published in 2000, and it predicted six things about Neanderthals that science at that point didn't yet know about. No one knows who the author is. She's like a porn Nostradamus, she . . ."

Fenella's already asleep.

Not many people know about *Primal Skin*. I only learnt about it thanks to a Neanderthal bone expert who I went out on a date with many years back. The author, whoever she is, anticipated Neanderthal language capabilities some seven years before experts announced them. She predicted that Neanderthals were redheads. She guessed that Neanderthal–human hybrids were possible, ten years before we discovered that modern Europeans and Asians contained 2–4 per cent Neanderthal in their DNA. And the book foresaw the discovery that Neanderthals were good artists, pre-empting finds of pigment, shell palettes, and cave paintings made by the species.

Neanderthal admixture aside, this particular erotic tome is special to me because it belongs to a curious subgenre of lit-

---

* I do, however, regret the time I was looking into the mating habits of hamsters and stumbled upon a website called xhamster.com. I had not heard of this site (I swear). Imagine my excitement: a whole site dedicated to hamster sex! It was just as I excitedly clicked on the link and realised my mistake that Fenella happened to lean over to see what I was looking at, which turned out, much to my surprise, to be a page full of human porn videos. We stared at each other. "This isn't what it looks like," I explained. "I thought it was going to be a website full of hamsters having sex."

erature I like to collect, that being: *books that have eerily predicted future events.*

There are many books in this exciting genre, and once you start reading them you can't help but ask the speculative question that many have pondered before: are these predictions all coincidental, or is it possible that the author has somehow recorded events of the future?

The answer is surely that with the numbers of books published every year, there's almost bound to be a fictional work that tells your story to an almost freakishly similar level of detail. Still, it does raise the hair on your arms when something so close to reality is discovered. Like the recently re-discovered works of lawyer and author Ingersoll Lockwood, who, were he still around, would no doubt be shocked to find himself being mentioned in a chapter about prescient books.

In 1889 Lockwood published his fictional book *Travels and Adventures of Little Baron Trump and His Wonderful Dog Bulger*, which tells the story of a young man named Wilhelm Heinrich Sebastian Von Troomp, who goes by the title Baron Trump. Trump is a precocious child, who likes to explain to everyone he meets just how brilliant he is. His arrogance is so great in fact that when one of his teachers charges him for the lesson they've given him, he sues them, arguing that they should be paying him, as *he* is the one teaching *them*. Trump claims to have a brain twice the normal size, and even creates original insults for many of the characters he meets along the way. As if these parallels to the real-life Trump weren't familiar enough, in the sequel, *Baron Trump's Marvelous*

Underground Journey (1893), Lockwood then goes on to write about Trump's adventures around Russia under the guidance of a mentor called "Don," who is known to be the master of all masters.*

Remarkably, it isn't even just these two books in which Lockwood managed to "channel future events." Another of his book's, *1900; Or, The Last President*, sees Lockwood writing about New York City in chaos when an outsider candidate is elected president. "The Fifth Avenue Hotel will be the first to feel the fury of the mob," the book says, coincidentally marking the location of Trump Tower some hundred years in the future.

Donald Trump isn't the only billionaire to appear in prescient works of fiction. As was discovered at the end of 2020.

THE ROCKET SCIENTIST WHO PREDICTED THE RULER OF MARS

In 1952, rocket scientist Wernher von Braun—the man who is largely credited with getting us to the moon with his invention of the Saturn V rocket, and who will forever remain controversial for his ties to Nazi Germany—wrote a science-fiction novel titled *Mars Project*. In it, von Braun included the potentially prescient detail when he wrote: "The Martian government was directed by ten men, the leader of whom was elected by universal suffrage for five years and entitled 'Elon.' Two houses of Parliament enacted the laws to be administered by the Elon and his cabinet."

* Don, of course, meaning "Mr." in Spanish (the character is a Spaniard).

It wasn't until December 30, 2020, that tech billionaire, and infamous mission-to-Mars enthusiast, Elon Musk learnt of this after someone tweeted it to him.

Musk clearly enjoyed it, later changing his Twitter bio to "imperator of Mars."

THE NARRATIVE OF ARTHUR GORDON PYM OF NANTUCKET BY EDGAR ALLAN POE (1838)

In 1838 an arguably unfinished novel by Edgar Allan Poe titled *The Narrative of Arthur Gordon Pym of Nantucket* was published. Unlike his other more gothic work, this was a pirate adventure. In the book four men are adrift at sea after being shipwrecked. One of them, called Richard

Parker, is killed and then eaten by the other three so that they may survive. Forty-six years later a ship called the *Mignonette* sunk in the South Atlantic, leaving four survivors on a lifeboat. In order to survive, the crew were forced to kill and eat one of their members. His name was Richard Parker.

ENOCH SOAMES: A MEMORY OF THE EIGHTEEN-NINETIES BY MAX BEERBOHM (1916)

Sometimes the books of the past not only correctly predict the future, but can actually form the future too. One case is *Enoch Soames: A Memory of the Eighteen-Nineties* by the author Max Beerbohm, a fictional short story that tells of an encounter Beerbohm had in London on June 3, 1897. In the story, Beerbohm is sitting with his friend, Soames, in a London Soho café, when the discussion turns to Soames's legacy. As a failed author, Soames has become despondent and depressed that his genius is going unrecognised within his own lifetime, and now wonders whether or not he might achieve posthumous fame.

The pair are then interrupted by a man who reveals himself to be the Devil, who makes Soames an offer: he will transport Soames a hundred years into the future, where he will arrive directly into the circular Reading Room of the British Museum at exactly 2:10 p.m. on June 3, 1997, giving Soames the opportunity to look himself up in the library's catalogue to see whether or not he has achieved post-death literary greatness. In return, however, the Devil will obtain Soames's soul, who will then spend all of eternity in hell.

Soames agrees to the conditions and promptly travels into the future.

When he returns a little while later, Beerbohm finds him drinking heavily, and in a troubled state. When pressed for what happened, Soames explains that he went straight to the catalogue that should have contained his work, as well as all the critical studies of it thereafter, but found nothing. Nothing, except for one lone mention of his name, which claimed that he was a made-up character, in a fictional work by Max Beerbohm. He explains to Beerbohm how his presence attracted much attention. His fashion, with his black hat and his waterproof cape, was now 100 years out of date. "They stared at me, I can tell you . . . I think I rather scared them. They moved away whenever I came near. They followed me about at a distance, wherever I went. The men at the round desk in the middle seemed to have a sort of panic . . ."

As he finishes telling his tale to Beerbohm, the Devil returns and drags him away. Beerbohm closes the piece by writing:

You realise that the reading-room into which Soames was projected by the Devil was in all respects precisely as it will be on the afternoon of June 3, 1997. You realise, therefore, that on that afternoon, when it comes round, there the self-same crowd will be, and there Soames too will be, punctually . . . The fact that people are going to stare at him, and follow him around, and seem afraid of him, can be explained only on the hypothesis that they will somehow have been prepared for his ghostly visitation . . .

And so it was, on June 3, 1997, roughly a dozen people waited in the Reading Room for this time traveller to arrive. They included a mystery writer from Malibu, who had flown over specifically to be there after having thought about it for 45 years; someone from Spain; a lady from Cambridge; and a librarian who clearly had no idea what was going on.

The Reading Room, interestingly, was not meant to be there on this day. It was no longer meant to exist. The new British Library had been built and the room was meant to have been shut down and relocated sometime in the 1980s. However, due to building delays, it had been given an extension until November 1997. As a result those who had waited decades to see if their time traveller would arrive were able to walk into the very room Beerbohm had described in his story.

The crowd were all hovering near a very specific set of books—ones that catalogued all of the library's contents from "SNOOD" to "SOBOS."

As the clock hit 2:10 p.m. someone said, "There he is," and they all turned to notice a man, who seemingly had appeared out of nowhere. They stared as he made his way to the catalogue to leaf through it and find his name. They were desperate to touch his cape, to make contact, but knew that they couldn't. Beerbohm had done it. His cheeky idea to manifest a scene in the future had worked, and as the dozen or so fans watched along, they suddenly found themselves *in the story itself*, playing the key characters as written by Beerbohm a century earlier. No one tried to speak to the time traveller—just as they didn't in the story—and instead they simply followed him around. Twenty minutes later, the crowd

had doubled, curious onlookers joining in as this time traveller desperately scanned the shelves of the Reading Room.

One of the people observing this curious man was Allan
Hailstone. "I was in the Reading Room working on the
Coincraft Standard Catalogue of British coins, of which I
wrote the section for British/English coins from 1658 to the
present day," Hailstone told me. "I was unaware of the
Soames connection until that day." Fortunately, Hailstone
had his camera on him, and managed to take what is so far
the only known photographic evidence of the event.

After a while spent scavenging through the shelves in
search of his name, "Soames" took a turn round a corner and
disappeared. His exit caused confusion. The door was
blocked, he hadn't left through there. Nor was there any
other way out, so far as the observers could see.

The only known shot of Beerbohm's time traveller.

If only Beerbohm could have witnessed this moment. Could he have asked for a better way to be alive once again as a footprint in the future than this? Who was to thank for making his time traveller appear? Though officially we don't know the answer, there was a very obvious candidate.

Sitting quietly in the reading room, watching on from a good vantage point was a man called Raymond Joseph Teller. Thirty-four years earlier, while still a student at school, a teacher would tell the story of Enoch Soames to the children in Teller's class. It was a story he would never forget. Teller went on to a career in magic, and, along with Penn Jillette, created Penn and Teller.

According to an interview written by Chris Jones for *Esquire* magazine, though Teller has never admitted to anything, Jones points out that he *might* have spent time sifting through casting books looking for the perfect Soames; that he *might* have visited a costume shop where he tracked down a waterproof grey cape and a soft black hat; and he *might* even have had an insider pull off the illusion of making his Soames disappear into the shelves—perhaps literally, hiding inside a hidden door. He *might* have made all that happen. But Teller has never confirmed it. Teller himself would later write that when his teacher (who didn't live to make it to the year 1997), asked his class the question of how many Enoch Soameses might show up on that day, he thought he was "merely musing . . . Later I understood. He was giving me a homework assignment."

FUTILITY BY MORGAN ROBERTSON (1898)

Perhaps the most prescient novel of all was written by Morgan Robertson in 1898. *Futility* is the fictional account of a British ship called the *Titan* that sinks in the North Atlantic one April after colliding with an iceberg, and there aren't enough lifeboats to save all 3,000 passengers: "Unsinkable, indestructible, she carried as few boats as would satisfy the laws. These, twenty-four in number, were securely covered and lashed down to their chocks on the upper deck, and if launched would hold five hundred people."

The book contained many striking similarities to reality: both ships were roughly the same size, with *Titan* measuring 880 feet, while the *Titanic* was 882.5 feet; both had three propellers and two masts; the *Titanic* had a capacity of 3,547 passengers, *Titan* had 3,000; the *Titanic* ran on 46,000 horse power, *Titan* on 40,000; the *Titanic* carried a measly 20 lifeboats, *Titan* had 24; the *Titanic*'s speed on impact with the iceberg was 22.5 knots, the *Titan* was travelling at 25 knots; the *Titanic* sank in April, so did the *Titan*, after both grazed an iceberg on the starboard side.

Interestingly, in a letter to the spiritualist Ella Wheeler Wilcox, Morgan Robertson wrote up his theory that perhaps his book was channelled from the future:

As to the motif of my story, I merely tried to write a good story with no idea of being a prophet. But, as in other stories of mine, and in the work of other and better writers, coming discoveries and events have been anticipated. I do not doubt that it is because all creative workers get into a hypnoid, telepathic and percipient condition, in which, while apparently awake, they are half asleep, and tap, not only the better-informed minds of others but the subliminal realm of unknown facts. Some, as you know, believe that in this realm there is no such thing as Time, and the fact that a long dream can occur in an instant of time gives color to it, and partly explains prophecy.

Morgan Robertson was replying to the spiritualist after she had contacted him wondering if he had knowingly predicted the sinking of the *Titanic*, as the story in his book *Futility* suggested he might have.

While it's intriguing to think that Robinson had predicted the doom of the *Titanic* via some sort of precognition, it's worth also considering this opinion from the popular science writer and sceptic Martin Gardner—that it's just a massive coincidence: "It is extraordinarily difficult for most people to grasp the fact that some improbable events are extremely probable, and in some cases absolutely certain." The likelihood of someone writing a book that accidentally predicts the sinking of the *Titanic* was quite high, when you look at what was going on at the time with transatlantic voyaging. It was a topic very much in the news, and therefore inspired much of the literature being produced at the time.

In reality, Robertson wasn't even the only one to make these supposed predictions about the *Titanic*. Even earlier was William Young Winthrop's *A 20th Century Cinderella; or, $20,000 Reward*, which makes reference to a ship called the *Titanic* that's built by the White Star Line company, the same company that built the actual *Titanic* (though no ships sink in this story). Perhaps the most interesting book associated with this niche "predicting the sinking of the *Titanic*" genre was one by a man called W. T. Stead.

THE WEIRD WORLD OF W. T. STEAD

In his short story *How The Mail Steamer Went Down in Mid Atlantic By a Survivor* by William Thomas Stead, published in 1886, a ship travelling from Liverpool to New York is half-way across the Atlantic when it collides with another vessel, which it doesn't see on account of fog. Before this happens the main character, Thompson, wanders the deck and takes note that there aren't enough life rafts on board to secure the number of lives on the ship. The story closes with an editorial line from its author, Stead, that reads: "This is exactly what might take place and will take place if liners are sent to sea short of boats."

What marks Stead out from the other writers is that this wasn't the only story he'd publish that had an eerie connection to the *Titanic*. In 1892—20 years before the *Titanic* sank—Stead wrote about another transatlantic sea tragedy, which had only a few survivors, on a ship called *Majestic*. It was presumably named after the RMS *Majestic*, which was captained by Edward Smith, who would go on to captain the *Titanic*.

W. T. Stead was an influential newspaper journalist in his day (often being called the father of modern investigative journalism). He was also a spiritualist. In the 1890s he started a magazine called *Borderland*, which billed itself as a

W. T. Stead.

"Quarterly Review and Index of Psychic Phenomena." As well as writing about the world of spiritualism, Stead began dabbling in it himself. He'd supposedly often communicate with *Borderland*'s assistant editor using telepathy, and would also experiment with automatic writing (where one is dictated to by a spirit from the other side). In 1909 Stead opened up a paranormal agency in the centre of London with a woman called Julia.

Located on the Strand in London, Julia's Bureau was named after its founder and operating director, Julia A. Ames. Describing the purpose of the venture, Stead explained that its objective was to "bridge the abyss between the Two Worlds."

Julia made for an interesting company director. A journalist and member of the Woman's Temperance Publishing Association, she was outgoing, thoughtful, and highly ambitious. She was also very dead. Julia A. Ames died 15 years before she supposedly opened her own bureau; having sadly passed away from typhoid pneumonia when she was just 30 years old, never to be aware of a London office set up and "run by her."

The bureau functioned by putting together a directory of "competent sensitives" (mediums), who would be paired up with the client if, and only if, they had been approved by Julia herself. Once approved, the client, accompanied by a stenographer, would be sent to the three mediums—a clairvoyant, a trance medium, and an automatic writer. All sittings were

Julia A. Ames, who in 1909 founded and ran a bureau in London that sought to reconnect the living with the dead, despite being already dead for 15 years herself.

held separately and there was no communication between the writers. Julia's Bureau ran for three years and in that time gave 1,300 sittings. Stead paid for it out of his own pocket, the enterprise costing him about £1,500 a year.

Given his interests in the world of telepathy and spiritualism, it's a tragedy that Stead never got to explore the idea that his book may have predicted the sinking of the *Titanic*. No doubt he'd have loved to have investigated the possibility that he had somehow tapped into the future and put down its events on paper. Perhaps he'd have set up a new London bureau designed to explore this phenomenon. Tragically, like Poe, Beerbohm, Winthrop, von Braun, and Lockwood before him, it was not to be. Stead would tragically die 26 years after publishing his story, on April 15, 1912, as a passenger on board the RMS *Titanic*.

CHAPTER 10

DID TIME TRAVELLERS SINK THE *TITANIC*?

THE THEORY OF THE *TITANIC*

It's bath time at the Schreiber house, and I've just introduced a new rubber *Titanic* bath toy for the boys to play with. After a quick ship-launching ceremony, we pop it onto the water's surface, and all watch as it immediately flips over.

"Bit insensitive for official merch," says Fenella.

I'd picked up the toy a few days before whilst in Northern Ireland visiting the Titanic Belfast museum gift shop. What an exciting visit that was. After all, it was here, in 1911, that the RMS *Titanic* made its way across a dockyard slipway lathered with soap, mutton fat, and sperm whale oil, and slipped down into the sea.

Titanic Belfast is a smart-looking building designed specifically to house the museum, which you can tell by the architecture. It's created to look like the front of a ship, with massive bow shapes protruding out from three of the four faces of the building's walls.

Most other *Titanic* museums around the world are less

classy, being designed to be outright replicas of the ship itself. There's the one in Pigeon Forge, Tennessee, which looks exactly like the *Titanic*, but built to half the size of the original. It's the largest *Titanic* museum in the world, and it aims to give the visitor a totally immersive experience. Upon entering, visitors are given a boarding ticket with the name of an actual passenger from the historic maiden voyage on it. At the end of the trip, they're told whether or not their ticketed passenger survived the trip. Unfortunately, sometimes the immersive side of things gets a bit too real. In 2021 three people were hospitalised after being hit by an iceberg at the *Titanic* museum. This happened as a result of a freak accident when its giant 15 feet by 28 feet wall of ice collapsed onto the visitors.

Bad luck seems to follow anyone re-creating the *Titanic* disaster. In 2008 a *Titanic* exhibit in Pittsburgh had to close on account of flooding. In 2018 the first British performance of *Titanic: The Musical* was stopped for health and safety reasons, after the ship hit the mock iceberg and plaster started falling onto the stage. (Another time, audience members got more than they had bargained for when a water pipe running across the ceiling of the theatre exploded across the first three rows of the audience. "Now we truly experienced the sinking of the *Titanic*," said one theatregoer.)

As you approach Titanic Belfast you notice numerous wooden benches circling the building. They're arranged in a Morse code sequence. If you follow the benches right around from the starting point, you'd read the distress message that the ship sent after it hit the iceberg. It's a nice touch.

"Why did the *Titanic* sink?" asks my son Wilf, aged four, from the bath. The question reminds me of the intrepid explorer Jack Grimm, who asked his mother this exact question when he was probably around the same age. She told him that the reason the ship had sunk was because everyone on board was a sinner and that the iceberg had been sent by God.

WHERE IS THE *TITANIC?*

In 1980 the first major scientific expedition to find the wreck of the *Titanic* was about to set off. Led and partially funded by multi-millionaire oil tycoon Jack Grimm, the exploration team was made up of a number of the world's top ocean explorers and scientists, including Dr. Fred Spiess, whom many regarded as the "father of deep-sea research," and Skip Gleason, the world-leading deep-sea scientist. For the trip, Grimm had secured a ship, the latest radar technology, and the funds for the search.

In the hours before departure, Grimm announced one final team member would be joining them on the search—a monkey, whom Grimm claimed was going to point out the location of the shipwreck on a map by using extra-sensory perception.* Spiess and Gleason were horrified. It was an insane idea, and one that would undermine both the serious-

---

* The monkey, called Titan, was to be a "consultant" and had been specially trained for the job.

ness of the expedition and their own reputations. They told Grimm, "It's us or the monkey." Grimm chose the monkey.

*　　*　　*

This wasn't the first expedition that Jack Grimm had funded, but it was the first where he and others considered that he might actually stand a chance of finding the "treasure." His previous expeditions included looking for Bigfoot (didn't find it), the Loch Ness Monster (didn't find it, but produced a grainy photo), Sasquatch (didn't find it), and an expedition to the North Pole to search for the entrance to the hollow earth (didn't find it). He had also made three expeditions to Mount Ararat in Turkey to search for Noah's Ark, and although no discovery was officially confirmed, Grimm claimed a piece of carved oak he recovered was in fact a piece of the ark, and would carry it on his person for the rest of his life. "This is the ark," he'd tell people. "That's my story, and I'm going to stick to it."

Grimm ended up launching a total of three expeditions to search for the *Titanic*. The first, which unfortunately did not yield any conclusive discoveries, was at least a success in that it did end up going ahead with its planned crew of scientists, Grimm having eventually been talked out of bringing the monkey. It was Grimm's second attempt that was to become the most notable of the expeditions.

As well as including the same leading oceanographers from the previous expedition, Dr. Fred Spies and Skip Gleason, the team Grimm assembled for this second attempt

at locating the wreck included an actor from the TV series *The Virginian*; a Christian Scientist who suffered from terrible seasickness but was unable to do anything about it as his religion didn't allow him to take pills; and a physics graduate called Bill Ryan, who claimed, among other things, to know where the lost city of Atlantis was.*

Grimm and his team desperately searched the ocean for any sign of the ship, but just like his previous expedition, nothing was showing up. The elusive wreck of the *Titanic* continued to remain hidden from him. As the final day of

---

* Ryan's claim to fame was that he had successfully verified Pliny the Elder's account of the eruption of Mount Vesuvius in 79 CE and the destruction of Pompeii. He thought that Atlantis was in the middle of the Aegean Sea and was demolished in 1450 BCE.

searching wound down, Grimm, in an act of desperation, had his camera crew lower their underwater camera into the ocean to film . . . just anything. For three hours as Grimm's boat made its way back to land, Grimm and the crew sat in silence, watching the footage, all in a depressed silence. It should have been an amazing moment—the footage they had just captured was filmed at a depth greater than had ever been previously captured. Yet no one was in the mood for that kind of trivia. As the hours passed they saw a foot-long shrimp, a seemingly new species of fish, and a starfish as big as a motorbike wheel pass by the camera lens. But no *Titanic*.

With the video footage entering its last 30 minutes, Grimm was on the brink of a breakdown, when suddenly a huge gasp went around the room. "What was *that*?" they all asked. Something large and steel-like had come into shot. Was it . . . a propeller? There was a brief flurry of arguments; some said it was, while others, like the guy who claimed to know where Atlantis was, refused to agree it was for fear of being ridiculed. After much debate, the captain of the ship was called in to pass his judgement on the footage. He immediately agreed that yes, it was indeed a propeller, and not only that, but one that was consistent with the size of the *Titanic*.

Grimm was ecstatic, and immediately set about announcing to the world that he had found the *Titanic*. However, as time passed, and more and more experts were shown the footage, sadly no academic in the field would corroborate it. Grimm never buckled on his belief that he was the true discoverer of the shipwreck, and just a few years later, an oceanographer by the name of Robert Ballard would go down in the history books as the discoverer of the wreck of the *Titanic*. And though he didn't rate Grimm as a good scientist or explorer, Ballard did acknowledge the invaluable assistance that Grimm's expeditions had given him. At the end of the day what Grimm had achieved was important work, including invaluable insight for Ballard in showing him where *not* to look.

RAISING THE *TITANIC*

Ever since the *Titanic* went down in the North Atlantic on April 15, 1912, there have been many methods proposed as to how to bring it back to the surface, the discussions starting as soon as just five days after it sank, in fact, when it was proposed that dynamite be used to get the bodies to float back to the surface. This idea was supported by Vincent Astor, son of John Jacob Astor, thought to be the richest man in the world and who perished on board. Vincent, however, was eventually deterred after learning that the extreme pressures at the depths of the Atlantic would have compressed all the passengers on the ship to jelly.

Other notable ideas for raising the *Titanic* included filling the hull up with ping-pong balls; injecting the vessel with 180,000 tonnes of Vaseline; and, most intriguing of all, turning the *Titanic* itself into an iceberg. This was to be achieved by constructing a wire mesh around the ship, pumping the area with 50,000 tons of liquid nitrogen and turning the ship into a big block of ice, which would enable it to float back up to the ocean's surface.

The technique of raising a ship via ping-pong-like balls was trialled by Danish engineer Karl Kroyer in 1964, after a ship sank with 5,000 sheep on it at a port in Kuwait—Kroyer successfully raised the ship after filling it with 27 million balls made of expanding polystyrene foam.

Kroyer later tried to patent this technique in Denmark, but his application was rejected when someone discovered that the cartoon character Donald Duck had already pioneered this method in a comic strip 15 years before. The idea was ultimately never tested out on the *Titanic*, because at 12,600 feet down the ping-pong balls would be crushed by the pressure.

The idea of turning the *Titanic* itself into an iceberg originally came from a man called Arthur Hickey (an unemployed haulage contractor from Walsall), who suggested freezing the inside of the ship and transforming it into a giant tube of ice. The thought was then expanded on by salvage hopeful John Pierce, who suggested erecting a nitrogen-filled netting around the ship to effect the same end.

Another clever idea came from the architect Charles Smith, who in 1914 proposed attaching electromagnets to a submarine, thereby letting the *Titanic* do the work of drawing in the submarine. Then there was Douglas Wooley, who proposed raising the ship using balloons, like in the film *Up*. Unfortunately, quite how the balloons would be inflated was a problem—the original calculation of taking a week was quickly shown to be massively optimistic; it would actually need ten years.

None of these ideas were taken up, perhaps because of the costs involved, although more likely because no one yet had any idea where the ship was, or even if it still existed in one piece. Serious consideration was given to the idea that the ship had already broken up or disappeared following an earthquake in 1929—according to calculations, the quake would have been more powerful than a hundred atomic bombs detonated on the sea floor, and might either have blown the *Titanic* up into a million small pieces, or the sea-bed would have split asunder and simply gobbled the ship up. Nobody knew for sure.

SO, WHAT REALLY SANK THE *TITANIC*?

We all know that the *Titanic* sank after colliding with an iceberg. What's fascinating, though, is that despite knowing this, for over a hundred years now, new theories continue to pop up trying to suggest that something more was going on: maybe it sank because there was a cursed mummy on board (there wasn't); or perhaps it never actually sank, but was swapped with its sister ship as part of an insurance hit job, though perhaps the oddest theory of all is the one that proposes that the real reason the *Titanic* sank is not because it hit an iceberg, but because so many time travellers visited it at the same time to witness the moment of the sinking, the weight of them all forced the ship under the water.

I first learnt of this theory while listening to astrophysicist Neil deGrasse Tyson's podcast Star Talk. It's a theory I love, because it has a fundamentally interesting thought behind it. That being that if we did ever crack time travel, the big moments in history are going to be absolute tourist hellholes: the Kennedy assassination, the construction of Stonehenge, the Roswell incident. These will all be jam packed with school excursions, drunken hen-do's, TV historians filming pieces to camera, and merch stands that will confuse the hell out of locals with T-shirts prefiguring an event that's about to happen.

HOW MANY TIME TRAVELLERS DOES IT TAKE TO SINK THE *TITANIC*?

How many humans would it take for this to happen? The answer is 5,682,646.

$$\frac{(404634 \; tons - 52310 \; tons) * 1000 \; kg \; tons^{-1}}{62 \; kg \; human^{-1}} = 5,682,646 \; humans$$

This calculation, devised by mathematician Emma Govan, is based on the average weight of a human being, not factoring in any time-travel equipment. Let's assume for simplicity that these tourists are using wristwatch time machines rather than each pitching up in their individual 5,000-tonne TARDISes or DeLoreans.

The problem with this theory is not the weight of the crowd but the size. The average volume of a human being is 0.062m³, so unless you liquidised everybody, there is no way a crowd of five and a half million is fitting comfortably inside the *Titanic*.

The majority of these time travellers will presumably

choose to materialise on the top deck of the ship, the best vantage point for seeing the iceberg hit the hull. But there isn't enough space there, which means they would simply pile up on top of each other in an ever-growing tower, rising 84 metres in the air, equivalent to 50 Kate Winslets standing on each other's shoulders (or 46 Leonardo DiCaprios).★

Time travellers aside, there have been some serious contenders presented by scientists and historians around the world as to what, outside of the iceberg, is to blame for the ship's sinking.

★ The theory goes that although the *Titanic* did originally sink due to hitting an iceberg, history has since been rewritten by the time travellers, who took the ship down before the iceberg ever got the chance.

NO. 1: THE MOON

On January 4, 1912, three months before the *Titanic* sank, the moon was unusually close to the Earth—closer than it had been for over a thousand years; and the closest it will be until the year 2257. According to the astronomer Donald Olson, who goes by the moniker "the Celestial Sleuth," when the moon reached its closest approach that night it happened to be a full moon, and the combined closeness and the fullness of the moon made it a "supermoon" event. It also happened that the sun and the moon were aligned at this exact time, which would have intensified their gravitational pull on the Earth, resulting in both higher and lower tides. It was an extremely rare event.

Old icebergs that have travelled far can sometimes run ashore, where they sit and melt until they're freed by the tide to float off again. According to Olson, on this particular night, off the coast of Newfoundland, a stranded block of ice might have been released by the moon's influence at high tide, and started travelling south. Three months later it found itself in a place it should never have been, on a night it never should have been there, and about to collide into a ship with which it should never have crossed paths. It was about to become the most infamous iceberg in history. To add insult to injury, it was particularly difficult to see the oncoming iceberg, since it was a moonless evening on the night of the famous collision; as if our constant satellite were hiding, ashamed of what it had done.

NO. 2: THE EARTH

In 2012 British historian Tim Maltin suggested that atmospheric conditions might have been responsible for the sinking. Maltin is the co-author of *101 Things You Thought You Knew About the Titanic . . . But Didn't*. It's a brilliant book, if only for the fact that I didn't even know that I supposedly knew 101 things about the ship. Maltin looked up testimonies from survivors, went through the ship logs, studied the weather records, and concluded that on the night of the sinking there were layers of warm and cold air, which caused mirages. These optical illusions may have hidden the iceberg until it was too late, interfered with the *Titanic*'s signals, and played havoc with any onlookers' perception of the location of the ship's distress rockets.

I remember reading about these optical illusions; they're known as "superior mirages." They occur as a result of a phenomenon called a "temperature inversion," whereby warm air sits on top of cold, causing light to bend in an unusual way, distorting reality and creating an illusion. Inversions most often appear in very cold waters like the Arctic, and can, for example, make ships in the distance appear to be floating above the horizon.

Such mirages can also take the form of "foggy walls." Well known to sailors throughout history, the Vikings called them *Hafgerdingar*, which translates from the Norse as "sea hedges." In the case of the *Titanic*, the sea hedge would have acted as a cloak of invisibility, making it impossible for the sailors to spot the monumental iceberg until it was too late.

Not only did the superior mirage cause the *Titanic* to be struck by the iceberg; it also screwed with its chances of being rescued. One ship that picked up the *Titanic*'s distress calls was the SS *Californian*. Looking out for the ship, the captain of the *Californian* spotted a vessel in the distance but decided it couldn't be the *Titanic*. The *Titanic* was 800 feet long and reported to be 10 kilometres away from the *Californian*; this ship appeared to be just 400 feet long and at only a distance of around 4 kilometres. It must be another vessel, thought the captain, but a vessel without a radio. It was, of course, the *Titanic*, but the mad mirages of the evening gave the illusion of it being half the size and half the distance away. The captain of the *Californian* decided to communicate using Morse code via its powerful lamp. It sent its signals to the ship but received no reply. This was because the mirage had, unfortunately, one last trick to play—the air of the thermal inversion caused a disruption in the lamp's light, so even if anyone had seen it on the *Titanic* it would have appeared to have simply been flickering lights from a distant ship.

NO. 3: THE SUN

According to the investigations of weather researcher Mila Zinkova, the sky on April 14, 1912, would have been lit up by the aurora borealis. Auroras are caused by blasts of electromagnetic radiation lobbed from the sun colliding with the Earth's atmosphere. While we mostly think of the beautiful northern—or southern—lights they produce, they can also cause havoc, in some scenarios end-of-the-world-level havoc.

The most severe solar storm on record occurred in 1859. Because there was little electronic infrastructure in place around the world at the time the damage was limited, although it was reported that the storm sent such strong currents along the newly built telegraph systems that the operators could disconnect their batteries and still be able to send messages. If we were hit today by another flare the size of the one in 1859, scientists claim it would cause up to $2 trillion of damage by crippling communications, from which it would take us four to ten years to recover.

According to Zinkova, a couple of things that these sun flares might have altered on the night of April 14, 1912, included the accuracy of *Titanic*'s compass and the consistency of its radio communications. As a result the crew would have needlessly adjusted the course of the ship, its new course sending it directly into an oncoming iceberg, one that it originally was never on course to hit.

NO. 4: THE ELEMENTS

A little-known fact is that the *Titanic* was on fire throughout its entire maiden voyage. In fact it caught fire ten days before it left port. The fire was in Bunker Number 6, where hundreds of tonnes of coal were stored. Indeed, there were crew members who spent the entire journey trying to put it out.

Based on this fact, engineer Robert Essenhigh of Ohio State University believes that in an attempt to extinguish the fire, the crew members accidentally helped to sink the *Titanic* instead.

The method used to extinguish the fire was to fight it with fire. The reason that the crew were unable to put out the flames was because the fire was located deep within the coal heap. To reach it, crew members were shovelling away the coal at the top into another bunker, and once they reached the raging flames, were shovelling the burning coal into the boiler—where it could happily burn away safely. This, however, would have created vast quantities of steam, which would have led to a much faster travelling speed.

It is widely argued that had the *Titanic* been travelling at a slower speed, the collision with the iceberg would have opened up fewer watertight compartments, which would have meant that the ship, though completely wrecked, wouldn't have sunk.

★　　★　　★

And so it was, if these theories are to believed, that the *Titanic* found itself on the night of April 14, travelling at a speed it shouldn't have been going at (thanks to a fire), on a course it shouldn't have travelling on (thanks to the sun), and slamming into an iceberg that shouldn't have been there (but was thanks to the moon) with a crew who couldn't see it coming at them (thanks to the haze-filled horizon).

I think we can all agree on one thing: that night in 1912 the *Titanic* was cosmically fucked.

CHAPTER 11
WHERE HAVE ALL THE PUBIC LICE GONE?
THE THEORY OF THE ENDANGERED

Did you know that according to a scientific paper published in 2006 by two STI doctors in Leeds, pubic lice appear to be going extinct because so many people are having Brazilian waxes? As a result, the lice don't have a natural habitat to exist in anymore. They're being deforested.

★   ★   ★

This discovery, made by Dr. Janet Wilson and Dr. Nicola Armstrong at the Department of Genitourinary Medicine at Leeds General Infirmary, came about after Armstrong and Watson combed through medical data from a period spanning seven years and noticed that there had been a decline in cases of patients reporting lice. Not only did they identify this trend for missing lice, but they also believed they had tracked down the culprits behind this sudden drive to mass extinction: seven sisters called Janea, Judseia, Jussara, Juracy, Jocely, Joyce, and Jonice.

The J sisters, as they're known, unwittingly started this terminal global decline in louse populations when they opened up a beauty salon in New York and introduced the Brazilian wax—a style of grooming that took off immediately. The first American recipient of the waxing was a 28-year-old woman called Sari Markowitz, who told author David Friend about the experience. Markowitz was in for some beauty treatment, when one of the sisters, Janea, pitches the concept of a "Brazilian" to her. Markowitz was intrigued and decided to give it a go. However, as the J Sisters didn't have a room specifically for waxing, it ended up being done on an office desk with everything pushed off. Markowitz, with her back on the desk, had one leg propped over a fax machine, the other being held by one of the J sisters (Janea), who spent the next six minutes waxing off most of her pubic hair. The next day Markowitz told her friends at lunch about her new "hairdo." One of those friends happened to be an editor at the magazine *Elle*, which then ran a story on the salon and the waxing, which is precisely when the hapless louse's fate was sealed.

WHAT HAVE BODY LICE EVER DONE FOR US?

For centuries now we've been trying to eradicate lice from our bodies, and yet have never quite managed it. Killing them has been at times an incredibly lucrative business; in the Victorian era, hospitals would employ lice destroyers, known as "bug catchers," who would be paid better than the hospital's surgeons themselves.* We carry three types of lice—head, body, and pubic. We picked the head lice up millions of years ago, and would have shared them with chimpanzees; body lice developed around 170,000 years ago; and pubic lice came from gorillas, although there's nothing to suggest that this was the result of any inter-species sexy time. Early humans simply picked them up when sleeping in abandoned gorilla nests.

You would imagine that when Armstrong and Wilson's paper—"Did the 'Brazilian' kill the pubic louse?"—was published, it would have sent shock waves through the world as we became aware of yet another endangered species. Surely the World Wide Fund for Nature would have promoted its plight, and placard-holding protestors would be standing outside beauty salons around the world chanting for the poor tiny creature's rights. But no. Nothing happened. The paper was viewed more as a humorous piece than as proper science, and even the paper's authors considered it to be merely an interesting speculative question.

Articles still appear rebutting the claim, insisting that "No, the pubic lice isn't endangered," explaining that the decline in the number of patients reporting the sexually transmitted infection is more the result of over-the-counter shampoos being made available in pharmacies and so we don't know how many cases there are anymore. Regardless, life on Earth is the only life we know of in this universe so far; it's precious.

* According to historian Lindsey Fitzharris, one "chief bug-catcher" destroyed 20,000 beds' worth of lice in his career.

It's simply unacceptable that we're shampooing a species into extinction.

Lice are important, and they can tell us a huge amount about our past. They've unknowingly acted as a mini Boswell to our Samuel Johnson. For starters, according to Mark Stoneking at the Max Planck Institute in Germany, it's thanks to lice that we now believe we know when humans started wearing clothes.

By using DNA sequencing, it has been worked out that around 170,000 years ago head lice on humans started diverging into becoming body lice. This was a seminal moment in the history of humans, as clothing meant we were able to successfully migrate out of Africa and start populating the world. Thank you, lice! We couldn't have discovered this any other way, because clothes from that long ago haven't survived. What other secrets of our past might they help us to uncover?

THE PUBIC LICE HUNTER OF ROTTERDAM

Fortunately not everyone turned up their nose in disbelief when the Armstrong/Wilson paper was released. Spotting the news over in Holland was the chief curator of the Natural History Museum in Rotterdam, Kees Moeliker. Moeliker is the best kind of curator: eccentric, funny, and someone who knows how to makes waves and attract attention to the things he's passionate about. He often appears on TV hosting his own wildlife shows, and is the author of multiple books, including one titled *The Butt Crack of the Tick*.* He's also known for a seminal scientific paper that recorded the first-ever case of homosexual necrophilia in the mallard duck.

As soon as Kees learnt about the Brazilian vs. lice paper, he had the museum put out a plea: if you have pubic lice, please get in contact, we need your donation (lice, that is, not money). This simple message attracted considerable media attention, giving pubic lice international column inches and inadvertently turning Moeliker into the world's first pubic louse hunter.

I've met and worked with Kees many times since I first learnt about his mission to save the pubic louse. His aim isn't

---

* "Technically speaking," Kees once told me, "ticks don't have a butt crack—they have an anal groove," although his publishers quite rightly thought that *The Anal Groove of the Tick* wasn't as marketable a title.

to actively keep them from extinction, I should add; he just doesn't want them to go the way of the dodo, an animal of which we no longer have any complete examples. Kees simply wants to build up a collection that he can keep in a jar for future researchers to study. Every so often, a decade-plus after he launched the appeal at his museum, he still gladly accepts donations. He told me proudly that couples quite often drive up to Rotterdam and hand him a bag containing trimmed pubic hair with examples of the deceased critters in them.

While this is a noble task, and one that future scientists of the world will no doubt be grateful for, it still doesn't help the lice themselves from disappearing into extinction. I wondered whether I should catch a few of their number and offer them shelter? Surely an itch is worth the trouble. I also considered how it could play to my advantage—imagine the excitement around the table before you arrived at a dinner party—"Did you hear the pubic lice guy is coming tonight?" If their plight got bad enough, I could probably be granted national park status as the last refuge for a dying species.

It turns out someone else has had this idea too, along with a much better way of doing it. Her name is Frida Klingberg, an artist based in Gothenburg, Sweden, and she planned to run a nature reserve for them. Klingberg managed to find a group of volunteers who all signed up to the project, which would see them each harbouring the lice on their bodies for a period of two to three weeks at a time, before picking out some of the lice and giving them to the next volunteer via a jar, for them to be infected with the species for the same period, then repeat.

The only snag in Klingberg's plan was that she couldn't find any pubic lice with which to kick off the project. "I searched for a few years, mostly through the media," she told me. "I never found any native specimens in Sweden to start the reserve, which also says something about the situation!" And just like me, she can't understand the underwhelming lack of attention that the problem attracts.

Why does no nature organisation fight for the preservation of this obviously threatened species? How shall then future generations [of people] be able to experience nature as we can today? How does the idea of function [for whom?] give a species some right to existence within nature preservation? How come no nature photographers do photos of lice? All photos are taken by "medicine photographers." Is the crab louse not nature?

Fortunately, there's one place that does respect the cry for help from the pubic/crab louse: an organisation that deals specifically with animals that have been ignored by mainstream organisations.

THE UGLY ANIMAL PRESERVATION SOCIETY

Founded in 2012, the Ugly Animal Preservation Society is the brainchild of biologist Simon Watt. His idea is that cuddly animals like the panda have been getting all the attention for far too long now, and that we should start focusing on the more aesthetically challenged type of creature. Simon believes that we've heard quite enough about snow leopards—what about the Canadian blue-grey taildropper slug, whose bum falls off when it gets too scared?

Admittedly, the Ugly Animal Preservation Society exists largely as a comedy night, but it has a serious conservation twist. Over the years I myself have performed at a number of events, championing the pubic lice whenever I can. For Simon, it doesn't matter if the paper published by Armstrong and Wilson is wrong, because defining what actually is endangered hasn't been agreed on, and the paper serves to highlight that.

The concept of what makes a thing endangered is tricky and requires agreement. For example, it's not rarity. There's a whole ton of stuff which is rare. Rare is the common state of most of life because it only exists in its own narrow confines. And if those narrow confines happen to be secure, then it is not endangered. Take polar bears. Some people would argue, and there's a legitimate argument to be had here, that polar bears are not endangered because in many, many places at least their numbers are on the rise. They're doing well. But if the ice goes, they're all gone. So perhaps the numbers are doing all right, but threats are increasing all the time.

Simon believes the pubic louse is a fantastic example of an endangered species, because it can spark a conversation about parasites.

There are only a few parasites on the endangered species list. So if you look at the International Union for Conservation of Nature red lists, you'll see the pygmy hog sucking louse and only a few others on it. And we of course know that is completely inaccurate. Every endangered species will have its own unique parasites, which will disappear if that species disappears.

Simon now uses the pubic louse as a mascot to help us understand the complexity of species living together, to show how nothing really goes extinct in isolation, as it drags a lot of other organisms—plant as well as animal—down with it. "Say an insect pollinator dies out, perhaps a specific flower that it feeds off may die out as well. I use it as a way of showing how things are worse than we know, even."

Life, says Simon, is an ecosystem. You knock one thing away, and the chain reaction can be great. It's our job to make sure we look out for *all* life, even the itchy ones.

If you—reading this now—do have pubic lice, congratulations! You're harbouring an endangered species. You're a hero. Don't burn them off in the shower with chemicals. Get in touch with Frida Klingberg and help her begin a reserve, or contact the Natural History Museum, Rotterdam—they need your donation.

CHAPTER 12
WILL WE EVER SPEAK DOLPHINESE?
THE THEORY OF ANIMAL COMMUNICATION

On the morning of November 1, 1961, a phone call was made to the California home of scientist Melvin Calvin, informing him that he had just won the Nobel Prize in Chemistry, but Calvin wasn't there to receive it. He was on the other side of the country, having quietly snuck off to a secret meeting at West Virginia's Green Bank Observatory, where he found himself listening to a man called Dr. John C. Lilly as he explained to Calvin and a small group of assembled scientists how he had recently trained a dolphin called Elvar to play fetch with a rubber ring in a unique way—instead of using his nose to catch the toy, Elvar had been taught to use his erect penis. Dolphins can achieve voluntary erections in just three seconds, Lilly told the crowd. By the time he'd thrown the toy ring into the pool, Elvar was able to gain an erection and collect the ring as it dropped to the bottom of the pool, returning it to Lilly.

The group of academics, silently listening to this man talk about his adventures with dolphins had gathered, in somewhat clandestine circumstances, for a very specific reason.

They were here to search for alien life. This was the very first meeting of what would become SETI, the Search for Extraterrestrial Intelligence.*

Dr. Lilly was the odd one out of the group, which consisted of world-leading experts in ballistics, biology, chemistry, exobiology, electronics, and physics. Still, everyone assembled was interested in what he had to say. The meeting had been arranged by biologist J. P. T. Pearman on behalf of the Space Science Board, and he, along with one of the greatest scientific alien hunters of them all, the astronomer Frank Drake (of the famous "Drake equation,")† had

---

* Strictly speaking, it wasn't a secret meeting (it was organised by the Space Science Board, after all), but the conference was definitely not openly discussed, as the scientists involved feared ridicule and didn't want to attract media attention. Since the Roswell incident in New Mexico 14 years earlier, a wave of alien-mania had taken over the United States, and thanks to multiple amateur scientists making claims on TV and radio, the search for extraterrestrials had become largely pseudo-scientific.

† Frank Drake, while not batshit himself, is a wonderful example of someone who deals with the batshit of others well. He once had his workplace vampire-proofed after one of the security team reported having seen a man with a black cloak walking around the satellite dish, and concluding that what he'd seen was a vampire. A few days later, when a cow was found dead in a local farm, with all of its blood drained from its body, word got around and the staff began to freak out. After that more and more vampire sightings started flooding in. Drake, despite his complete scepticism, researched how to rid an area of vampires, even calling up his vampire bat expert friend Donald Griffin at Cornell University for advice. Griffin, who was well read on folklore, advised that Drake get everyone to eat loads of garlic. And so Drake arranged a meeting with his staff, where he ordered for all meals served in the observatory to have increased amounts of garlic in them, and that extra-garlicky dishes be introduced to the menu generally. Following this, the vampire reports vanished from the area.

drawn up the list of invitees. These included Su-Shu Huang (who coined the term "habitable zones," meaning the distance from a star that planets need to be in order to support water on their surface), Philip Morrison (a nuclear physicist who worked on the Manhattan Project, and transported the core of what would become the first-ever detonated nuclear bomb in the US to its test site in the back seat of his Dodge Sedan), Bernard M. Oliver (the vice president at Hewlett-Packard R&D Labs), scientist Otto Struve (whose eyes looked in different directions, supposedly a consequence of his method of staring with one eye into a microscope, and with the other consulting a nearby numerical table), biochemist Dana Atchley, the soon-to-be Nobel-anointed Melvin Calvin and, of course, perhaps most importantly of all, a young Carl Sagan, who would go on to achieve huge fame as a science communicator and host of the popular TV series, *Cosmos*.

Lilly was invited to join the group after one of the organisers jokingly pointed out that the only person missing on the list of invitees was someone who had actually spoken with extraterrestrials. It was suggested that someone already had, and that was Lilly.

At the time it was thought that if dolphins were intelligent to the same level as human beings, it would mean that two separate intelligences had evolved on Earth and that intelligence as a concept was therefore not a unique event. And if that were the case, intelligence might be abundant in the universe. However, it was also pointed out that as bright as dolphins were, they probably had no interest in astronomy, and even if they did, what were they going to do? Build telescopes and rockets with their flippers?*

MONKEY ORGASMS AND FLOTATION TANKS

Dr. John Lilly was a hugely influential neuroscientist and polymath who is rarely spoken about today. Described by some as being as handsome as a movie actor and not someone who was plugging electrodes into his own head to experiment with pleasure and pain (something Lilly routinely did as an academic), he was courted by multiple government agencies and was at the cutting edge of scientific advances in numerous areas.

His first notable experiments involved working out how to help pilots with decompression (using himself as the test subject) before moving on to the National Institute of Health, where he helped map the brain by figuring out how each section interacts with the rest of our bodies. He began his experiments on monkeys, designing a pain-free method to thread hypodermic tubing into their brains. He then inserted

---

* Interestingly, this point of underwater intelligence is a leading theory in why we may not have discovered spacefaring aliens yet. The so-called water world hypothesis proposes that while there's lots of life in the universe, we haven't met any of it because all the aliens live underwater. The hypothesis states that Earth is peculiar due to its position within a habitable zone—we're very near the edge of one, and it might be the case that this position has resulted in the planet having more land mass and an oxygen-rich atmosphere, meaning that living organisms are able to survive on land. Living above a water surface may be incredibly rare, so while extraterrestrial life does exist, it will never be able to get to us, because it's stuck swimming on its planet.

electrodes, enabling him to stimulate a range of emotions from pain to anxiety at the push of a button and without damaging any of the brain tissue. He also discovered the bits of the brain that were in charge of giving the monkeys erections and orgasms. (One of his studies showed that if you gave a monkey a button that, when pressed, would give it an orgasm, the monkey would hit that button once every three minutes, for up to 16 hours in a day, before passing out in euphoria.)

From here, Lilly started to focus more on human brains, turning himself into his own test subject again. In 1954 he became interested in human consciousness, and wondered what would happen to the brain if it were deprived of sensory stimulation—no sound, smell, sight, touch, or anything else. Was the brain only active because of these stimuli? What if you removed them, and the brain had nothing to react to? Would it just shut down? To answer these questions he designed a sensory-deprivation box to lock himself in to see if his consciousness would shut down once inside. If it did, would he still be alive?

This wild idea is what led to the invention of flotation tanks, used globally today for mental well-being, although Lilly's box wasn't really a flotation tank, of course. "That's a cover story," he would say. "It's really a doorway into the universe." (Something you won't find advertised in your average spa pamphlet.) His sensory-deprivation experiences led to him contacting three interdimensional beings that ran the local branch of a much larger universal institution called the Earth Coincidence Control Office (ECCO). They were, according to Lilly, responsible for orchestrating long-term coincidences in one's life. According to Lilly's idea, ECCO would have been responsible for putting W. T. Stead on-board the *Titanic* and they also would have guided Tu Youyou's father into choosing her name from a poem. "ECCO runs our lives," Lilly claimed, "though we won't admit it."

Around this time Lilly became interested in the minds of other species. Did they have consciousness? A self? Focusing his attention on dolphins in particular, a creature that seemed to demonstrate high levels of intelligence, he wondered whether he could learn to communicate with them. So he decided to move in with some and find out.

THE DOLPHIN HOUSE

Lilly believed that humans needed to acknowledge the superior mind of the dolphin, and proposed setting up a Cetacean Nation. He wrote a manifesto that read:

> *To insure the survival of cetaceans, in light of the continuous onslaught by their terrestrial counterparts, human beings, it is essential that cetaceans be recognized for what they truly are: non-terrestrial intelligent lifeforms . . . To attain this goal, it is essential that the cetaceans attain a status in human society in which they are recognized as the intelligent lifeforms that they are. It is with this goal in mind that a Cetacean Nation is now being initiated. The eventual goal is to have cetaceans represented as a nation within the framework of the United Nations.*

Using NASA funding, Lilly aimed to teach dolphins to speak the English language so perfectly that they would be given a chair at the United Nations to speak on behalf of all marine mammals.

NASA agreed that he was on to something and thought that helping to decipher different languages might be useful in the event of contact with aliens. So it approved a grant to him through its biosciences programme.

Lilly believed that humans and dolphins should be living as one. However, he worried that if they were as intelligent as he believed them to be, they were probably incredibly pissed off with us over our treatment of not only them, but of all creatures on Earth. A solid point. I've often thought that if we do ever get to make contact with plants or animals, we're probably not going to like what they've got to say to us.

To begin the process of making amends with them, Lilly planned to sail out into the ocean and attract pods of dolphins, so he could serenade them with music as a message of peace. The best show of companionship, however, was his idea to co-habitat with them, and in order to demonstrate how that might be achieved, in 1959 Lilly bought land to build an ocean-side laboratory on, on the Caribbean island of St. Thomas, using his NASA funding as well as other charitable donations. He partially flooded the building, installing ramps on the side that allowed ocean water to wash in so that a constant circulation kept the marine environment fresh and replenished. His idea was that there would be rooms for dolphins, rooms for humans, and then rooms for both dolphins and humans, like the dining room, where the dinner table would have water coming halfway up the table leg, so that both dolphin and human could eat in each other's company. He even worked on a flooded car design for the dolphins, so that they could transport themselves between locations.

Lilly began his experiments by trying to teach dolphins to speak English, which attracted much curiosity from the scientific community. Carl Sagan, who first met Lilly at the SETI meeting a few years later, would make trips to St. Thomas so that he could catch up on what Lilly was up to. On his first visit, he was introduced to Elvar (the dolphin with the special way of playing fetch), whom he was left with on his own. Sagan started tickling the friendly dolphin's belly, and after he stopped, he was shocked by Elvar's response. He could have sworn he heard the dolphin say "More" to him. Lilly would later confirm that this was one of the English words that Elvar knew.

Sagan is possibly the catalyst for the most controversial

aspect of the language classes between human and dolphin that would take place over the next few months. One night while he was out to dinner on the island, he started chatting to the hostess of the restaurant, a woman called Margaret Howe. Sagan, in an attempt to flirt with Howe, told her about the Dolphin House and offered to introduce her to the team, and eventually gave her a job at the facility.*

HOWE TO TRAIN YOUR DOLPHIN

Howe soon moved into the house and began working with Peter, one of the dolphins living there. Deciding to bunk up in one of the dolphin-friendly areas of the house, Howe set up a bed in the middle of a flooded room, and surrounded it with shower curtains to maintain a bit of privacy and dryness. Margaret's job was to teach Peter English: how to pronounce words correctly and let him know what they meant. She was in no way scientifically trained, fortunately the only qualification required of her was that she read *Planet of the Apes* before starting. He believed that it was ECCO that brought them together and had total faith in her abilities, so he didn't interfere at all with her lessons, only ever attempting to commu-

---

* I should point out that this story comes from a brilliant William Poundstone biography on the life of Carl Sagan. Poundstone got it from an interview with Lilly and he also found it in Sagan's writings. Margaret Howe, however, denies it, saying she heard about the Dolphin House while working at a hotel on the island and went there on her own initiative, where it was Gregory Bateson who generously folded her into the research programme on a volunteer basis.

nicate with her about the job via telepathy from the floor above while floating in his isolation tank.

If you search online, you can listen to the tapes recorded during these English lessons. Howe was a stern teacher. She tried as much as possible not to communicate with Peter if he spoke to her in Dolphinese, using his clicks and whistles. She only responded when he spoke in English. You can hear her trying to communicate certain words, with Peter mimicking and matching her syllables, forming sentences like, "I'm a good boy."

After about a month Peter was said to be speaking mostly using his very basic English, and it started to look as if interspecies communication might be on the horizon. Unfortunately, as sometimes happens, sex got in the way.

Margret Howe chatting with a dolphin.

Peter started becoming troublesome. He was entering puberty, and was quickly discovering that penises weren't just something you used to play fetch with. Howe would be mid-lesson with Peter when he'd get an erection, and then class had to be dismissed.

To begin with this was a huge problem, and it looked like it wasn't going away. But then it became something that Howe got to thinking about. What if she could help satisfy the dolphin's sexual needs, and, in her words, "strengthen the bond between dolphin and human?" So she decided to lend a helping hand.

I found that taking his penis in my hand and letting him jam himself against me he would reach some sort of orgasm, mouth open, eyes closed, body shaking, then his penis would relax and withdraw. He would repeat this move two or three times and then his erection would stop and he seemed satisfied.

When reports of these incidents were published, the scientific world turned on both Lilly and Howe. Howe was subject to global humiliation, with her story sensationalised in the press and, years later, even written up as a steamy tale in *Hustler* magazine. Howe was so distressed by this that she went around shops trying to buy up every copy so that no one would see it.

Pretty soon the entire project was shut down, and for decades now, people have been ridiculing Howe for what she did.

With the experiment over, Margaret moved out of the

house, and Peter the dolphin, in a state of depression, would sadly commit suicide, by drowning himself. The house would eventually be de-flooded and Margaret would once again take up residence there, now married to the man who had photographed the whole dolphin experiment.

Years later Lilly would once again try to experiment with dolphin communication, this time using computers. He believed it would take five years to speak to them, and five years to create a human–dolphin dictionary. But neither happened. His ideas, once respected by some of the greatest scientific minds of the time, soon became nothing more than a curiosity. From there on Lilly became a true fringe scientist, dropping deep into the rabbit-hole of psychedelia, fascinated by the mind-bending drugs of the 1960s.

★   ★   ★

On the day that Melvin Calvin was told he'd won his Nobel Prize, all the scientists at the secret alien-hunting conference gathered alongside him for a spontaneous party in West Virginia. Cracking open a bottle of champagne,* Calvin made a toast, declaring that this ground-breaking group would henceforth be known as the Order of the Dolphin.

A few weeks later they'd all receive a special present in the post from Melvin—a silver tie pin made from a reproduction

---

* Frank Drake had considered sending the observatory's chauffeur to pick up the alcohol, but decided against it in the end. A great shame, because if he hadn't the champagne would have been delivered by a driver called Mr. French Beverage.

of a 300 BCE coin from the Greek colony of Taras depicting a boy riding a dolphin. It was the official membership badge of the new Order.

And so it was that the founding of SETI, the most concerted attempt to date in the search for life in the cosmos, would log as its first ever members ten eminent scientists and, thanks to Calvin, one dolphin named Elvar.

CHAPTER 13

SHOULD OFFICE PLANTS BE INVESTIGATING MURDER CASES?

THE THEORY OF PLANT COMMUNICATION

Whenever King Charles III participates in a tree-planting ceremony he gives one of the branches a handshake and wishes it well. "I happily talk to the plants and trees, and listen to them," Charles once told the BBC. "I think it's absolutely crucial." For decades we've laughed at his attempts to communicate with his plants, yet recent scientific discoveries have shown there may actually be something a bit more "intelligent" going on than we realised.

Have we misjudged the ability of plants? We've recently learnt they have their own "internet"—known to botanists as the "wood wide web"—which an astonishing 80 per cent of all plants use as their "provider" and where they have been observed committing the equivalent of cyber-crime, as well as doing online shopping. They also, it has been discovered, appear to know who their family are, apparently recognising their siblings, thereby avoiding competing with them for resources and sending them messages through the WWW, warning them of danger.

One person who believes there's something more going on with plants is Monica Gagliano. Gagliano is a Research Associate Professor in Evolutionary Ecology at the Southern Cross University in Australia and published a book titled *Thus Spoke the Plant*. Despite having only one author name on its cover, the book, according to Gagliano, was actually co-authored with a collection of "plant people," who dictated their parts of the book to her. A "plant person" is what Gagliano calls the plants she studies, believing them to have some form of cognition. The book isn't a metaphorical collaboration; Gagliano claims she genuinely co-wrote the book with the plants, labelling it a "phytobiography."* If what she claims is true, it is the first book ever co-written by the vegetal world.

I first became aware of Gagliano thanks to a *New York Times* article in which she told the interviewer that the only reason she got into studying plant acoustics was because a friend assured her she would be given a grant on "sound communication in plants" if she applied. That friend was an oak tree.

Gagliano started talking to plants after a series of lucid dreams led her to Peru, where she spent time with shamans doing the hallucinogenic ayahuasca, as well as other spiritual practices.

---

* The first chapter is titled "Oryngham," a word that means "thank you for listening" in plant language. Though Gagliano says you can't really speak the word, it's more a feeling.

It was there that the plants started speaking to her.

Ten years on, and Gagliano now studies plants, publishing peer-reviewed papers in the new field of plant bioacoustics, which she pioneered. Her research is focused on showing that plants can learn new behaviours (something thought to be impossible) and that they are able to move towards water when they "hear" the sound of it.

Gagliano now is a star draw at alternative conferences looking into plant consciousness, and an ambassador for those who believe in the exciting thought: what if nature is sentient?

Gagliano's not the first to make us wonder about the "mind" of plants, though. Back in the 1970s a book was released that convinced us that there was more to the natural world.

THE SECRET LIFE OF PLANTS

In 1973 a highly contentious book called *The Secret Life of Plants* somehow escaped its fate of glorious obscurity in the University of Rejected Sciences and improbably found itself somewhere it should never normally have been—right at the very top of the *New York Times* bestseller list, and selling millions of copies worldwide.

This can very occasionally happen, much to the annoyance of many in the academic world. Written by Peter Tompkins (author of *Secrets of the Great Pyramid*) and Christopher Bird (a former CIA operative and alumnus of Harvard, where he had read Eastern European studies and Polynesian anthropology), *The Secret Life of Plants* promised to have readers reassessing everything they thought they knew about the natural world, as well as helping them to start appreciating its many unknown, occult forces.

The material that the authors gathered together in the book read like some far-fetched science fiction: it included claims that seeds could communicate with distant galaxies; it showcased maverick inventors, like electrical engineer Thomas Galen Hieronymus, who invented a device that could supposedly enable farmers to eradicate crop-eating insects, not by spraying pesticides on their fields but by beaming the energy signature of pesticides pasted onto photographs of their fields instead. However, it was the story of a CIA polygraph expert that exploded into the consciousness of the American and British counter-culture, inspiring a relationship with plant life that continues to this day.

THE MAN WHO SPOKE TO PLANTS

The year was 1966, and a man named Cleve Backster was about to make first contact with the vegetable world. He didn't plan for it, of course. Perhaps if he'd known that this was the moment plants and humans would finally communicate he might have approached the natural world with a message of peace. As it happened, contact was established via a sinister threat of burning.

The moment occurred in the early hours of February 2. Backster was in his office pouring himself a cup of coffee when he found himself staring at the *Dracaena fragrans* potted plant sitting in his office, and wondering what would happen if he hooked it up to one of his lie-detection machines.

Backster was not a botanist and he didn't even particularly like plants. His background was in interrogation. As a young man he'd worked for the US Army Counter Intelligence Corps, where he made a name for himself by using hypnosis and truth serums to get the enemy to reveal their secrets.* In 1948 the CIA became aware of his efforts and hired him as an interrogations officer. It was while working for them that he became interested in learning about lie-detection machines.

The polygraph, which had only been around for a couple of decades at this point, was still viewed as a rather futuristic

---

* One visiting US Army general was said to have been astounded by Backster's abilities after Backster hypnotised the general's secretary and got her to dig out a classified document and hand it over to him.

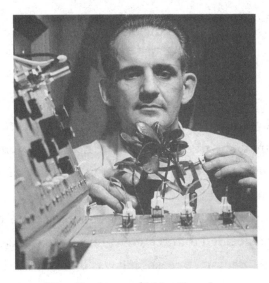

Cleve Backster and his office plant.

invention. According to contemporary accounts it was quite an intimidating machine to your average criminal, many of whom apparently appeared to believe that it was some sort of an un-cheatable magic box.

Backster spent a few years at the CIA before leaving to open his own operation: the Backster School of Lie Detection, with an office in New York City. There he'd teach FBI agents and NYPD detectives how to use the machines.

It was in his office, in the early hours of that fateful Wednesday morning while looking at the *Dracaena fragrans*, that he thought to himself, *I wonder how long, once the roots have been watered, it takes for the water to reach its leaves?* He realised that he might be able to find out by hooking up one of its leaves to a polygraph machine. When humans are connected to a polygraph, one of the things we're being measured for is the change in the electrical resistance of our skin; the theory is that if you're lying, you sweat, and that decreases electrical resistance. Backster assumed that as the water rose from the roots and replenished the leaves, the polygraph would show the same results. What he didn't expect was for the trace made by the pen on the lie detector to pitch downwards. *Curious*, thought Backster—it was not dissimilar to how a human might react.

He wondered if he could get a better reaction out of the plant, so he decided to threaten it. This isn't as bizarre as you might think. Backster's reasoning was that when using a polygraph on humans, one of the best ways to provoke a response in the person is to threaten them. Not being able to use words to threaten the plant, Backster needed to see if physical pain would work, so he dipped one of the plant's leaves into a hot mug of coffee. But the plant didn't give any reaction on the polygraph. Perhaps, he thought, he should come at the plant with a stronger threat, and so he decided to burn the very leaf to which he had attached the electrodes.

This was when the universe shifted for Backster. As soon as he had the thought of burning the leaf, the polygraph shot up. It was as if the plant had read his mind and was reacting in fear.

After buying more plants, Backster started testing every possible way in which they might react emotionally to him—first with experiments when he was in the same room as them, then when he was away. He wandered about with his notebook along the streets of New York, writing down every

distressing thing that happened, from getting into an alterca-
tion with a street vendor to almost being run over by a car.
When he returned to his office he was amazed to find that his
plants had spiked at the precise times that he was stressed.

As his experiments continued, Backster started to believe
that his plants were growing quite fond of him. For example,
one time when he was out of the office, he recorded the time
of the exact moment that he had the thought of returning to
see them all. When he finally got to the office, he noted a
spike on the polygraph readings that matched the exact time.
It was as if they were excited dogs watching through a window at home as their owner returns from work.

Backster soon decided to bring in an assistant named Bob
Henson to help with the increasing number of experiments
he was performing. Together they designed a test in which
they employed standard police interrogation tactics. Picking
as their subject a *Philodendron cordatum* plant that had not yet
met either of them, they subjected it to the classic good cop/
bad cop routine. Henson would first enter the room to terror-
ise the plant, then Backster came in and calmed it down by
addressing it in loving tones. Backster would later claim that

The moment of contact.

the experiment worked, noting that any time he entered the room the plant would become calm, but whenever Henson showed up it showed clear signs of distress.

As Backster's observations continued, he kept accumulating many curious discoveries: he found that plants would feel threatened if a dog entered the room; he noted that if a plant became too overwhelmed by a threat then it would "pass out." Backster also discovered that plants felt intimidated by the presence of someone with a history of plant-harming. In one example, a supposedly well-known, but unnamed, scientist asked to see Backster at work. When Backster hooked up a plant to the polygraph to demonstrate his findings to the scientist, he failed to get any reaction from the plant. So he tried another one, but still nothing. Confused by the lack of response, Backster thought to ask if the scientist by any chance injured plants for a living. "Injure them?" she replied. "In my experimental work I grind them up by the bushel." No wonder the plants didn't respond, thought Backster, the scientist was a plant killer.

At this point Backster was starting to get very excited about his experiments, but the academic community remained unmoved. As far as they were concerned, his discoveries weren't proper science. Any attempts to replicate his findings failed, and many claimed that the responses being registered by the polygraph were simply down to things like the build-up of static electricity in his lab.

But Backster didn't care what they thought. He was too busy working on an idea that he hoped would revolutionise the world of criminal investigation—his plan was to create a new breed of plant-based police officers.

PLANT WARFARE

Backster had the idea for an elite force of vegetable officers after conducting an experiment in which he tested his plants to see if they could pick out a murderer from a line-up of six suspects. To do this, he asked six students, one by one, to enter a room that contained two potted plants, and have one of them "murder" one of the plants by tearing it out of its pot and stamping all over it. To make sure that no one knew who the murderer was, including Backster himself, the six participants were each asked to draw pieces of paper from a hat, with only one of the pieces containing the instruction to kill. After the grisly task was completed, the surviving plant, which had witnessed the crime, was then attached to a lie detector as the six students re-entered the room one at a time. As the first five students wandered into the room, the plant showed no emotional reaction, then as the sixth student entered the room the plant began to display "wild stress." When Backster asked if he was the killer, the student admitted that yes he was. The experiment had worked.

Backster was soon able to test this newly discovered plant ability in the real world when he was called up by police in New Jersey, who needed his help in identifying a killer. According to the story in *The Secret Life of Plants*, a woman had been found dead in a factory, and the police had no suspects and no witnesses. The idea was that Backster would

interrogate every single person who worked there, by hooking them all up one by one to a lie-detection machine. However, when he arrived at the scene of the crime, Backster spotted something that all the police officers and investigators had somehow managed to miss. They had told him there had been no witnesses to the murder. This was wrong. There were in fact two witnesses to the murder, and both were still in the room, inside a couple of pots.

One by one, the first batch of factory workers were presented to the plants, who gave no reaction. How Backster managed to convince the police into agreeing to this method of interrogation, I have no idea, but according to the story, at the end of the day, Backster requested that both plants be placed in protective custody overnight, as their lives might be in danger given that the murderer was now undoubtedly aware of them. The next day, the rest of the factory workers got their moment in front of the plants, but neither plant managed to single out the assassin.*

THE THEORY OF PRIMARY PERCEPTION

As time passed, Backster started developing his theory of "primary perception," the idea being that perhaps the plants were engaging in some sort of telepathic communication with humans. He soon began to wonder if it wasn't just office plants that displayed this kind of sentience. And so he introduced bananas, onions, lettuces, and oranges to the polygraph machines, to see just how widely this unrecognised consciousness occurred within the natural world. They all seemed to register a positive reaction. Just imagine how extraordinary this must have felt to him. Assuming he fully believed in what he was claiming, Backster must have felt like the Doctor Doolittle of fruit and veg.

The applications and possibilities for our relationships with the natural world were suddenly endless. Imagine if it were true that plants could somehow be paired up with humans in telepathic connection. He started to dream bigger

---

* Backster would later discover that the plants were on a hiding to nothing, as the murderer was someone who didn't work at the factory, which is why they gave no reaction. Curiously, the story of Backster and the Factory Murder has been removed from every subsequent reprint of *The Secret Life of Plants*, following its initial release. Why was it removed? Did the police get in contact and demand it be taken out because they didn't want the public freaking out about their methods? Perhaps the same can be said for Backster? Or was it perhaps entirely made up?

about his plans for police use, believing that plants could even be used as covert assets in jungle warfare, where they could relay intel on the position of the enemy back to base. And what about space travel? Why send a human to the far reaches of the solar system when instead you could send a potted plant and have it relay information to mission control telepathically? Were there now any barriers preventing us from exploring its strange new worlds with this new breed of astreenauts?

THE TOMATO WHISPERER

Backster wasn't the first person to try to communicate with plants. Many before him had made attempts to get to know the "vegetal soul," as Aristotle called it. Charles Darwin said in his book *The Power of Movement in Plants* that plants "act like the brain of one of the lower animals; the brain being seated within the anterior end of the body, receiving impressions from the sense organs and directing the several movements." He thought plants were shaped a bit like a human doing a handstand—brains at the bottom, genitals in the air. His experiments on them included getting his son to spend hours playing the bassoon to his mimosas, to see what effect it might have on them. He later wrote:

> The day before yesterday & today I observed (but perhaps the observation will prove erroneous) that certain sensitive plants were excited into movement, by a prolonged note on the bassoon & apparently more by a high than a low note.

He eventually decided, however, that nothing was coming of it and abandoned the idea, calling it his "fool's experiment."

Maybe he should have just read to them instead . . . In 2009 the Royal Horticultural Society conducted a month-long study to see if tomato plants grew taller when being spoken to by a human. Ten random people were selected and paired up with a different plant, for which they each recorded an audiobook of their choice. This was played to the plant on a loop via a set of headphones placed around the plant pot. At the end of the month-long experiment the plant that was found to have grown the most, by over half an inch, was the one listening to *On the Origin of Species*, which was being read to it by the great-great-granddaughter of Charles Darwin.*

THE SOUNDTRACK OF PLANTS

Not many, if any, theories get their own soundtrack, but plant sentience did.

In 1979, Stevie Wonder's *Journey Through the Secret Life of*

---

* Sarah Darwin's plant grew 1.6cms higher than the tallest of the two control plants in the experiment. Of the rest, the ones that grew tallest were being read to by women. It must be noted that the experiment was hardly scientific (the sample size was far too small, for starters), Sarah Darwin herself believing it to be a joke, having been asked to take part on April 1. One participant in the study wrote to me saying that while it captured people's imaginations, they were sure everyone involved wished it never really happened. This hasn't deterred me from my new hobby of streaming YouTube videos of Sarah Darwin reading extracts from her ancestors' book to my kitchen pot plants.

Plants was released, the soundtrack to the documentary film of the *Secret Life of Plants* book. As part of the album pre-launch, the record label Motown sent out copies of the paperback edition of the book to record stores, along with packets of flower seeds, with the promise that by the time the flowers had sprouted the album would have arrived. An American chemist created a specific scent for the album that would give it a plant-y smell, although analysis by the Motown technical department in London showed that there was one chemical in the perfume that actually corroded vinyl, so, sadly, it was not included on the British release. The al-bum was launched in the New York Botanical Garden, where critics were invited to listen to both sides of the LP while eating vegetarian food.

The album actually arrived quite late in the day, given the trend for plant albums in the early and mid-1970s. Following Backster's sentience claims, many tribes within the American counter-culture latched on to this new idea of plant love, and music made specifically for plants sud-denly became terribly chi-chi. Some artists even specifi-cally produced albums for plants that were sold (fairly) exclusively in plant shops. Mort Garson's *Mother Earth's Plantasia*, released in 1976, was only sold at two places: a Los Angeles store called Mother Earth, where if you bought a houseplant, then the album was given to you for free, and, oddly, a mattress company, which also gave you one gratis with the purchase of any new product. According to the liner notes, *every pitch is scientifically designed to affect the stomata, or breathing cells, of your plants, opening them ever so slightly wider and allowing them to breathe ever so slightly freer and thus, grow ever so slightly better. Talking to them? Well, we've always felt that talking to your plants is going to do more for you than it does for them.*

The *Secret Life of Plants* film and soundtrack's success prolonged Backster and his lie detector machine's time in the limelight, and he was by this stage touring colleges and international venues. One attendee I spoke to described one of his talks as "sort of like a Trump rally, I suppose . . . Created a lot of buzz, as the stuff he was talking about seemed so incredible."

His critics, however, continued to mock his ideas, from the scientists who claimed he was a charlatan to the parapsychologists who have tried to discredit him by claiming he was simply altering the polygraph results via telekinesis.

Reading interviews Backster gave in the 1980s and '90s is rather interesting. They often show journalists arriving as sceptics, then leaving, not as converts, but at least less sure about what they thought. When journalist Derrick Jensen met with Backster some 30 years after his initial discovery, Backster had moved on to experimenting with other forms of primary perception, and tried to demonstrate to Jensen that yoghurt could respond to emotions during the interview. Placing some yoghurt in a test tube, he attached electrodes to it and started recording.

Jensen admitted to being sceptical, albeit a little excited. When Backster briefly left the room, Jensen tried to provoke a response from the yoghurt. He thought of disturbing ideas like deforestation and child abuse—but he got nothing. Abandoning his plan, he instead took a walk around the lab. While staring at the walls he noticed an advert for a shipping company and found it made him angry. Realising this was an impulsive moment of high emotion, he went back to check just in case the yoghurt had felt it too. It had—there was a clear spike on the chart.

As well as yoghurt, Backster also tested the method on human sperm. According to Backster, this worked too. Collecting the semen from a test subject, he successfully showed that sperm was able to identify its donor. The sperm literally knew who its daddy was.

"In this experiment, the sample from the donor was put in a test tube with electrodes, and the donor was separated from the sperm by several rooms," he wrote. "Then the donor inhaled amyl nitrite, which dilates the blood vessels and is conventionally used to stop a stroke. Just crushing the amyl nitrite caused a big reaction in the sperm, and when the donor inhaled, the sperm went wild."

However, Backster didn't continue with these experiments, despite the extraordinary ramifications of his discovery, as he was worried that sceptics would mock him about them, asking him about his "masturbatorium."

BACKSTER'S LEGACY

I wonder if one day we'll discover that Backster was actually on the right track and we establish some form of two-way communication with the plants of our world. Cleve Backster died in 2013, just one year after Monica Gagliano started chatting with mimosas and only a few years before scientists started making new major discoveries in plant communication.

But are they intelligent? My personal hope is that even if Backster had some faulty methods, he might still have been right about his core idea. And after spending some time reading his story, I can't help but look at plants differently now.

I particularly noticed this when I walked through Kew Gardens not long after one of the pandemic lockdowns. Founded in west London and later gifted to the public in 1840, Kew is billed as the "largest and most diverse botanical and mycological collections in the world." As I wandered around with my family, I spotted one woman in the distance hugging a tree. I couldn't see her face, but I bet it was in bliss. Usually I'd have thought her weird; now I found myself envious of her connection with nature.

As we continued our family walk among the many wonders of Kew, I stumbled across a sign that read, "The oldest potted plant in the world?" The plant growing behind it was over 240 years old and had travelled over from South Africa on the top deck of a ship so that it could be naturally watered by the ocean's rain on the way. My, what stories this veteran would have to tell. This plant is so old that it has been given an artificial crutch just to keep it held up. Again, I thought about Backster and his *Dracaena fragrans* in a pot in his office. Before moving on I reached out my hand, shook one of the plant's leaves and wished it well.

CHAPTER 14
CAN WATCHING URI GELLER ON TV GET YOU PREGNANT?
THE THEORY OF MAGICIANS

In 1974, Uri Geller was served a paternity suit by a woman in Jönköping, Sweden. She wasn't accusing him of being the father; but rather claimed that while watching him on TV, the power of his metal-bending skills was so great that the same power that had caused spoons to bend had also bent her contraceptive coil, rendering it broken.

The incident occurred in the same year Geller released a pop-music album in Europe. During the promotion of it, strange things were reported to have happened when DJs played songs from it over the radio. They started receiving complaints from its listeners. One station in Switzerland reported that it received hundreds of calls from people claiming their cutlery and keys were bending on their own in their houses. "If this kind of reaction continues, it will be an important corroboration of the theory that there is a new force in the world, that it can be triggered in others, and that it should receive serious and immediate attention," wrote Geller in his autobiography.

Today, Geller has a comical feel about him, but back in the day, many believed he had access to mystical powers. According to Geller, many governments would consult him as a result. Among the claims are that Geller spoke to the Norwegian defence minister, who asked him whether or not he could influence rockets; and that the American Secret Service took him to an arms talk in Vienna to project the word "peace" at Gorbachev's head. According to Geller it worked, and the next day Gorbachev agreed to disarmament.

Perhaps my favourite story of Geller's, which he wrote up in his autobiography, is about the time he was on a cruise with the actor Gary Cooper's daughter. While on board he

was challenged by the ship's band to use his mind to stop the ship. Accepting the challenge, he got everyone to stand on the deck and concentrate on stopping the vessel. Suddenly, according to Geller, the ship got slower and slower, until it stopped completely. Uri himself was surprised and everyone else was scared. They asked the ship's officer what had happened, but he had no idea. Hours later, when the ship was on the move again, they again asked the same officer what the problem had been, and he explained that it turned out the captain had stopped the ship on purpose. The reason? The ship's main fuel pipe had suddenly bent.

In 2009, Geller purchased a 100-by-50-metre island off Scotland called Lamb Island. It was said to have a history of witch trials, but the main reason for his purchase is that, according to Geller, there is buried Egyptian treasure, brought over by Scota, the daughter of the Egyptian pharaoh Cingris, who, it should be noted, never existed. Neither of them did. It's not even in Egyptian mythology—it's Irish and Scottish mythology. Nevertheless, Geller believes that he will find the treasure through dowsing (which is when you search for things underground with a Y-shaped stick). Geller himself has revealed that he has buried treasure of his own there, in an attempt to boost the powers of the island. Somewhere on the island, he says, is a crystal orb that once belonged to Albert Einstein.

Like Novak Djokovic's pyramids, Geller has contributed to the local economy with his mystic island theory, as locals now take tourists on trips around the island and tell them about the Geller-inspired folklore. And it may well be the case that Geller bought this island for mystic reasons. But I have a theory that he was following in the footsteps of the most successful magician ever, who also bought an island, but who has made an even bigger discovery.

HAS DAVID COPPERFIELD DISCOVERED THE ELIXIR OF LIFE?

In 2006, the magician David Copperfield spent $50 million purchasing an island in the Bahamas. He didn't find the island as you might expect, by leafing through some sort of *Rich Bastard* catalogue; rather, he discovered it the old-fashioned way—by taking a map of the world and drawing two lines on it. The first was a line that began at Stonehenge and ended at the statues of Easter Island. The next line he drew between the Great Pyramids of Giza and the great Pyramid of the Sun in Teotihuacan. It just so happened that the two lines crossed paths, in a sort of giant batshit X marks the spot, over an island in the Bahamas.*

As luck would have it, the island was for sale. Once he'd purchased it, Copperfield bought up the other 10 surrounding islands, and spent $40 million doing renovations to the main island, called Musha Cay, which now functions as a luxury holiday destination for the super-rich. "Comprised of 700 lush acres covering 11 islands with 40 secluded sugar sand beaches, five spectacular guest houses," is how the re-

---

* I've tried making these lines cross on the map so that they land on the Bahamas, but so far, no luck.

sort is marketed. However, it was a press release, sent out by Copperfield himself, that attracted the most attention to the group of islands. According to Copperfield, he was trekking through one of the islands one day with a cutlass when he noticed a particularly vibrant spot. "We found this liquid that in its simple stages can actually do miraculous things," Copperfield claimed to Reuters. "You can take dead leaves, they come into contact with the water, they become full of life again. Bugs or insects that are near death come in contact with the water, they fly away. It's an amazing thing, very exciting."

Copperfield claimed to have discovered the elixir of life, and hired biologists and geologists would experiment with the water to find out what effects it would have on humans, he said. However, no results were ever produced. Silence followed and

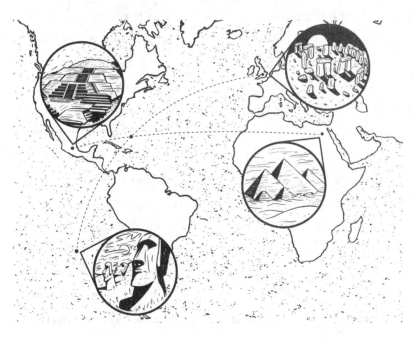

due to the nature of it being a privately-owned billionaire's island resort, investigating the fountain of youth independent of Copperfield has not been possible. However, someone did try. In his book *The Book of Immortality*, journalist Adam Leith Gollner describes how he managed to blag his way out to the island to see if he could get Copperfield to reveal its location. He learnt that Copperfield had discovered since his press release that the fountain of youth was not something that you could dip a limb into and have it rejuvenated. It was more that the animals and plant life there seemed youthful.

Gollner also became privy to other odd things happening on these islands, like a haunted beach Copperfield was designing where, Gollner was told, Sherpas were going to make it snow. He desperately tried to get more information from the magician, but it didn't materialise. Copperfield was more interested in telling Gollner about his island, which the magician was instrumental in designing, deciding on literally everything— from the furniture, all the way down to what the design of the user's manuals for phones should look like. Gollner in desperation left to investigate the islands for himself, sneaking off and conducting his own experiments by dipping brown leaves into various bits of water to see if they would turn green. By the time he left the island, he was none the wiser.

Has David Copperfield really discovered the secret to immortality? Or is he taking us for a ride? Those close to him insist he believes that it may be the source of eternal youth. Until we find out the truth, I wonder how many journalists, like Gollner, will find themselves trekking through the jungles of Copperfield Bay, searching for the proof of immortality.

Perhaps tricking otherwise rational journalists to snoop around an island in search of the elixir of life is his greatest trick yet.

CAN MAGICIANS' TIGERS PERFORM EMERGENCY SURGERY?

David Copperfield isn't the only great Las Vegas magician who has kept us guessing about a real-life mystery. On October 3, 2003, world-famous magicians and entertainers Siegfried & Roy, along with their tiger Mantacore, took to the stage at the famous Mirage Theatre in Las Vegas to perform their resident act to a sold-out crowd. As it happened, it was Roy's birthday on this particular night, and deciding to have a bit of fun, he was improvising more than usual. Holding the microphone to Mantacore's mouth, he asked the tiger to say hello to the audience. Mantacore responded by biting Roy's sleeve. Somewhat shocked, Roy swatted at the tiger, yelling at him to let him go. Upon being released, Roy tripped over Mantacore's back leg and fell to the stage floor. When Mantacore spotted Roy on the ground, he leapt onto him and bit deep into the entertainer's neck and vertebrae, puncturing several arteries and cutting off the blood to the right side of his brain in the process, then dragged him offstage.

Fortunately a back-up crew of animal trainers leapt into action and eventually managed to wrest Roy free from the tiger by spraying the animal with fire extinguishers. Roy was quickly rushed to hospital but was not in a great state. On at least one occasion he was considered medically dead, but his life was fortunately saved during surgery. Roy would later report that he experienced an out-of-body moment during surgery. "I stepped out of my body and looked over the surgeon's shoulder, and I sat while he was cutting me up," he said. "And my mom is sitting in a chair, and in front of her is one of my lions I had before, and my Siberian tiger was laying there, and my brother who had passed on years and years ago. And I know everything is going to be fine."

It was a painful road to recovery post surgery. Roy suffered a stroke and had to be brought back into surgery, this time his brain having swelled to such an extent, a quarter of his skull had to be removed to relieve the pressure. This part of his skull was then sewn into his abdomen so that the tissue remained alive before it was retransplanted.

Meanwhile rumours and theories were beginning to circulate about what had really happened on the night of the attack.

Later, when Roy finally spoke to the press, he presented an unusual theory: that Mantacore hadn't tried to kill him. In fact the opposite was true: the tiger had actually noticed Roy was suffering from a sudden medical emergency, and decided to perform life saving surgery on him. Had Mantacore not been there, said Roy, the illusionist might have died.

Roy suffered from hypertension, and what we were being asked to believe was that Mantacore could sense this and knew exactly where to bite in order to relieve the problem with a spot of precision bloodletting. "He did what every cat would do. He picked me up by the neck and carried me to the side. He relieved the blood pressure or I would be brain dead. I would be a vegetable," said Roy.

And it's not even the best theory out there.

★   ★   ★

Siegfried & Roy's career as magicians began on a cruise ship. After becoming tired of pulling rabbits out of hats, one day, while the ship was docked, they snuck a cheetah on board and began performing with it (stories differ as to whether or not they were kicked off the ship as a result). They continued with this act for many years, finally achieving fame at a party for Grace Kelly when their cheetah Chico leapt off the stage and wandered through the celebrity-packed room. Despite what everyone thought at the time, the move was not planned.

Siegfried & Roy with their tiger, Mantacore.

Chico had simply spotted the door to the kitchen and fancied a bite to eat. Unfortunately, history doesn't record how terrified the kitchen staff were when a cheetah wandered into the grill section.

After that the pair became popular with celebrities, politicians, and even Pope John Paul II, who reportedly gave them a fragment of Saint Francis of Assisi's shin bone as a gift.

Eventually they decided to take on a residency in Las Vegas, where they performed for decades with a show that went on to generate over $1 billion in ticket sales. They also created the Mirage's Secret Garden, where they kept over 60 of their animals, including elephants, leopards, and tigers, including Mantacore.

Mantacore was a white Bengal tiger, which, unlike normal tigers, has a white coat and few or no black stripes. They're often referred to as "ghost tigers"—animals purported to be so rare it is said that only one is born in the wild every hundred years. Siegfried & Roy loved Mantacore—the star of their show—and, they said, he loved them back.

So what the hell happened that night in 2003?

Steve Wynn, the man who had originally recruited Siegfried & Roy to play the Mirage, believed he knew the answer. After spending hours analysing video footage of the incident, he revealed that Mantacore had become distracted by a lady with a particularly big beehive hairdo.

"For whatever reason, Mantacore was fascinated and distracted by the guest sitting ringside," said Wynn. "Mantacore got down on all fours and put his twenty-six-inch head four inches away from the woman. She thinks this is adorable and part of the show, and reaches out to try and rub him under his chin. Roy is talking and sees this move [which is] way wrong all the way around. As usual, the heroic fellow that he is, Roy jumps between the woman and the tiger."

Wynn's hairdo hypothesis then evolved into a murder theory, with others claiming that the woman had deliberately tried to trigger Mantecore into killing Roy, not only by attracting him with her big beehive but by soaking her hair in exotic animal urine, the smell of which might have turned the tiger aggressive.

Other theories held that Mantacore had been triggered by Roy's mouth odour (he had apparently eaten something odd before the show), that the tiger was upset by ultrasonic sounds, and even that he had snagged his testicle on his cage before coming out on stage to perform with Roy. The motivation for such an attack, said the theorists, was possibly homophobic, or it might even have had something to do with furious animal rights activists who wanted to send a message.

Curiously, the case was investigated by the counterterrorism unit for the Las Vegas Metropolitan Police Department. They did background checks on everyone who worked on the show, on as many people who attended the show as they could locate, and, some reports claim, on Mantacore the tiger himself.

No official conclusions were ever reached, and Mantacore was allowed to return to the Mirage Gardens, where he lived out his life, dying aged 17 in 2014. So will we ever know what happened that night? Perhaps not. Roy never changed his story, and, sadly, he passed away from Covid in 2020.

One last theory remains, however. This one was said to have been believed by Siegfried & Roy's good friend, the actress Shirley MacLaine. It goes like this: Horn wasn't there the night of October 3, 2003, to be attacked by Mantacore the tiger, because he had, in fact, died years before, and ever since then had been replaced by a surgically modified lookalike. The Roy Horn who passed away in 2020 was a clone.

CHAPTER 15
DO GHOSTS FLY BUSINESS CLASS?
THE THEORY OF CURSES

"Okay, here we go," says Fenella. "Let's hope the plane doesn't crash."

I turn to stare at her. "Are you fucking nuts?"

We're on the runway at Heathrow Airport, about to take off on a Qantas flight bound for Sydney, Australia.

"Why would you say that?" I whisper angrily.

I'm a hugely nervous flyer and yes, even though I know her words won't actually have any effect on the flight, I still find myself, against my better judgement, needing to find something wooden to touch.

I quickly think of the comedian Tim Minchin to calm my anxiety. Years ago, Tim was a guest on the BBC Radio 4 show I used to make called *The Museum of Curiosity*. Each episode, guests are invited to "donate" anything they want to an impossible museum and Tim donated the concept "tempting fate." "You think your words are going to somehow rewire the plane, cause a malfunction, so that it crashes?" I remember him saying. It was such a good point, but, ironically, a point that no one got to hear, as the BBC forced us to edit it out of the show at the last minute because a commercial airline had just crashed into the Atlantic. My nervousness is so great on flights that I once stopped reading a biography of Buddy Holly after hitting a particularly nasty patch of turbulence, thinking it might help. What was I expecting? The pilot to get on the Tannoy and say, "Could whoever is reading books about pop stars who died in plane crashes back there please cut it out?"

Deciding I was being stupid, I apologised to Fenella, and in an attempt to show how comfortable I was, told her about a recent discovery. "I hope we're not on a cursed plane. Did you know some people think those exist?"

Silence. "Why the fuck would you tell me THAT?" she finally says.

CURSED AIR

On December 29, 1972, Eastern Air Lines Flight 401 was making its way from New York to Miami when, quite out of the blue, the plane crashed into the Florida Everglades. A black-box recording would later reveal the crash occurred as a result of the cockpit crew being distracted by a conversation about the plane's landing gear indicator light not working. While they were discussing the issue, part of the autopilot disconnected and the plane slowly started to descend. By the time the pilot, captain Bob Loft, realised what was happening, it was too late.

This was the world's first ever major aeroplane disaster involving a twin-aisle airliner. In total 101 people lost their lives, though remarkably 75 of the passengers survived largely thanks to the fact that the plane had crash-landed in a swamp, which absorbed a lot of the energy of the impact. The swamp is quite the hero in this story, even possibly continuing to save lives once passengers had jumped out of the plane, by coating their injuries in mud, which may have helped stop many from bleeding to death (though perhaps not entirely a hero, as the bacteria would also cause a few deaths later on).

Months later, bizarre stories started circulating about crew members on other Eastern Air Lines flights claiming to have seen ghosts on board. There were the flight crew members who claimed to see the reflection of a ghost in an oven door while heating up some meals; another saw a ghost staring down at them in one of the overhead baggage compartments; and perhaps oddest of all, there was the cabin crew who claimed a ghost had joined them in the cabin, warning them of an electrical fault that, upon investigation, proved to be true. As the stories continued to filter in, new details started emerging about the identity of these ghosts—which had now been identified as 401's captain Bob Loft and his second officer, Don Repo. But why were they appearing on these random flights? What connected the pair from one fatal flight to all of these other airliners?

Sometime later the connection was made. When Flight 401 crashed into the swamp it suffered major damage, but the plane wasn't entirely destroyed. And often, once investigations looking into the cause of the crash have finished their vital work, many of the plane's surviving parts are salvaged and re-used in other aircraft. That's when it clicked: other planes were experiencing ghostly apparitions because they had been refitted with replacement parts from the doomed Flight 401. When it was noted that many of these parts had been refitted to one plane in particular, Flight 318, which happened to be of one of the planes reporting many of the ghostly encounters, people really started to get scared. Three senior pilots were reported as having had their plane exorcised by a priest. While others who had claimed an encounter were reportedly given access to a company therapist. In an attempt to curb fears, employees of Eastern Air Lines were warned they'd be dismissed if caught telling others that the cursed parts of Flight 401 were haunting other planes belonging to the airline.

CAN A PLANE BE CURSED?

The aircrafts that sourced parts from Flight 401 weren't the first to experience paranormal phenomena. There was the *Lady Be Good*, a military plane that went missing in 1943 while on a combat mission during the Second World War. The plane, which carried a crew of nine, was thought to have disappeared while over the Mediterranean. In fact it didn't crash into the sea at all, but was discovered 15 years later in the Libyan desert by a team of explorers. When they looked inside, the plane was empty of bodies, with everything in place; tidy and serene, with a Thermos of tea still sitting inside the cockpit that was, according to the explorers, still good to drink. For a while what happened to the crew remained a mystery. Later, though, their

bodies were found. It turned out that they hadn't died in the crash, but instead had managed to safely parachute before the plane went down. The crew would then each die at various different times as they wandered aimlessly in the desert, having taken the wrong direction towards civilisation.

The plane itself had landed much more gently than you'd expect a pilotless plane to do, so it was brought back to base and stripped, and as many of the parts as possible were reused in other American military craft. Then the strange phenomena began.

The first plane to experience problems was a Douglas C-54 Skymaster that had been fitted with some transmitters from the *Lady Be Good*. As it was making its way to land it suffered propeller difficulties and only made it down safely after various items from inside were lobbed out to help with the weight of the plane. Next a Douglas C-47 Skytrain, which had inherited the radio receiver from the *Lady*, crashed into the Mediterranean. And last, a bomber that had been fitted with armrests salvaged from the *Lady* went down in the Gulf of Sidra, taking with it the lives of ten men. The plane was never fully recovered, although a few small items later washed up on shore. According to the National Museum of the United States Air Force, one of those items was an armrest from the *Lady Be Good*.

HUESTON, WE HAVE A PROBLEM

If you ever get to fly into Savannah airport in Georgia and are of a superstitious nature, make sure to look out for the most active runway, Runway 10. Some say it might be cursed. The airport is built on farmlands, and after the Second World War the airport needed expanding. In the way of this extension was a private cemetery owned by a family called the Dotsons, which was made up of over a hundred burial plots. After much negotiation with all the great-grandchildren, the family reached a compromise. The airport could relocate the cemetery and all those buried in it, except for four people—the original owners of the farm, Richard and Catherine Dotson, and their relatives John Dotson and Daniel Hueston. As a result, the tarmac of Runway 10 now incorporates the gravestones of Richard and Catherine in the runway itself.

Online, there are suggestions that pilots have experienced paranormal encounters with the ghosts of the Dotsons. However, this rumour largely comes from a remark made by a pilot called Lisa Ruedy, who has flown in and out of the airport, and once wrote: "It's said that if you are coming in to land just after sundown, two figures will appear just along the north side of the runway."

I managed to track Captain Ruedy down via her Instagram account and she was more than happy to expand on her remark: "That specific quote actually came from a flight attendant that I flew with to Savannah on a work trip," she said. "He was from the area, so prior to the flight while we were waiting for passengers to board, he said he wanted to tell us a ghost story. He really got into it, dimmed the lights in the cabin and even held a flashlight under his chin like we do as kids." The attendant was joking, of course, "though he seemed like the type of person who would believe in ghosts," she added. "We had a short layover in Savannah, so I looked up the history about the graves online and learnt you could request a taxi from the air traffic control tower to see the tombstones if it wasn't super busy. So we did! ATC calls it the 'Graveyard Tour.'"

CURSED OCEAN

It isn't just cursed airports and aeroplanes you need to worry about. Oceans are also said to be cursed, most famously the Bermuda Triangle. I recently opened a map to look for it, but of course, it wasn't there. It's not an official part of any map.

Instead, it's an imaginary space in the Atlantic Ocean with ill-defined boundaries—ranging anywhere between 500,000 and 1.5 million square miles—that assumes a triangular shape whose corners touch Bermuda, Florida, and Puerto Rico.

I think, despite my fears, that I would quite like to fly over it. It's a celebrity patch of ocean, after all! I'd feel a bit star-struck, I imagine, as I looked down at it from my window. I certainly would be looking out for all of the interesting possible ways planes have been said to have gone missing while passing through the area. This would include looking for giant water tornadoes, which supposedly do occur and rise high up into the sky, although they never usually rip planes apart, as has been suggested happens in the Triangle. I'd also be looking for a doughnut shape in the clouds below us and checking to see if it was following us—a phenomenon known as electric fog. There are also hexagonal clouds to keep an eye out for—clouds that supposedly just shove a plane down from the sky. Then, of course, there are the UFOs, and the wormholes that lead into a parallel universe. It would be—I don't care what you say—a fascinating way to pass the time, in the same way that looking out for Nessie is, when you're on the banks of Loch Ness.

My favourite theory, however, is that what may have sunk all of those ships in the Bermuda Triangle was giant ocean farts. These farts, or "Burps of Death," as they're referred to by those who work at sea on oil rigs and so on, are huge expulsions of methane that have been trapped on the ocean floor, housed within pockets of subterranean rock. If they become dislodged they can be very dangerous, expanding as they travel towards the ocean's surface. Once they reach it, the bubbles created by the methane can reduce the density of the top layer of the ocean, causing ships to lose their buoyancy, some have claimed, and make them disappear below the surface altogether.

According to a paper published in the *American Journal of Physics* in 2003 by Australian scientists Joseph Monaghan and David May, it could very well be that what has been sinking so many ships in the Triangle are these giant methane farts. They pointed to a shipwreck off the east coast of Scotland as a potential example of a deadly methane encounter. In 2000 a fishing trawler was spotted on the ocean floor in a site known as Witch's Hole. (I was most disappointed to discover that "Ship sunk by massive fart from Witch's Hole" isn't a headline to be found anywhere online.) The trawler didn't display any obvious damage and was lying in a horizontal position. Sonar surveys found the ocean floor in that area to be a very "farty" patch of sea, with a particularly high level of methane some 150 km off the coast.

A paper written by US Geological Survey (USGS) geologist Bill Dillon also supports the possibility that giant methane bubbles could have the power to take down ships. Mapping conducted by the USGS shows that there are large amounts of gas hydrate in the sea-floor sediments on the continental rise off the western portion of the Bermuda Triangle. "If you release enough gas you generate a foam having such low density that a ship would not be able to displace enough to float," wrote Dillon. The only real problem with this idea, added Dillon, is that these large methane explosions haven't occurred in the area for a good 15,000 years.

What's more, according to Monaghan and May, it's not just ships that are in danger from these methane explosions. As the bubble expands, the gas continues to travel into the atmosphere. "In the Bermuda Triangle, methane gas is known to be present and the release of that gas could cause not only boats to sink, as shown in our study, but also aeroplanes to crash," May told *The Age* newspaper. The theory is that these gases could rise into the sky and create a mixture of air that contained up to 15 per cent methane. If a plane flies in its path, the engine's exhaust would make contact with the gas and cause a huge explosion.

In truth the Bermuda Triangle is no more dangerous than any other patch of air and ocean on Earth. One of the most travelled shipping lanes in the entire Atlantic Ocean, it has been estimated that roughly 50 ships and 20 aeroplanes have been lost there, in an area that covers 700,000 square kilometres. Many experts have pointed out that the number of ships and planes that go missing there is pretty much the same percentage as anywhere else in the world. It isn't even, according to a survey by the WWF, on the list of the 10 most dangerous bodies of water in the world for shipping.

THE GHOST OF FLIGHT 401

Despite Eastern Air Lines' best efforts to suppress the story of the ghostly sightings, the story eventually caught the eye of journalist and author John G. Fuller. Fuller was already an influential character in the world of esoteric literature, having written *The Interrupted Journey*, which tells the story of Barney and Betty Hill, a couple who claimed to have been abducted by aliens while driving home from a holiday and who put forward the idea that medical experiments were being conducted on them. The book—and their story—remain one of the most influential in UFOlogy.

So, as you can imagine, the bosses at Eastern Air Lines weren't exactly overjoyed when they heard news of the publication of *The Ghost of Flight 401*. And they were quite right not to be. Fuller got his information from a spy on the inside, a flight attendant called Elizabeth, who would eventually become his wife, and his book not only became a bestseller but was also adapted into a TV film.

As time passed, however, it became increasingly clear that the stories of these ghostly encounters were being made up by airline staff, or at least (not to get conspiratorial) that's what we've been told. And once the stories of the ghost of Flight 401 started to get discredited, the sightings slowly began to vanish too. Though some pointed out that sightings stopped being reported at roughly the same time that the company ordered the repurposed parts to be stripped from all of its planes.

Were there actually ever any ghostly encounters on any of those planes? Were pieces from Flight 401 definitely repurposed to be used on other airlines? Many people, like journalist Robert J. Serling, who has published a book investigating these events, say no—none of it ever happened. While others, like Don Repo's son, Jay, who himself had a ghostly encounter with his father, continue to believe every word of it.*

Regardless of what you believe, here's something to think about, next time you're on a plane: often when someone dies and is cremated, if that person has any metal in them—say as part of a hip replacement or from any other reconstruction—the metals are then collected afterwards from the ashes and sent off to be recycled for further use. Some of those metals will often end up being used to make new aeroplane parts, which then get fitted to commercial aircraft. So the next time you're on a plane, remember this: though you may never find yourself as a passenger on a haunted airline, you will conceivably be flying on something that's now partially made up of a bunch of dead grannies.

---

* Jay claimed his father made himself known on Jay's wedding night, when he and his bride arrived in a Miami hotel room. As he opened the empty closet of their room to hang up some clothing, Jay was astonished to find that, sitting there on the floor of the closet, was a pair of Eastern Air Line wings.

CHAPTER 16

ARE WE ONLY HERE BECAUSE OF AN ALIEN PICNIC GONE WRONG?

THE THEORY OF LIFE ON EARTH

There's a theory that the reason life on Earth began is because billions of years ago some aliens pit-stopped on our ancient planet for a picnic, and then didn't tidy up properly after themselves. The cosmic garbage theory, as it's known, was first proposed by Professor Thomas Gold of Cornell University in the 1960s. It proposes that when the aliens were shaking out their picnic rug, bits of extra-terrestrial cookie crumbs landed on the ground, and the microbes within the crumbs went on to spark the genesis of life on our planet.

What Gold was proposing was a version of a theory known as panspermia.

Panspermia is the idea that life didn't arise on planet Earth through a series of chemical reactions, but arrived from outer space, possibly by latching on to space dust. Gold didn't invent this idea; it was actually being proposed as far

back as the ancient Greeks. The philosopher Anaxagoras (circa 500–428 BCE) wrote about it when he twice mentioned *spermata* (Greek for seeds) being part of the universe. And though he doesn't explicitly state that this was how life originated, scholars have subsequently suggested that this is what he meant.*

Did we originate from outer space? The celebrated physicist Lord Kelvin seemed to think so, writing in 1871:

---

* Anaxagoras was brilliant; he also proposed that the sun was a star and that the light of the moon was a reflection from the sun. He also believed the Earth was flat. According to his theory, the way our flat Earth functioned was not dissimilar to how a puck sits on an air-hockey table. He believed the Earth was being floated by a current of air that lay underneath it, which, when disturbed, caused earthquakes.

We must regard it as probable in the highest degree that there are countless seed-bearing meteoric stones moving about through space. If at the present instance no life existed upon this Earth, one such stone falling upon it might, by what we blindly call natural causes, lead to its becoming covered with vegetation.

All such theories involve life finding its way to Earth by travelling a vast distance to get to us. This poses many problems, not least how any life forms might survive the radiation of space. So what Gold was proposing—a version of panspermia where aliens physically plopped down onto our planet and left the organic material here—makes more sense, to me at least.

DESIGNED BY ALIENS

One even more radical idea in this field comes from Francis Crick, the co-discoverer of DNA, and biochemist Leslie Orgel, a leading researcher in the study of the chemical origins of life on Earth. In 1973 Crick and Orgel published a paper proposing that not only might life on Earth originate from space, but also that it was *deliberately seeded* by aliens.

Their theory was originally outlined in the scientific journal *Icarus*, with Crick subsequently expanding on the idea in his book *Life Itself*.

It now seems unlikely that extra-terrestrial living organisms could have reached the Earth either as spores driven by the radiation pressure from another star or as living organisms imbedded in a meteorite. As an alternative to these nineteenth-century mechanisms, we have considered Directed Panspermia, the theory that organisms were deliberately transmitted to the Earth by intelligent beings on another planet.

Although Crick proposed this as a mechanism for the introduction of life, he was unsure whether it was definitely true as the science wasn't entirely up to speed.

We conclude that it is possible that life reached the Earth in this way, but that the scientific evidence is inadequate at the present time to say anything about the probability. We draw attention to the kinds of evidence that might throw additional light on the topic.

Crick believed that because there's a commonality among all lifeforms on Earth, we must have descended from a single origin. He believed that the extraterrestrials would have sent their bacteria in canisters, instead of bringing them along themselves, as it makes far more sense to seed the universe in that way.*

---

* As part of Crick's proposal for directed panspermia, he includes a brilliantly egotistical point, suggesting that while the aliens had done an amazing job of seeding life on Earth, they'd have had better success if they had consulted with him first. Crick reckons he'd have done a better job by including two types of organism, eukaryotes and prokaryotes, which would have sped up the process of evolution, instead of forcing the Earth to have to slowly develop these over the course of many millions of years.

THE ORIGIN OF FAECES

Another scientist/author to propose a galactic-origin story for humanity is Arthur C. Clarke, who, just like Gold, speculated that all life on Earth ultimately came from a passing alien vessel. In Clarke's theory, however, it wasn't picnic snacks that sparked life but stray faeces, ejected from an alien craft that then plummeted to Earth. In his article "Toilets of the Gods," Clarke wrote:

> *Space scientists recently completed an examination of orbital debris, recovered after circling the Earth for several years. They discovered that much of it was coated with a thin film of what was delicately described as "faecal matter," attributed to astronaut's sloppy sanitation. . . . It's a humbling thought that we may have arisen from dumped [alien] sewage; the first chapter of Genesis would certainly require drastic revision.*

What a thought: all life on Earth may be here, simply because someone used us as a toilet. Whoever/whatever they were, I hope it would amuse them to know that when a human begins to form in the womb the thing we begin as is an anus. A fitting tribute to our creation story.

CHAPTER 17

WHERE CAN I GET A GOOD PINT OF ALIEN MOONSHINE?

THE THEORY OF EXTRATERRESTRIALS

Somewhere in Buckingham Palace (or perhaps one of the other Royal residences), there's said to be a room full of UFO miscellanea, including multiple well-thumbed issues of *Flying Saucer Review*, a map pinpointing numerous alien hotspots and a big file of unpublished papers containing first-hand interviews with many people who have claimed to have had encounters with aliens. Altogether these make up the private collection of the late Prince Philip, the Duke of Edinburgh and amateur alien hunter.

Prince Philip is said to have first become interested in extraterrestrials in the 1950s. This was possibly thanks to the influence of his maternal uncle, Lord Louis Mountbatten. Mountbatten, also a known subscriber to *Flying Saucer Review* magazine, was not only well read on the subject, but had also contributed to the literature of it by writing up his own report about a UFO that once landed on his estate in

Hampshire in front of a bricklayer called Fred Briggs. Briggs claimed that the hovering UFO opened up, and out emerged a man in overalls and a helmet.*

Mountbatten was said to be so obsessed with the subject at one point that he even had his own theory as to what UFOs really were, which was this: *UFOs aren't the vehicles, but are the aliens themselves.* Mountbatten speculated that they might even be from a planet that has evolved a conscious species of metal discs. "I know this sounds ridiculous," he wrote to the editor of the now defunct British newspaper *Sunday Dispatch*, whom Mountbatten had also requested to have a team put together to look into the more compelling UFO cases, "and I

---

* There have been reports that when aliens abduct people, they present themselves in familiar forms so that the abductee is less scared.

am relying on you to . . . not make capital out of the fact that I've put forward such a far-fetched explanation."

Although little more can be discovered about Mountbatten's "sentient UFOs" theory from his own hand, we're fortunately offered a glimpse into his thinking on the topic thanks to his daughter Patricia Mountbatten, in whose archive we learn they were:

> *both convinced that they come from another planet but we mutually and independently came to the conclusion that they were not "aeroplanes" with silly little almost human pilots but are themselves the actual inhabitants: Martians, Venusians, Jupiterians or what have you. Why should life in another planet with entirely different conditions in any way resemble life on our planet? Their inhabitants might be "gaseous" or circular or very large. They certainly don't breathe, they may not have to eat and I doubt if they have babies—bits of their great discs may break away and grow into a new creature. The fact that they can hover and accelerate away from the earth's gravity again and even revolve round a V2 in America (as reported by their head scientist) shows they're far ahead of us.*

Other references to Mountbatten's interest in UFOs can be found in his diaries. One entry describes a meeting with Prince Bernhard of the Netherlands, who claimed he and his chauffeur had once seen two UFOs performing aerial acrobatics, as if they were trying to copulate with each other, before both shot off into the sky. Bernhard, who didn't believe in UFOs, was left baffled by the encounter.

Lord Mountbatten's interest in the subject apparently waned before his assassination in 1979. But according to reports, Prince Philip continued to be interested right until the end—his hot summer read of 2019 was said to have been *The Halt Perspective*, a book covering the Rendlesham Forest Encounter, often referred to as the British Roswell Incident.

What's perhaps most interesting is that, like his uncle, Philip wasn't just a passive consumer of UFO literature. Very subtly, Philip basically permitted an in-palace *X-Files* unit to exist. And secreted somewhere in one of his family homes are the results of those investigations. We don't know much about it, except from what has been written by his one-time equerry Air Marshall Peter Horsley, whose autobiography *Sounds from Another Room* gives insight into some of the investigations.

Horsley was given permission by the prince to go off and meet with those who had claimed to have had encounters. He spoke to everyone from RAF pilots and high-ranking military officials to people with titles like "Gentleman Usher to the Sword of State." Horsley heard stories of objects said to be travelling at 1,000 miles an hour and had actual meetings with "aliens" himself. In his book, he wrote about one particular meeting with a man called Mr. Janus, who briefed him on the future of humanity, including intergalactic space travel, the harnessing of the rules of gravity and anti-gravity, and the workings of robot-controlled spaceships. He told Horsley that the human body was not unique to Earth, and that many civilisations in the universe were peopled with beings of the same general appearance. These aliens were rather discreet, to put it mildly, and very rarely landed on Earth because they didn't want to interfere with us. All in all, quite wild ideas to be circulating around the upper echelons of British society in the 1950s.

Mr. Janus also asked if he could come to Buckingham Palace to meet Prince Philip, saying that the prince was "of great importance in future galactic harmony." This wasn't a completely wild request; Horsley had been bringing anyone with a credible story to Buckingham Palace so that he could interview them and get their story down properly. There was also another reason for bringing them to the palace. Horsley was using Philip as a human lie-detector machine. He believed it was virtually impossible for military personnel to lie to the prince and so if they stuck to their story once at the Palace it meant that they must be telling the truth.

They interviewed everyone, from the captain of a commercial airline who claimed to have seen a UFO while flying over the North Atlantic to a schoolboy called Stephen Derbyshire who had taken two photos of a UFO in Coniston, Cumbria.

Another person who had contact with Prince Philip over his interest in extraterrestrials was the author and amateur UFO sleuth Timothy Good. Good is the author of the hugely influential (in its bit of the bookshop) book *Above Top Secret*, and it's thanks to him that we know of at least two volumes in the UFO section of Prince Philip's bookcase. One, which Good co-authored, is *George Adamski—The Untold Story*, which chronicles the life of Adamski, who was famous in the 1950s as the world's first contactee who claimed to have flown to the moon with aliens; the other, a book by Adamski himself called *Flying Saucers Have Landed*, about which

Philip said, via Major the Hon. Andrew Wigram: "There are so many reasons to believe that they [UFOs] do exist: there's so much evidence from reliable witnesses. The book *Flying Saucers Have Landed* has a lot of interesting stuff in it."

WHERE IS EVERYBODY?

Four scientists had just sat down to lunch at Los Alamos National Laboratory in New Mexico in the summer of 1950 and were happily chatting away when one of them suddenly blurted out, "But where is everybody?!"

That blurter was Italian physicist Enrico Fermi. Fermi couldn't understand it. If there was life in the universe and it arose long before we showed up, it could have had the same aspirations for space travel that we now do, and so would have already cracked intergalactic travel. So "where the *fuck* are they?" he asked (the "fuck" is mine).

"They are already here among us," replied one of the other lunch companions, Leo Szilard. "They just call themselves Hungarians."

Szilard was most probably making a humorous, if oblique, reference to the recent popular claims by people like the pioneering UFO theorist George Adamski that aliens had already populated our world, most usually disguised as Nordic people.

However, so far as I can tell, this theory of aliens appearing in human form wasn't actually in the mainstream at that time, so it's interesting to wonder how Szilard would have heard of it. This leaves us with another possibility: he was answering honestly. I'm surprised Szilard has never been accused of being a reptilian off the back of this comment. I mean, come on, his name is literally an anagram of "lizards."

OUR REPTILIAN OVERLORDS

Alien lizards are of course something conspiracy theorists like to claim are populating our world. Many people believe these reptilians are from a binary star system called Alpha Draconis, although one academic thinks he's discovered their real origin. Writing in his book *A Culture of Conspiracy: Apocalyptic Visions in Contemporary America*, author Michael Barkun proposes that "In all likelihood, the notion of a shape-changing serpent race first came from the imagination of an obscure pulp fiction author, Robert E. Howard." Howard (1906–36), most famous for creating Conan the Barbarian, published a story called "The Shadow Kingdom" in August 1929 in which he described "snake-men" who had human bodies and serpent heads, and the ability to shape-shift into human shapes. His story also includes the somewhat chilling fact that "they were thought to have been destroyed, but they returned insidiously, insinuating themselves into positions of power."*

* By the way, here's a bit of advice: if you ever find yourself going for a pint with someone claiming to be a reptilian, make sure to sit indoors. I once had a beer with a self-proclaimed reptilian. Or rather, he was only half-reptilian. It was a hot spring day and we were sitting at an outside table at the Barge Inn in Wiltshire when my new friend started shivering. "Sorry, can we move inside?" he said through trembling teeth. "It's just that I'm cold-blooded and feel the wind much more than you do."

A few years ago, while filming an interview for a UFO documentary I was presenting for Channel 4, I found myself standing under a bridge in north London talking to a conspiracy theorist called Max about his belief that the world is being run by a group of reptilians, the boss of whom is known as Pindar, which translates as "Penis of the Dragon." "Many famous people are reptilians in disguise," he told me, and were they to return to their lizard base form, they'd look sort of like dinosaurs. "Are they wearing a human skin suit?" I asked. "No," he replied. "They don't shapeshift. They just alter your vision so you think they're human beings." Max mentioned some very famous names, from presidents like Barack Obama to business entrepreneurs of the past like McDonald's owner and CEO Ray Kroc. "Seriously, Ray

Kroc was a reptilian?" I asked. "He wasn't even trying to hide it," said Max. "Ray Kroc . . . hello . . . Ray Krocodile!'

One person who appears to be a strong believer in reptilian overlords is Alice Walker, the Pulitzer Prize–winning author of the novel *The Color Purple*. When Walker appeared as a guest on the BBC Radio 4 show *Desert Island Discs* back in 2004, she was given, as all guests are, the choice of taking one book with her—along with the mandatory spiritual/philosophical text and the works of Shakespeare—to a deserted island on which she was to be stranded. Walker chose *Human Race Get Off Your Knees: The Lion Sleeps No More* by conspiracy theorist David Icke, in which he pushes his belief that not only is the planet run by lizards in human body suits, but also that the moon is artificial and is beaming down messages to influence our minds.

Pulitzer Prize–winning author, Alice Walker.

This wasn't the only time Walker would publicly advocate Icke's work. She'd later go on to select another Icke book when being interviewed by the *New York Times*'s "By the Book" column. When asked what was on her bookshelf she spoke about *And the Truth Shall Set You Free* by Icke, saying, "In Icke's books there is the whole of existence, on this planet and several others, to think about. A curious person's dream come true."*

NORDIC ALIENS

The idea that aliens are secret reptilians wearing Nordic skin is one that's very popular today.

A few years back I met the aforementioned prominent UFO researcher and Prince Philip pen pal Timothy Good, who claimed to have come across at least four of them. When he's not disclosing top-secret information about extraterrestrial visits, Timothy plays cello for musicians like Phil Collins and has appeared as a session musician on many albums.

---

* If you visit her website, you'll find many blog posts in which she fawns over the conspiracy theorist. There's one where she has posted YouTube videos of his for her readers to watch; there's a recommendation of interviews between him and conspiracy theorist Alex Jones to watch ("I like these two," she writes under the video, "because they're real, and sometimes Alex Jones is a bit crazy; many Aquarians are. Icke only appears crazy to people who don't appreciate the stubbornness required when one is called to a duty it is impossible to evade"); there's her brief account of having spent a day listening to a ten-hour presentation by Icke; and she even writes about her wish that Malcolm X were still around so that she might hear him and Icke having a chat.

The problem when talking to an investigator like Timothy Good is that so much of the information he conveys is unverifiable, typically having been passed on to him by an "unnamed source from high up in the military."

I was lucky enough to be invited to Timothy's home once for an interview I did for a Channel 4 documentary. Timothy was incredibly kind, interesting, and good humoured. His house looked like an aristocratic version of Fox Mulder's shambolic office in *The X-Files*, and every photo on his walls told an interesting story. There's a picture of the lunar surface, only it was coloured a shade of green. "That's the fields of vegetation on the dark side of the moon they don't tell us about," said Timothy. Signed and dedicated photos from Apollo astronauts dotted the walls (and the way Timothy would look at them as he spoke suggested that some of his top-secret authorities might very well have been among these moonwalkers). Another photo I spotted looked incredibly— what's the word?— ... *glamorous*, as if the UFO were posing for it. "It was," Timothy admitted when I put it to him. "Often those who make contact with extraterrestrials have asked for photos of the ships mid-flight, and if asked politely, they will comply."

We were chatting about aliens who had visited Earth when Timothy explained his belief that they had been visiting for thousands of years, and that in fact Jesus Christ himself was an alien.

JESUS WAS AN ALIEN*

I wasn't sure if Timothy was taking the piss, so I asked him to repeat the sentence.

"I believe," he said slowly, "that Jesus was a human–alien hybrid."

In his book *Alien Contact*, Good wrote: "Supposedly, Jesus and two other spiritual leaders were genetically engineered, in the sense that they were implanted in people on Earth and their births were closely monitored."

This theory possibly originated in 1968 when Dr. Barry Downing, a UFOlogist and Presbyterian minister, published his book *The Bible and Flying Saucers*. Downing, who was born in 1938, proposed that Mary's immaculate conception was in fact alien insemination, with an embryo being implanted into Mary, and that the Star of Bethlehem was a UFO, guiding the Three Wise Men telepathically.

The question of the Star of Bethlehem is something that has occupied the minds not just of conspiracy theorists but of scientists too. What precisely was it in the night sky that guided the Three Wise Men towards their destination? Despite the fact that most scientists would view this event as entirely made up, some have wondered what might have attracted these three Magi, who were, after all, said to be scholarly men—the world's first ever astronomers, in fact. One

---

* Heads up: most UFOlogists absolutely hate this theory, believing that it cheapens the field.

professor, David Hughes, published a book in 1976 in which he suggests a solution:

> *The Star of Bethlehem was probably a triple conjunction of Saturn and Jupiter in the constellation of Pisces, the significance of which was only obvious to the Magi of Babylonia. This occurred in 7 BC and events indicate that Jesus Christ was probably born in the Autumn of that year, around October, 7 BC.*

Another idea is that the star was a comet. This is my own particular favourite theory regarding the birth of Jesus. Comets are made of ice, and when they get close to the sun they start to melt, creating a highly dramatic tail of debris that follows them. As a result, when seen over the horizon, the comet appears to be pointing down, which might have looked to the magi like a giant arrow, as if advertising "Virgin Birth happening HERE." There's a record of a bright comet in 5 BCE by astronomers in China, which could be a candidate for the guiding star.

The "Jesus as an alien" hypothesis is often ridiculed; however, it does have its fans, even modern ones, like former front man of the punk band Blink-182 Tom DeLonge. "Things were written in text thousands of years ago, like hearing voices in your head, a burning bush that was talking," DeLonge told journalist Rich Pelly. "The ancient texts may have called it God, but I'm just saying it's not that simple. The star of Bethlehem—was that a star or a craft? Because a star is really big. It wouldn't be hovering over a manger."

It turns out that while we were all giggling away to his album titles like *Take Off Your Pants and Jacket*, Tom was in the background beavering away, reading top-secret disclosures that had been "leaked." In an interview with the *Guardian*, he explained that he used his first cheque, after Blink-182 signed with a major label, to buy a computer so he could delve deeper into his research. It was the reason that after six albums with the band he eventually left. Being a touring musician and a serious UFO researcher simply weren't compatible.

When Pelly asked him, "What's the most convincing piece of evidence you've seen as to the existence of aliens?" DeLonge explained that he couldn't answer as he had to observe "national security issues."

WILD THINGS THEY DON'T TELL YOU

Another prominent rock star/UFO hunter was the lead singer of the Troggs, Reg Presley, who, late in life, unexpectedly was able to self-fund his own attempts to find ET thanks to a million-pound royalty cheque that hit his bank account after Wet Wet Wet covered his song "Love Is All Around" for the *Four Weddings and a Funeral* soundtrack.

Presley was largely interested in crop circles. UK crop circles, we now know, were at the start largely the work of a couple of pranksters called David Chorley and Douglas Bower, both landscape painters, who in 1978 came up with the idea for the hoax after a drink in the pub. For 13 years they sneaked around the fields of southern England with ropes, string, and some planks of wood, constructing up to 30 new circles every growing season. They finally revealed that they were the creators of the circles in 1991, silencing a decade of wild UFO theories that had built up around them.

"So case closed on aliens creating crop circles, right?" I remember once asking a UFO conspiracy theorist.

"Yes," replied the expert, "they were built by pranksters."

"Good," I said, thinking that was the end of that.

"But something very interesting has been discovered about these pranksters is that they themselves are the ones being pranked . . . you see, it used to be thought that UFOs were coming down from the sky and creating these patterns. But that's not the case. The crop circles are portals, like a stargate. But the UFOs need the portal to be built. And what many of these pranksters who come at night to build them don't realise is that they've been instructed by the UFOs to build them. And so as soon as they're finished, a UFO will emerge from the crop circle, leaving the prankster astonished but too embarrassed to admit what happened to anyone."

For years, I'd not heard this theory anywhere else, until I found a blog recently by a man named Darren, who was hitchhiking along a sliproad in Bristol when he was picked up by a passing car that was being driven by none other than Reg Presley. When Darren brought up the point that crop circles were built by "randoms" in the night looking to trick UFOlogists, Reg told Darren:

> *"That's what they want you to believe"... and then his eyes went wide. "Do you want to hear the truth?" Indeed I did. "It's the aliens. The aliens have approached the locals to do their work for them. Wouldn't you get someone to do the dirty work? What the aliens do is they make this special drink the farmers love. They pay the farmers this drink for the work done." "You mean like moonshine?" I asked. He nodded. "Alien moonshine."*

Crop circles can be good money. When Reg Presley went to see his first crop circle (he was a sceptic at the time) he had to pay the farmer a £1 entry fee. Reg would later learn that the farmer had collected £7,000 in total from amateur UFOlogists and others who were curious.

One concern from crop-circle believers is that once the crops recover from being pressed into the ground, they eventually begin to grow vertically again. Then the wheat or barley or what-have-you is harvested and enters our food chain and who knows what secret alien ingredients ET is subtly sneaking into our diets.

According to Reg, a team of scientists analysed the wheat from a crop-circle field.

> *They say that every living thing has its own energy structures and that by analysing certain samples of body tissue, by the energy they find they can tell the condition of the different organs of the body. Now, because you can do this with any living thing, they decided (out of idle curiosity) to put the wheat through the same procedure. They discovered that the actual crystalline structure had changed. It was as if a high energy had passed through the wheat. It seemed to me to be undeniable evidence that something out of the ordinary was occurring. This, if nothing else, deserved some attention from the government.*

Sadly, Reg Presley died aged 71 in 2013, and the footprint he tried to leave in the world of UFOs didn't outlive the one he left with his band, the Troggs. However, just like the aliens who accidentally scattered their cookie crumbs on Earth, Presley did manage his own bit of unintended consequence—a legacy he'd never know he inspired. It would go on to be voted one of the greatest moments in British television history.

A VERY BRITISH INVASION

Reg Presley's inability to ever stop talking about aliens would lead to one of the UK's most popular ever TV pranks. Many years ago he was sitting in a pub with a British sitcom comedy writer called Richard Turner.* Rich, who was initially excited to be sharing a pint with one of the great legends of rock 'n' roll, quickly found himself getting bored as Reg banged on about his strange beliefs.

"The chat probably only lasted for about half an hour, but it felt like twice as long," said Rich. "He was only interested in talking about UFOs, and boy, was he interested in them! It was like hearing a Jehovah's Witness going on and on about the End of Days. I was annoyed at how he seemed—to me, at the time, nearly 30 years ago—to be so easily fooled by shit like 'energy' and 'auras.' I knew a little bit about UFO stuff, but I'd never previously heard about it in connection with all the New Age spiritual/magical ideas that were popular at the time."

A few years after his encounter with Reg, Rich found himself in a brainstorming room for *Beadle's About*, a 1990s British TV show hosted by Jeremy Beadle that pulled off some fairly outlandish pranks on the public. While sitting there thinking of ideas, Rich was reminded of his chat with Reg, and thought, *Wouldn't it be funny to actually get someone to believe they were meeting a real-life alien?*

The team loved the idea, and the prank was eventually set up to take place on a Dorset farm owned by a lady called

* He's also co-creator of *The Museum of Curiosity*.

240

Janet Elford. The premise of the skit was that a mysterious meteorite had crash-landed on her farm, and inside the meteorite was a space capsule containing an alien. Smoke machines were dug into the ground, yellow and black caution tape was set up around the incident, with Janet's family having arranged for her to be away while all of this was happening. When she returned to her farm she was greeted by the local policeman and fireman, who were both in on the act. An actor in the scene put Janet at the centre of the drama, convincing her that the reason this particular meteorite had crashed on her farm was because it was in some way intrinsically connected to her. As she and the man stood looking at the crash site, phase two of the prank began, and a terrible, cheap, completely fake-looking alien suddenly emerged. Remarkably, Janet was so caught up in the moment that she needed little convincing that the alien was genuine. As far as Janet was concerned, she was about to became the *first* human being ever to make official alien contact.

"What do you want from us?" asked Janet a number of times in a sympathetic voice. No answer was forthcoming from the creature, and it eventually attempted to beat a swift retreat. Sensing that she was about to lose her chance to get any form of response, Janet desperately hurled one last question at the retreating alien.

"Would you like a cup of tea?" she asked the alien.

And that's why I think the day when contact occurs, the day when aliens finally land on Earth, the person wheeled out to greet them should be neither a scientist nor a government official. It should be a British farmer.

PART III

YOU CAN'T HAVE THE THEORY OF EVERYTHING WITHOUT THE THEORY OF EVERYTHING ELSE

Batshit makes the world go round, and its footprint can be found everywhere you look. You won't always notice it, but it's usually there, hiding in plain sight. Just look at Milton Keynes, a city that has been endlessly mocked for being soulless and dull.

What most people don't realise is that the city was designed by architect Derek Walker, who drew up plans while under the influence of a book called *The View over Atlantis* by John Michell. Walker positioned the city's main street (Midsummer Boulevard) so the rising sun on the Summer Solstice would beam direct down its length, and even designed the sewer systems using the route of an ancient leyline that he had just walked.

Batshit also helps communities to flourish. There are dozens of towns in America making good money off the name of Bigfoot, though curiously the only place actually called "Bigfoot" isn't one of them.* There's Willow Creek, for ex-

* Bigfoot, Texas, is not, as you might expect, named after the mysterious beast, but, as one of the stories has it, is instead named in honour of a local sheriff who was said to have had really big feet.

ample, which, with a population of just 2,000, has become a mecca to monster hunters thanks to the notorious encounter filmed by Roger Patterson and Bob Gimlin at Bluff Creek in 1967. These days its local museum turns over at least $180,000 annually.

Bigfoot is a substantial money-making industry and few commodities remain unexploited by the big mythical beast. In my house alone (and I don't even live in the US) we own a Bigfoot board game, a Bigfoot stuffed toy, multiple books on Bigfoot, Bigfoot bandages in our first-aid box, and in our garden a Bigfoot statue is expected soon (though I'm still in negotiations with Fenella over that one; she's arguing for a tasteful statue of the Virgin Mary instead).

You can buy Bigfoot watches (or a "Sasquwatch,") and you can even get Bigfoot erotic fiction, something that came to light during the 2018 US Congressional campaign when Virginia politician Denver Riggleman was accused of penning some by the candidate running against him. Posting screengrabs taken from Riggleman's social media, his opponent Leslie Cockburn showed that Riggleman appeared to be teasing the imminent publication of his novel *The Mating Habits of Bigfoot and Why Women Want Him*. Although he denied the novel was real, Riggleman had previously published a non-erotic Bigfoot novel, titled *Bigfoot Exterminators Inc.: The Partially Cautionary, Mostly True Tale of Monster Hunt 2006*. He has subsequently published his memoir *Bigfoot . . . It's Complicated*, in which he denied he was ever going to talk about about the cryptid's sex life, and then immediately devoted a chapter to describing the size and shape of the creature's genitals.

The Virginia Republican really should publish the novel as there's damn good money to be made in Bigfoot erotica, as demonstrated by another Virginia. In 2013 US author Virginia Wade published her series of Bigfoot sex books, starting with *Cum for Bigfoot*.* In 2012 her titles were downloaded over 100,000 times, some months generating $30,000. Today she continues to produce monster erotica, but they've got a bit more of a New Age feel about them, like 2018's *Namaste with Sasquatch*.

In 2021 Oklahoma made it compulsory to obtain a Bigfoot hunting licence, but you could claim a $25,000 reward if you caught one. Other cities have similar rules as there are just so many heavily armed Bigfoot hunters in the States, roaming the forests looking for them. When *The Return of the Jedi* was filming in California, this became a genuine concern for the production crew, and Peter Mayhew, who played Chewbacca, had to be accompanied by crew members in hi-vis vests so that he wasn't shot by these lunatics.

A good theory of this type can make you rich. According to a 2018 *Forbes* article, Scotland generates around £60 million a year from Loch Ness Monster tourism. Again, I have been one of those who have contributed—I bought a T-shirt.

It's often the case that those caught up in such outlandish

---

* Here's a sample: "It's fucking Bigfoot," hissed Shelly. "He's real, for fuck's sake." Horror filled her eyes. "With a huge cock."

theories have no choice but to exploit them, just to keep the wolf from the door. This is something that often happens to people who gain questionable notoriety. I remember once reading about John Wayne Bobbitt, whose wife chopped his penis off following an argument—he had to lean into exploiting his situation just so he could make money to help deal with his legal and medical bills. He did so by forming a band called the Severed Parts. He also appeared in the adult films *John Wayne Bobbitt Uncut*, *Frankenpenis*, and *Buttman at Nudes a Poppin' 2*.

What's more, in the 1960s, if you were to travel to Dealey Plaza in Dallas, Texas, the site of the John F. Kennedy assassination, you might have found an old woman standing at the bottom of the Book Depository building selling signatures for five bucks that read "Marguerite Oswald, mother of Lee Harvey Oswald." Marguerite Oswald, who strongly believed her son was innocent, was often low on funds and would stand there appealing to anyone who believed her son was innocent too. She would also later release an LP titled *The Oswald Case: Mrs. Marguerite Oswald Reads Lee Harvey Oswald's Letters from Russia* (available on Spotify, if anyone is interested).

Incidentally, as I write I'm currently watching live footage from a 24-hour livestreaming camera that's positioned on the sixth floor of Dealey Plaza. The view is from Oswald's vantage point, from the position he shot JFK. In the distance you can see an "X" on the road, marking out not treasure, but the spot on the road where the bullet hit the president. Every so often the camera cuts to adverts. That's right, even this webcam is monetised. As I watch today, the killer's view of the assassination is currently being sponsored by a "Buenos Aires is back" travel ad.

In 2019, when the Madrid football team UD Móstoles Balompié was taken over by former player Javi Poves, he had the team re-branded as Flat Earth FC. In a video explaining the move, Poves explained:

> *Two years ago, I started to have a different vision of the world by observing water . . . when I started to ask myself, how does water curve? No one gave me a valid answer. They told me, "It's because of gravity." Yes there is gravity, but at what scale does it curve water? Because it isn't curved in a glass of water, nor in my bathtub, nor in my neighbour's swimming pool.*

With the name change, Poves believes his football club became the first to make people think. Poves also claims the name change helped them to join the top ten Spanish teams with an international following. (Sadly, for merch nuts like me, Poves has since left and the team has been renamed.)

Entire countries have even got involved in exploiting wacky theories about them for financial gain—in Bermuda, for instance, the government once minted official coins in triangle shapes. The $1, $3, and $9 coins were minted in 1996 and show a map of Bermuda, a sinking ship, and a compass on their reverse side. These coins now get listed on eBay for roughly £1,500. The last of these triangular coins was minted in 2007.

And over in Shingo, Japan, you can buy "Christ Hometown

The tomb of Jesus Christ.

Sake" with teacups with crosses on them, and Christ-themed fudge. This is done to celebrate the town's main claim to fame—that Jesus Christ didn't die on the cross in Jerusalem, but escaped to Shingo, where he died and was buried there, aged 106.

According to the story, Jesus was replaced at the crucifixion by his brother, who died so that Jesus could live. Jesus then fled to Japan, a place he knew well having studied there in his 20s. His journey involved travelling through Siberia to Alaska, where he boarded a boat that took him all the way to Japan. To integrate himself with the people of Shingo he assumed a Japanese name, Torai Taro Daitenku, and began farming garlic. He then married a woman named Miyuko, with whom he had three daughters.

Jesus' grave in Shingo was protected for many generations

by the Sawaguchi family, who had always been told that a man of importance was buried there. What gave further credence to the story is that both the head of the Sawaguchi family and his sister had blue eyes, which singled the family out as being Christ's descendants. There were other curious things going on too. The townsfolk practised customs that aren't really seen anywhere else in Japan, such as newborn babies being swaddled in clothes embroidered with the Star of David and having a cross painted in black ink on their foreheads.

There's now an annual "Christ festival," which has been going on since the 1960s, and in 1997 the erection of a small museum exhibition hall, where visitors can learn interesting facts, such as the town's former name "Herai," which derives from the word "Hebrew." Every year over 20,000 people make a pilgrimage to Shingo to pay their respects at the grave of Jesus Christ, a plot that's lovingly maintained by the town's local yoghurt factory.

The only person not exploiting this rise in tourism for financial gain is the Shingo resident who is said to be the actual living descendant of Christ, a Japanese man called Junichiro Sawaguchi, a government worker who comes from a long line of garlic farmers. Sawaguchi is well aware that people believe he's the direct descendant of Jesus Christ, but you haven't heard much from him about it because, as a Buddhist, he's really not that bothered about it.

In this final part of the book let's have a look at some of the theories that have accidentally shaped the world today . . .

CHAPTER 18
HOW ISAAC NEWTON HOLLOWED OUT THE EARTH
THE THEORY OF THE HOLLOW EARTH

I was walking through London St. James's Park one rainy Thursday when I realised that I was just around the corner from one of the greatest scientific institutions ever founded— the Royal Society. As it happened, I'd just spent the week desperately trying to find the location of a portrait featuring a remarkable scientist who worked there as a clerk in the 1600s, and it suddenly occurred to me that perhaps the picture was simply hanging on one of the Society's walls, and so I decided to just pop in and ask if I could hunt the walls for it. Once inside, the bemused receptionist, who spent some time trying to decide if I was a loon, eventually called to the Society's library to see if someone could help me. I was met a few minutes later by a man called Jon. "Oh, it's you," he said with a cheery smirk, "I remember you from last time."

I was surprised he remembered me, as the last time I was there was years ago. I was there to investigate a theory that had been discussed amongst members of the Royal Society back in 1745, about whether or not drinking gin was causing women to spontaneously combust.

There were two documented cases from the time that reported stories of women downing some gin and then going up in smoke, as well as a few cases having been reported about other European women doing the same, only with brandy. The matter was taken seriously enough that it was mentioned in the Society's staff meetings, and recorded in their minutes. (Sadly I wasn't able to track down the answer.)

"How can we help this time?" asked Jon.

"I'm trying to find a portrait of Edmund Halley," I told him.

Halley had become a new hero of mine. Without him the world would have been a very different place. Without him, we may possibly never have known of Newton's greatest calculations.

On January 24, 1684, Edmund Halley was having drinks with fellow Royal Society scientists Robert Hooke and Christopher Wren when a question came up about gravity, and how it acts when distances between two objects are closer or further away. Hooke claimed to know the answer to his own question, but refused to say what it was. Wren, tired of Hooke's arrogance, laid down a prize of 40 shillings if the other two could prove the answer within the next two months. Halley decided he'd consult the scientist, Isaac Newton, for a possible answer the next time he was in Cambridge.

Newton obliged, and as it turned out he had already answered the question, and said it was scribbled down somewhere on some sheets of paper in the mess of his house.

Three months later Newton got the answer to Halley, who was astounded. Not only had Newton answered the question, but he appeared to have come up with a whole new science. Halley encouraged Newton to write his Principia Mathematica, which was arranged by Halley to be published by the Royal Society.

Sir Isaac Newton's *Philosophiæ Naturalis Principia Mathematica* is regarded as one of the most important scientific books ever published. It contains theories in it that have shaped the modern world. However, it almost never saw the light of day, thanks to a book called *The History of Fishes*.

As the Royal Society prepared to publish Newton's work, they suffered a huge financial blow after they pumped all their resources into the Fish book, which bombed on release. As a consequence, Newton's book was cancelled.

Fortunately, Halley, who was working as a clerk for the Royal Society at the time, stepped in and personally raised funds so that the book could be published, even sinking in his own wages to help get it released, which it did the year after, in 1687.

What would life be like today if Halley had not believed in Newton to such a degree? Would we have ever known of Newton's work at all? How long would we have taken to catch up to the theories his brilliant mind had unravelled? Every theory needs a champion, and Newton's Laws of Motion were lucky Halley would find them. He made sure they saw the light of day, and at great personal cost. The Royal Society, who were still suffering from their previous book, hadn't paid Halley for 18 months. Finally, after requesting to be paid many times, Halley was offered compensation. He was to be given £20 on top of his £50 annual salary. Though unfortunately, they didn't actually have any cash, so they offered to pay him in unsold copies of *The History of Fishes* instead.

Interestingly, Halley was not only the person to first see Newton's theory of gravitation, but he was also the first person to directly prove it when the comet he said would return to Earth (known simply as Halley's Comet) did so exactly when he predicted. Sadly this event happened 16 years after his death. But there was something else that was born out of Halley's involvement in Newton's book. Something that's rarely spoken about. Halley had been studying polar magnetism after noticing some odd compass readings, due to the shifting magnetic poles. In his quest for an answer he then noticed something in Newton's book. Newton had written about the density of the moon, and got it very wrong. Halley however took it as fact, and wrote: "Sir Isaac Newton has demonstrated the Moon to be more solid than our Earth, as 9 to 5; why may we not then suppose four ninths of our globe to be cavity?" Off of this he concluded that it would make sense the inside of our planet must be a series of concentric shells, and that each of these was rotating at different speeds and directions. Then in a bizarre move, Halley went on to say that the areas in between each shell was spacious, and had a luminous atmosphere that could support life. In that very moment, Halley created Hollow Earth Theory, and it was all Newton's fault.

Over 100 years later, one man would take the idea of the Hollow Earth, and inadvertently start the ball rolling on a project that would lead to the founding of one of the greatest scientific institutions ever.

SYMMES'S HOLE

Captain John Symmes Jr. was a clever man. So far as I can tell, he did something that no other person about to drop their batshit theory onto the world has ever done—he attached a doctor's note to the theory certifying that he wasn't insane.

It was on April 10, 1818, that Captain Symmes, a retired army officer from Sussex County, New Jersey, at great personal expense printed out and posted 500 letters to the world's leading authorities proposing an expedition to the North Pole to search for the entrance of the Hollow Earth.

> *To All the World!*
>
> *I declare the earth is hollow, and habitable within; containing a number of solid concentrick spheres, one within the other, and that it is open at the poles 12 or 16 degrees; I pledge my life in support of this truth, and am ready to explore the hollow, if the world will support and aid me in the undertaking.*
>
> *Jno. Cleves Symmes of Ohio, Late Captain of Infantry.*

Further down the note he also wrote:

I ask one hundred brave companions, well equipped, to start from Siberia in the fall season, with Reindeer and slays [sic], on the ice of the frozen sea: I engage we find warm and rich land, stocked with thrifty vegetables and animals if not men, on reaching one degree northward of latitude 82; we will return in the succeeding spring.

J. C. S.

The attached note, signed by a number of prominent physicians, stated that not only was Symmes a good Christian gentleman, but a great dad too. The appraisal ended with the line, "He is considered sane by all who know him."

⋆   ⋆   ⋆

Despite the great astronomer Edmond Halley being the obvious inspiration for Captain Symmes's Hollow Earth theory, Symmes never properly acknowledged him. He claimed to have reached the idea about the state of the Earth's interior on his own through a series of observations he'd been making. He believed that the driftwood found on coastal shores had escaped from the inside of the planet, floating up out of the giant hole and into the outer world. He also believed that the disappearance of schools of fish was evidence that the ocean continued into the Hollow Earth. They travelled in through one hole and out the other, which, he said, explained fish migration.⋆

⋆ This is not dissimilar to the theory of seventeenth-century scientist and minister Charles Morton, whose proposed explanation for the disappearance of birds over the winter was that they migrated to the moon and back

He became an expert in his own theory, quashing anyone looking to ridicule it. And ridicule it they did, as no one of any scientific credibility gave the Hollow Earth any real consideration. But he didn't care. Symmes travelled the United States, talking to crowds, looking for intrepid explorers to join him while trying to raise funds.

One person who saw great merit in his theory was a newspaper editor from Ohio called Jeremiah N. Reynolds, who believed in Symmes's idea to such an extent that he quit his job and joined Symmes on his tour of the country. So many people became interested in the theory that letters began arriving at Congress asking for Symmes to be taken seriously and an expedition mounted. Eventually Congress started acknowledging the idea, with two motions being raised in the House of Representatives.

The two continued to speak at sold-out lectures, becoming known nationwide. Eventually, however, Reynolds started to spot flaws in the theory and slowly lost his belief in what Symmes was saying, causing the two to part ways. Reynolds also recognised that when they were pitching their idea across the nation, getting to the poles for the sake of exploration had been the thing most were intrigued by. Perhaps Congress would approve a trip if they believed the motive was a little more scientific, thought Reynolds. He carried on without Symmes, eventually attracting the attention of President John Quincy Adams, who wrote in his diary of November 4, 1826:

once a year (he estimated it would take them 60 days to get there flying at an average speed of 125mph).

Mr. Reynolds is a man who has been lecturing about the Country, in support of Captain John Cleves Symmes's theory that the Earth is a hollow Sphere, open at the Poles—His Lectures are said to have been well attended, and much approved as exhibitions of genius and of Science—But the Theory itself has been so much ridiculed, and is in truth so visionary, that Reynolds has now varied his purpose to the proposition of fitting out a voyage of circumnavigation to the Southern Ocean—He has obtained numerous signatures in Baltimore to a Memorial to Congress for this object, which he says will otherwise be very powerfully supported—It will however have no support in Congress. That day will come, but not yet nor in my time. May it be my fortune, and my praise to accelerate its approach. *

*   *   *

* In recent years John Adams has been accused of wanting to fund the expedition because he believed there was a city of "Mole Men" living in the interior of the world. The story originated in an article on the website Cracked. It was then picked up and copied by various websites, including the *Smithsonian Magazine*'s. Journalist Howard Dorre pointed out this was a particularly terrible bit of misinformation, as the Smithsonian Institute, the largest museum in the world, owes its very existence to John Adams, who expedited its creation. Dorre asked for a retraction. It was the second time Dorre had to correct the institute for spreading false information about John Adams. The first was when the Smithsonian's *The Presidents: Visual Encyclopedia* attributed the quote "If your actions inspire others to dream more, learn more, do more and become more, you are a leader" to Adams, when, of course, it should have been credited to the person who really said it, country music star Dolly Parton.

After years of persistent campaigning Reynolds's efforts finally paid off, and the Adams administration approved the funds needed for the expedition. However, the entire project fell apart when Adams lost his office in the 1828 presidential election to Andrew Jackson, who then cancelled the expedition. Reynolds turned to private investment, doing well to secure the funds, and his expedition was launched. Unfortunately, it didn't go well. The crew didn't like Reynolds, staged a mutiny, and abandoned him in Chile, where he remained for two years.

Upon his return to the United States, Reynolds turned his attention to writing a book called *Mocha Dick, Or the White Whale of the Pacific*, based on local Chilean stories about an

The grave of John Symmes Jr., which includes a Hollow Earth on its top. The grave is part of the Smithsonian's collection.

indestructible whale who had survived a hundred encounters with sailors trying to kill it, harpoons supposedly sticking from out of its body long after the attacks. If the title (and plot) of his book sound familiar, it's because it is. Published in 1839, it would go on to inspire a fictional account in a book with a strikingly similar name and plot called *Moby-Dick*.

Eight years after the first expedition, and after much additional lobbying by Reynolds, the original government-funded expedition pitched to President Adams all those years ago was finally approved by Congress and set off on the long-awaited mission. The expedition was missing one thing, however: Reynolds, who was not invited as a result of being so offensive to so many in his desperate attempts to get the mission off the ground. No one wanted him on board. Upon its return in 1842, the expedition brought home with it a global collection unlike anything previously seen. On just one trip they gathered a third more items than Captain Cook managed in three trips: over 4,000 ethnographical pieces, over 60,000 animal and plant specimens (including 2,150 birds, 1,000 living plants, and 300 species of fossil), each item being meticulously stored in colour-coded and numbered boxes.*

The United States was not endowed at this point with appropriate places to house such a collection, and a temporary home was given to it. However, as luck would have it, a huge inheritance from a British man called John Smithson had just

---

* A completely wasted effort, it would turn out, as the curator who received the boxes didn't receive any information about the colour coding or numbers, and so had to unpack it all to find out what was in it.

been received by the US government. The funds were used to set up a new establishment, the Smithsonian Institute, with the items acquired by the expedition making up its initial collection.

*   *   *

Once Isaac Newton realised his mistake concerning the calculations for the density of the Moon, he quickly revised his book and fixed it. For some reason though, Halley couldn't let go of the idea that the Earth was hollow, and maintained his belief that there were huge cavernous spaces, with luminous atmospheres, and all sorts of creatures living there.

And that was why I desperately wanted to see the painting of Halley that day in the Royal Society, because despite being

The portrait of Edmond Halley, which hangs on the walls
of the Royal Society.

the man who rescued modern science, who helped us to see the seminal work of Newton, and whose reputation as one of the greats of science remains unchallenged—he just couldn't help himself. There, hanging in the heart of rational science is something completely unscientific. In the portrait, Sir Edmond Halley is seen to be staring out, a look of calm and contentment on his face. In his hand, he is holding a single sheet a paper, upon which is a series of hand-drawn concentric circles—the theory of the hollow Earth.

CHAPTER 19
HOW TO DISCOVER THE KNOBS OF MARS
THE THEORY OF NTOMARHIYDIONHGARNAYGNIAR

In 1610 the astronomer Johannes Kepler received a letter from fellow polymath Galileo Galilei that read:

SMAISMRMILMEPOETALEUMIBUNENUGTT
AUIRAS

Although Kepler had no idea what it meant, he was honoured to receive it. It signalled respect—he was now on Galileo's "I've discovered something, but I'm not telling you what" list. In the seventeenth century it was commonplace for scientists to send their contemporaries and rivals confusing letters written in gibberish. Robert Hooke did it, as did fellow leading scientific figures Isaac Newton, Christiaan Huygens, and Christopher Wren.

These long nonsensical words were in fact anagrams, which if successfully decoded would reveal the sender's latest theory. What Galileo was doing was telling Kepler that he had found something. He hadn't fully ironed out the details of it yet though, and so wasn't ready to publish it, BUT just in case Kepler happened to discover the same thing, this letter would be proof that he, Galileo, got there first. These were letters designed to call dibs on a discovery.

When Kepler received his letter from Galileo, as well as being excited, he was nervous. He had been on the brink of proving that Mars had two moons for some time, but hadn't quite managed it. Now he was worried that Galileo, famously a discoverer of planetary moons, was trying to beat him to it.*

And so he took Galileo's anagram and began trying to unscramble it. After having played around with it, Kepler successfully deciphered the code, which revealed:

Salve umbistineum geminatum Martia proles.
Or: Be greeted, double knob, children of Mars.†

Kepler took this as the final proof that he was right about his theory, and immediately made his announcement to the Holy Roman Emperor Rudolf II, for whom he worked as the imperial mathematician. It was to be another great astronomical discovery to add to his already impressive CV—which

---

* Among the reasons Kepler believed Mars had two moons were (1) he had done some mathematical modelling and (2) he reckoned because Earth had one moon and Jupiter had four, which meant Mars, which was in between both planets, must have two.

† There are many ways to translate this sentence, including "Hail flaming twins, offspring of Mars" and "Hail companionship, children of Mars."

included showing that the solar system moved in elliptical orbits; proving the Copernican idea that the Earth revolved around the sun; and discovering the three major laws of planetary motion. It wasn't just scientific achievements he had to boast about; Kepler also proved to be one of the great lawyers of the seventeenth century—despite only engaging in one case, when he had his mother, Katerina Kepler, acquitted of being accused of occasionally turning herself into a cat.

Accusations of witchcraft were rampant in the sixteenth and seventeenth centuries, with some 50,000 people being executed as a result of it in Europe alone. That number would surely have been at least halved, though, if only each of the accused had their own Kepler to represent them. Having packed away his scientific work, Kepler set about proving his mother's innocence against accusations that included: being raised by an aunt who was a witch and was burnt at the stake (not true); making and selling magical potions (also not true, though it can't have helped that she'd boil her food in a big black pot and that among the ingredients in her cupboards at home was a bag of bat wings),* and, of course, the above-mentioned shapeshifting. Eventually, Kepler won the case and his mother was set free.

Rudolf II, looking for absolute verification of Kepler's discovery about the moons of Mars, went to Galileo to confirm that this was definitely what he was hiding in his anagram. It wasn't. Kepler had got it completely wrong. What he had hidden was this:

Altissimum planetam tergeminum observavi.
I have observed the highest of the planets three-formed.

The anagram related to his proposed discovery that the planet Saturn had two moons. He had come to this conclusion after pointing his telescope at Saturn, and seeing something blurry around the planet that looked to him like a pair of ears. He described it in a letter to his patron Cosimo de Medici with the drawing oOo. Galileo was wrong—what he was looking at was the rings of Saturn. Unfortunately, his telescope was too primitive to give him a good enough view of them.

What's curious is that Kepler didn't recognise that his

* Joking.

translation of the anagram was wrong. So desperate was he to beat Galileo to the discovery, he was unable to see that he had decoded the message incorrectly.

Kepler would die in 1630, having never confirmed how many moons Mars had. And it wouldn't be until another 267 years later that someone would manage it. In 1877 the American astronomer Asaph Hall finally made the discovery. There were two.

Deimos and Phobos, as they're called, are roughly 1 millionth of a per cent the size of Mars, making it incredibly hard to spot them, which explains why they eluded every astronomer from Kepler until Hall.

Incidentally, Kepler wasn't the only person to accidentally predict the correct number of satellites orbiting the red planet before Hall came along. Another curious occasion came about in 1726, when Jonathan Swift's book *Gulliver's Travels* somehow managed it too. In the book, the scientists of Laputa had:

> *likewise discovered two lesser stars, or satellites, which revolve around Mars, whereof the innermost is distant from the centre of the primary planet exactly three of his diameters, and the outermost five: the former revolves in the space of ten hours, and the latter in twenty-one and a half.*

The mystery as to how Jonathan Swift could have predicted that Mars had two moons has been debated for a long time. These days, it's largely believed that he was aware of Kepler's claim and was parodying the anecdote about the misinterpreted anagram. But what no one can explain is how on earth, a century before Asaph Hall got there, Swift had so nearly managed to describe their size, their distance from the planet Mars and the time it took for them to orbit the planet as well. Deimos takes 30.3 hours to orbit Mars, which the Laputians had at 21.5 hours, while Phobes takes 7.7 hours to orbit Mars, which the Laputians had at 10 hours. And whereas the real moons have an orbital distance of between 1.4 and 3.5 Martian diameters, the Laputians had it between 3 and 5.

Many have theorised that perhaps Swift had read some bit of literature since lost that suggested these numbers, or that he consulted his friend Dr. John Arbuthnot, a Scottish physi-

Jonathan Swift, author and soothsayer?

cian and polymath, to calculate them. But one scientist, V. G. Perminov, the Soviet Union's leading spacecraft designer for the Mars and Venus missions, had a different idea about how Swift got the information.

In the introduction to his book *The Difficult Road to Mars*, Perminov wrote it was

> *possible that the English fiction writer [J.] Swift managed to find and decipher records that Martians left on Earth. Based on these records, long before the Martian moons were discovered, Swift predicted that Mars had two satellites. One of them he named Phobos (fear), the other he named Deimos (horror), and rather precisely predicted the parameters of their orbits.*

This bold statement, which appears in the introduction to an otherwise very dry scientific book, also states: "Perhaps Martians once arrived on Earth and left some evidence of their visit. Perhaps they built huge runways in South America, maybe constructed a chemically pure iron column in India (now chemically pure iron can be produced only in the laboratory), and built the mysterious Egyptian pyramids."

I don't think we will ever know how Swift got his information, but his bizarre accidental guess will forever be entwined with the two Mars moons' narrative, as today the majority of craters and ridges on the knobs of Mars bear names taken from the characters and locations of Swift's novel.

CHAPTER 20

THE PRESIDENT WHO STOPPED HIS OWN ASSASSINATION

THE THEORY OF DESTINY

THREE EMPTY SEATS

On December 9, 1980, David Bowie took to the stage at New York City's Booth Theatre to play John Merrick in the Broadway production of *The Elephant Man*. That night, as he stood on stage, looking out at the audience, Bowie would have been conscious of three empty seats in the front row.

It was to be an incredibly emotional show for Bowie. "I can't tell you how difficult it was to go on," he'd later tell a friend. "I almost didn't make it through the performance."

At approximately 10:30 p.m. the night before, and just a 30-minute walk up the road from the theatre, the unthinkable had happened: John Lennon was gunned down by a crazed fan called Mark David Chapman. Chapman killed the former Beatle for the simple reason that he wanted to take the life of someone with great fame.

Fame. The word that, ironically, united Bowie and

Lennon, when just five years earlier they used it as the title for their only song-writing collaboration, which would go on to become Bowie's first No. 1 hit single in the States. The experience had made friends out of the pair of them, and now that Bowie was back in New York they had arranged to see each other again. That night in fact. Two of those empty front-row seats were meant for John Lennon and Yoko Ono. The third empty seat was for Mark David Chapman.

★   ★   ★

The tale of the three empty seats is a story Bowie personally told to his friend, a veteran American DJ called Redbeard. They had just finished a radio interview in Redbeard's Manhattan studio when Bowie told the anecdote. Sadly the microphones were off, and so we'll have to take Redbeard's word for it. Bowie was told by the police officers who'd searched Chapman's New York apartment that they had found among his possessions an *Elephant Man* theatre programme with Bowie's name circled in black pen. "I was second on his list," he told the DJ.

Had Bowie been murdered that night on stage, not only would he have been the first major celebrity to be gunned down in a theatre since the assassination of Abraham Lincoln, but weirdly it would also have happened in a theatre named after the brother of Lincoln's murderer, John Wilkes Booth. The Booth Theatre opened in 1913, just 48 years after Lincoln was shot dead in the Ford Theatre, Washington, DC, and I'm just going to put it out there—that feels a little bit too soon. I appreciate that Booth's brother Edwin, after whom it's named, was a hugely famous actor in his day,* but it stills feels somewhat insensitive. Add to this the fact that in the second ever year of productions, the Booth Theatre put on a run of *Our American Cousin* (the very same play Lincoln was watching when he was murdered), and I think you'll agree—this theatre was taking the piss.

According to the book *Nowhere Man* by Robert Rosen, on the morning of December 8, 1980, Mark David Chapman was sitting in his hotel room with a Bible in his hand, reading passages from the Book of John, or rather the Book of John *Lennon*, Chapman having scribbled the singer's surname onto the page. According to Rosen, there was one passage in there that particularly pissed Chapman off: John 14:20, which reads, "I *am* in My Father, and you in Me, and I in you." Chapman believed Lennon was a phony, and that he had directly stolen this passage for his song "I Am the Walrus." It was for religious reasons, in fact, that Chapman was now in New York to kill Lennon.

Who could have predicted that in 1966, when John Lennon sparked global controversy for suggesting that The Beatles were bigger than Jesus, 14 years later one man/ dickhead would still be so angered by it, it would reportedly be the catalyst that would drive him to kill Lennon. For Chapman, killing Lennon was a mission from God. "My desire to kill John Lennon at that point was so strong, there was no law that could have kept me from getting my hands on a gun," he'd later tell an interviewer. Chapman believed it was

---

* So loved, in fact, that even after his brother took the life of the president, his acting career continued to be a success.

his destiny to kill Lennon. Many coincidences kept presenting themselves to confirm this. Like the fact that the gun he bought in a Hawaii shop to kill Lennon with was sold to him by an extremely helpful store clerk called Mr. Ono.*

Lennon's death at the hands of 25-year-old Chapman led to global mourning. One person who was particularly affected was another 25-year-old, a struggling musician from Dallas, Texas, called John Hinckley Jr. "John Lennon is dead, the world is over," he'd later drunkenly record himself saying as he ranted one night into a tape recorder. But Lennon wasn't his only obsession. Having seen the 1976 movie *Taxi Driver*, Hinckley had developed a deep fixation on its young star Jodie Foster. Wanting to do something to impress her, Hinckley decided the best way to achieve this was to kill the recently inaugurated fortieth president of the United States, Ronald Reagan.

Hinckley travelled to Washington, DC, where he started

---

* Names are powerful and can be very influential on your life decisions. There is a theory called nominative determinism, a term coined by New Scientist journalist John Hoyland, which refers to the theory that "a person's name is given an influential role in reflecting key attributes of their job, profession, or general life." Hoyland came up with the term after spotting many examples of it (including an article on urinary infection in the *British Journal of Urology* by J. W. Splatt and D. Weedon). What must Chapman have thought the moment Robin Ono sold him that gun? There is an opposite to this effect too, which I'm going to call nominative deterrentism. It's when a name can actively affect your chances of landing a job. For example, the lead actor in the 1985 biopic *John and Yoko* suffered from the effects of it when, after being cast in the lead role, was fired once Yoko Ono discovered his name was Mark Lindsay Chapman. Yoko reportedly thought it was "bad karma."

tracking Reagan's movements (listening to David Bowie's "Heroes" on repeat while he did so), until finally he found his chance to shoot the former Hollywood B-movie star.

THE PRESIDENT WHO SAVED HIMSELF

On March 30, 1981, John Hinckley Jr. stepped out from a crowd of onlookers with a gun in his hand and a John Lennon pin in his pocket, and fired six rounds at the US president as he was walking out of the Washington Hilton Hotel. The moment the shots rang out, Reagan's Secret Service detail leapt into action. One agent, Jerry Parr, grabbed the president by the shoulder and bundled him into the back seat of the waiting presidential limousine, diving in after him. As they sped off, leaving the other agents to deal with the assassin, Parr searched the president for injuries; however, neither he nor Reagan could find any.

Little did the president know that he had in fact been shot, and that the bullet, lodged in his rib, was going to kill him in a matter of hours. Or at least, that would have happened had Reagan not coughed up a little bit of blood. Parr recognised that something was very wrong and, going against all protocols, immediately diverted the limo to the nearest hospital. Doctors would later tell the president that had he arrived even just five minutes later, he'd have died. Parr's decision to rush him to hospital saved the president's life.

Parr was heralded as a hero and received numerous honours for his swift response, including a congressional commendation.

Interestingly, the only reason Parr was there that day to save Reagan's life, was because as a kid he became obsessed with a film that his father took him to see at the cinema called *Code of the Secret Service*. The star of which was . . . Ronald Reagan.

"Did you know you were an agent of your own destiny?" Parr later asked Reagan, as the president lay recovering in his hospital bed. Parr, a religious man, truly believed that he had been set on a course by the universe that would eventually lead him to rescuing the president. And who can blame him?

It does seem, on the surface at least, that something mystical was at play here. Even the president himself had inklings that an assassination attempt was perhaps on the cards. Just a month earlier, Reagan had visited the Ford Theatre in Washington, DC, with his wife Nancy, and would later write: "I looked up at the presidential box above the stage where Abe Lincoln had been sitting the night he was shot and felt a curious sensation . . . I thought that even with all the Secret Service protection we now had, it was probably still possible for someone who had enough determination to get close enough to the president to shoot him."

Parr wasn't the only person who believed he was supposed to save Reagan's life that day. A few days after the shooting, Reagan's wife Nancy received a phone call from TV star Merv Griffin, who informed her that the astrologer Joan Quigley had predicted that March 30 (the day Reagan was shot) was going to be a dangerous day for the president. Nancy was horrified—had she been more vigilant, consulting with an astrologer about these matters, she would have stopped the shooting from taking place. Nancy immediately employed Quigley so that nothing like this would happen again. The First Lady and the astrologer would speak up to eight times a day, and Quigley was consulted on everything from what times Air Force One should take off and land to the finer details of Cold War negotiations with the countries of the Warsaw Pact.

CHAPTER 21
THE MAN WHO DIDN'T
FALL TO EARTH
THE THEORY OF INCREDIBLE LUCK

The White House has seen a number of presidents who were a touch batshit over the years. Franklin D. Roosevelt suffered from triskaidekaphobia (the fear of the number 13), and would avoid travelling on Fridays if he could; Jimmy Carter claimed to have seen a UFO while serving as Governor in Leary, Georgia, in 1969, even submitting a report to the International UFO Bureau in Oklahoma City;* and when Harry S. Truman was in power, he reputedly hung a horseshoe on the door of the presidential office to ward off evil and bring good luck.

---

* Many explanations were given for what Carter's UFO may have been—everything from coloured clouds as part of a military experiment, to just being the planet, Venus. Regardless, the sighting had a huge effect on him: "One thing's for sure, I'll never make fun of people who say they've seen unidentified objects in the sky. If I become President, I'll make every piece of information this country has about UFO sightings available to the public and the scientists." Carter never disclosed any information once in office.

Truman wasn't the only president to believe in luck. William McKinley, the twenty-fifth president, believed in it too, big time. McKinley's luck was powered via red carnations. McKinley first became attached to carnations after winning a debate while wearing one in the early days of his political career. He always made sure to be wearing one for all his important moments—from his first congressional win in 1887 to his presidential campaign in 1896. Once he became president, McKinley sported one at all times.

McKinley was so interested in the idea of luck that he even became the member of an unlucky club. The Thirteen Club was founded in 1882 by a man called Captain Fowler, a Civil War veteran. The club, made up of 13 men, would meet on Friday the 13th at 7:13 p.m. To get to the dinner table each man would have to walk under a ladder, then spill salt in front of them without throwing any over their shoulder afterwards. Open umbrellas would surround the dinner table, and the members would joyfully break mirrors as they dined.

Unfortunately for McKinley, his luck ran out in 1901. While chatting with members of the public in Buffalo, New York, he met a 12-year-old called Myrtle. So impressed was he with her that he handed her his own red carnation, something he seldom did. "I must give this flower to another little flower," he said, handing over his lucky bloom. Usually he'd replace the flower as soon as possible, but this time he never got the chance. Just moments later, McKinley was gunned down by an assassin standing a few people away from Myrtle. The president was rushed to a hospital, where he was operated on. Unlike Reagan, though, who had top doctors to save his life, the only doctor available to perform surgery on McKinley was a gynaecologist, and the president died eight days later.

Poor McKinley. If only he'd kept hold of his red carnation, maybe he'd have lived for many more decades. But is there such a thing as luck? Would the red carnation have changed anything? To say someone is lucky is quite often a contradiction in terms. Usually for someone to become notably lucky, more often than not they've first had to have something incredibly unlucky happen to them. So what does that make them, really?

Someone who is often cited as being the luckiest person to live sure had to go through some major horrors to be granted that title. His name was Frano Selak, of Croatia.

Selak's run of luck/bad luck began in 1962, when he was riding on a train from Sarajevo to Dubrovnik and it derailed and plunged into a river. Seventeen people perished, but Selak somehow survived and was carried back to shore. Then, the next year, Selak took his first ever plane ride. The trip was going well until mid-flight, when the door to the plane burst open, and Selak got sucked out of the plane. He only survived because, as luck would have it, he landed on a haystack. Sadly for the rest of the passengers, the plane crashed, killing all 19 others on board.

In 1966, having decided never to fly in a plane again, Selak was riding a bus when he ended up fighting for his life once again as it shot off a bridge and into a river. "By this time my friends had stopped visiting me," he told journalists. The accidents kept on coming; in 1970 Selak was driving his car when it suddenly caught fire—fortunately, he was able to escape just before the vehicle blew up. Three years later, while driving another car, a freak hot oil accident caused giant flames to start pouring out of the air vents, burning all the hair off his head. In 1995 he was hit by a bus.

Finally, in 1996 he luckily escaped a head-on collision with a truck while on a mountain road, though in doing so, he rather unluckily then hit a guardrail, which sent his car plunging down a 300-foot cliff. *Luckily*, he was not wearing a seatbelt, so he was able to leap out of the car, catch hold of a branch of a tree on the side of the mountain and watch as his car plummeted into the depths below. Was Frano Selak lucky? He didn't think so, telling journalists, "I always think I was unlucky to have been in them in the first place, but you can't tell people what they don't want to believe."*

THE IMPOSSIBLE PILOT

Grahame Donald, or Air Marshal Sir David Grahame Donald, KCB, DFC, AFC, to give him his full title, was a Royal Navy and RAF pilot who served in both world wars. A war hero and a thoroughly decorated pilot, he also claimed to have achieved something seemingly impossible mid-flight.

The story, recounted by Donald himself in Joshua Levine's *On a Wing and a Prayer*, goes like this:

As I was approaching the airfield at 6,000 feet, I decided to try a new manoeuvre which might prove useful in combat. It

* The reason we largely know about Selak's dubious story is because of the multiple interviews he gave after he, rather luckily, won hundreds of thousands in the lottery.

Air Marshal Sir David Grahame Donald,
KCB, DFC, AFC.

was to be a half loop and then I would roll at the top and fly off in the opposite direction. I pulled her up into a neat half loop but I was going rather slowly and I was hanging upside down in the air. With an efficient safety belt that would have been no trouble at all—but our standard belts were a hundred per cent unsafe. Mine stretched a little and suddenly I dived clean through it and fell out of the cockpit. There was nothing between me and the ground. The first 2,000 feet passed very quickly and terra firma looked damnably "firma." As I fell, I began to hear my faithful little Camel somewhere nearby. Suddenly I fell back onto her. I was able to grip onto her top plane and that saved me from slithering straight through the propeller which was glistening beautifully in the evening sunshine.

As impossible as it sounds, what Donald is claiming here is that after he fell out of the cockpit, the Sopwith plane continued the loop the loop without him, which meant that by the time he had plunged those 2,000 feet, the plane continuing its loop was there to meet him.

The ride wasn't a smooth one just yet however; when Donald gripped the plane, it went into a dive at 140 mph. Donald somehow held on, with one foot and one hand gripping on to the inside of the cockpit. His attempts to level the Sopwith only caused more problems, sending the plane into a spin. Eventually, just 2,500 feet from the ground, Donald managed to wiggle his foot onto the control stick and ma-

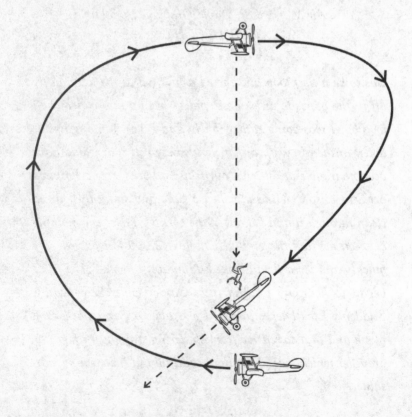

noeuvre the plane into a smooth glide. The only snag was that it was upside down. Donald was able to flip the plane back over, and, with 800 feet left, was able to bring it down to the ground safely. After making his miraculous escape, Donald was saddened to see that no one had witnessed this incredible feat. For some reason everyone had gone missing. He later learnt why:

> *Every man-jack of the squadron had mysteriously disappeared. After a minute or so, heads began to appear all over the place— popping up like bunny rabbits from every hole. Apparently, when I had pressed my foot on the control stick, I'd also pressed both triggers and the entire airfield had been sprinkled with bullets. Very wisely, the ground crew dived as one man for the nearest ditch.*

This story seems utterly implausible. But I believe it and, according to a number of pilots I spoke to, it isn't impossible.* Mark Welsh, a pilot with over 30 years' experience, thought it was unlikely. "To fly a loop you have to actively pull back on the stick. If he fell out at the inverted position there's nothing that would cause the aircraft to fly the second half of the loop on its own. It would just waffle off inverted until it crashed." "It's not literally against the laws of physics," said British Airways pilot James Richardson. "Most aeroplanes will recover from the top of a loop without the need for any further

---

* Full disclosure: about 90 per cent of the pilots I asked said it was impossible.

control inputs, and stabilise into a dive such as the author suggests. If there's little or no wind, it's even fairly plausible that the path of the aircraft and the erstwhile pilot could even intersect. I'll admit it stretches credibility a little, though!"

It seems that if it did happen, it was by sheer luck. And luck, or unluck, or whatever you call it, is what led Dennis Collier to survive seven days of aerial hell.

THE LUCKIEST MAN ALIVE

Dennis Collier is a licensed pilot, and in late 2021 he spent $110,000 on a Seawind 3000—a small amphibious aeroplane. The plane had been built by an 88-year-old retired pilot called Lynn Swann and, despite it not having flown in two years, looked to be in good shape generally. In total the plane had only clocked up 20 hours of flying time and a few bits clearly needed repairing, but nothing major. Dennis planned to fly his new plane from Los Angeles to Boyne City, Michigan, a flight that should have taken him seven hours. It ended up taking a bit longer . . .

Flight no. 1: Dennis decides to take the plane out for a test flight while Swann goes off to pick up some supplies. Unfortunately, as he comes in to land, the wheels (landing gear) remain up and he crashes into the runway. Records from the Federal Aviation Administration (FAA) confirm this fact. Somehow, Dennis is OK. Swann tells Dennis that he is lucky, and it could have been much worse for him. Luckily Swann has installed a block of wood underneath the front of the plane and that must have taken the brunt of the crash.

Flight no. 2: Despite this initial crash, Dennis decides to patch up the damage and immediately takes the plane out again for another test, flying to New Mexico. Arriving there at 3:20 a.m., Dennis makes his descent and stalls the engine, causing him to crash beside the runway, taking out a runway light and a sign. The plane is smashed up but Dennis, somehow, is still fine. The FAA are informed by the local airport staff.

Flight no. 3: Dennis fixes up the plane and takes off once again, from New Mexico. He crashes again. This time he needs to speak to the FAA. For some reason they agree to continue letting him fly. Dennis parks his seaplane in an empty aircraft hangar and fixes the plane himself.

Flight no. 4: Following the patch-up, Dennis manages to take off once again, making his way to Chicago. After a few hours in the air he suffers a problem with the left wing, which forcibly pitches his plane upwards. Dennis struggles with the controls, and it takes him four attempts to land. When he finally manages to do so it's incredibly rough and his plane skids off into the grassland, but he just about manages to steer it back onto the runway. He's now in an airport in Nebraska, somewhere he'd absolutely never intended to be. This time he finds himself shaking with fear from his experience. The airport managers, a married couple, manage to calm him down and look after him for the night, suggesting that maybe he shouldn't fly the plane again.

Flight no. 5: Dennis is back up in the air later the next day. The plane is pretty banged up by now, but Dennis believes his patching-up work should have fixed all the issues. This quick flight is just a little test to make sure everything is working before he heads back to Nebraska. He crashes the plane.

Flight no. 6: Having discovered the problem is some crossed wires, Dennis fixes those and takes off for Nebraska. The flight is going well as he flies over Mississippi, and he's only five hours out of Nebraska when he hears a "clunk." Dennis radios to a local airport that he can see about five miles off. He needs someone to spot him as he approaches and let him know if his front wheel is down. No one responds. And his front wheels aren't down. Dennis lands the plane holding off on the back wheels for as long as possible, before bringing the nose of the plane smashing down into the tarmac and skidding hundreds of yards before coming to a rest.

Flight no. 7: People are now properly concerned because, despite all the problems, and breakages, Dennis still plans to get off the ground in his Seawind for one final leg of the journey—to reach Boyne City, now just a 25-minute flight away. The FAA are justifiably worried that Dennis's landing gear will once again malfunction and cause another crash. To placate them, he promises that this time he'll keep the landing gear down for the duration of his 25-minute flight. He takes off, and the flight is going well until he smells burning. The engine splutters and Dennis decides to turn around to make an emergency landing at another local airport an achievable distance away. However, the wing is playing up and Dennis is forced to make an emergency water landing in Lake Michigan. Thankfully, this being an amphibious plane, it's designed to land in water.

"I glanced back over the water and realised I could judge my altitude by the glittering of the sun over the small ripple of the water," Dennis later said. "Time seemed to slow and I was transfixed on the beauty of the sun over the water . . . I could see it coming and it was really close."

Unfortunately, he forgets he still has his landing gear down, and upon hitting the water, it causes an almighty crash, flipping the plane vertically. Finally, the amphibious plane that was designed to float then sank to the bottom of the lake.

Dennis has since retired from flying. When asked by journalist Francis X. Donnelly what his next plans were, he revealed that he had found work at Disney World ferrying tourists around on a boat. Remarkably, they have made him the ship's pilot.

CHAPTER 22
THE SECRET TO WORLD DOMINATION
THE THEORY OF UNPALATABILITY

Two million years ago, we were a fairly unremarkable ape. Of all the many mind-expanding facts in Yuval Noah Harari's blockbuster book *Sapiens*, that's the one that completely rocked my world. There was nothing special about us. Nothing to suggest that we'd rise to become the dominant species on this planet. We had no weapons with which to defend ourselves, we hadn't yet discovered how to make fires and we lacked the cognitive brilliance to outwit our predators. So how did we do it? How did we survive, when all around us were man-eating carnivores? According to the late palaeoanthropologist Louis Leakey, the reason was this: we were too smelly to eat.

"I seriously believe," Leakey said to a conference room full of leading academics, "that one of the things which protected many early primates, including early man, in the defenceless days before he had weapons or tools, and when he was living on the ground, was that he was unpalatable to the carnivores."

Leakey, who presented this theory in 1965 at an international conference co-sponsored by the Brain Research Institute at UCLA, was first struck with the idea after he and a companion were forced to sleep in the Serengeti plains following a car breakdown. As they lay on the ground, five lions came along and each sniffed both of the men's heads, before deciding "nah" and moving on. What had they sniffed that they didn't like? After reporting the incident to his students, Leakey learnt he wasn't the only one to have experienced this: "In 1931 I had two students in my first camp at Olduvai, and a lion came, sniffed at them as they lay in their cots, and walked through their tent. He was a hungry lion but he didn't touch them; they were not good food."

Leakey and his team looked into the literature of humans being killed by "man-eaters" and concluded that even when a human was killed, they weren't immediately eaten. Hyenas, for example, said Leakey, can't stand our smell, and will wait for a human to go putrid before touching the carcass, some 40 hours after he or she has died. That's how terrible our natural smell is to predators apparently—they have to wait for the maggots to set in.

The cases that Leakey and his team unearthed suggested that if a lion or leopard were to eat a human directly after a kill, it would be as an act of desperation—the animal was either ill or wounded, or perhaps their food sources had been depleted by humans in the area. Expanding his research, Leakey looked at other primates and discovered that they don't get eaten much either (all apart from the family of Old World monkeys, known as Cercopithecidae; this includes mandrills, which leopards seem to love, although Leakey had no idea why).

Closing his speech to the academics at UCLA, Leakey said:

> Whether man's natural immunity to large carnivores is smell by itself—they certainly sniff at us—or whether it is a combination of smell plus knowledge of how flesh tastes, I do not know, but I am convinced that a major defence mechanism of the earlier stages of protoman . . . and early man was . . . not being good food for large carnivores.

The argument was widely panned by his peers, and rarely appears in the scientific literature, though you'll find quite a lot of papers pointing out that generally speaking animals are disgusted by us. Cockroaches, for example, have been observed cleaning themselves after making contact with humans. And according to scientist Diane Akerman, bats are pretty disgusted by us too. In her book *A Natural History of Sense* she tells a story about putting a large Indonesian flying fox in her hair, curious to see if it would get entangled in it. When placed on her head the bat began to cough, and once she set it back into its cage it spent some time licking itself clean of the smelly human odour.

Mostly, though, Leakey's theory of unpalatability was discredited: "The idea is ingenious, but from an ecological point of view it's inconceivable that a readily accessible source of meat would remain unexploited for 10 or 20 million years," wrote Professor Adriaan Kortlandt, a Dutch ethologist, in his paper "How might early hominids have defended themselves against large predators and food competitors?" Kortlandt thinks we might have survived, not by being revolting to eat but by waving thorn bushes at our predators. Lions are apparently terrified of them.*

THE LEAKEYS

The Leakey family was brimful of serious scientists, archaeologists, and soldiers, but several of them were slightly batshit too. Louis, in particular, was full of mad theories. Unfortunately for his contemporaries, he was also at the forefront of major discoveries and progressive scientific thinking.

Louis was among those who pioneered the study of our closest primate relatives. However, he believed this could only be done by single women who lacked scientific training. Lucky us that he still managed to see this idea through, as his selected protégées were three women called Dian Fossey, Jane Goodall, and Biruté Galdikas, "the Trimates" as he called them, or "Leakey's Angels" as others called them. So trusted was Leakey by these three, that when he told Fossey she'd have to get her appendix removed before heading out to Rwanda, she did so, before receiving a follow-up letter explaining that he was only joking.

* Kortlandt tested his theory by attaching some thorn branches to "an electrically operated helicopter-like rotor with four blades" to prove it. Turning it on any time lions appeared looking for food, he found that it scared them away.

*Mary Leakey with the Laetoli Footprints, which she and
her team found after a game of "throw the elephant shit
at each other."*

Louis Leakey discovered more hominid fossils than anyone else, barring just two people: his son Richard, who grew
up fossil-hunting with his family and went on to become a
celebrated palaeoanthropologist himself, now holds the record for most finds; and Louis's wife, Mary, who actually
found most of the fossils he took the credit for finding.

Over many decades, Louis and Mary's discoveries, and
those made by their assistants, included a fossilised tooth of
a species of hominid named *Homo habilis*. This was a hugely
important find as it helped show that humans evolved originally in Africa rather than Asia (as was believed at the time),
pushing back the date of the origin of humans by a million

years. They also discovered the first fossilised ape skull to be found, a 25-million-year-old species named *Proconsul africanus.**

The Leakeys' biggest discovery, however, was the 1.75-million-year-old skull found in the Olduvai Gorge, Tanzania, which purported to be the link between "South African near-men" and "true man as we know him." Rivals were bemused by the mad rate the Leakeys and their "hominid gang" discovered new and important fossils. They called it "Leakey luck." The truth is, it wasn't luck. The Leakeys had a shit-hot team and were aggressively proactive, productive, and on the move. They made their luck.

LEAKEY LUCK

Mary Leakey, who continued on making huge discoveries after Louis had passed away, noted the importance of their luck when she and her team made one of the greatest anthropological finds to date in Laetoli (Tanzania): the discovery of the oldest example of bipedal human footprints, which they found while playing a game of "throw the elephant shit at each other." During the game a team member fell down and noted that he was lying on a hard surface which appeared to contain ancient animal footprints, including those of rhinoceros.

---

* The skull received so much publicity that when it arrived in England it was met by photographers and TV news crews, and given protection in the form of two plainclothes policemen, who were told never to let it out of their sight.

It was to prove to be an incredible find; and it wasn't just a few footprints. The area ended up containing over 18,400.

Two years into the process of excavating the site, Mary Leakey discovered a heel print that seemed to belong to a hominid. Later she would write: "The discovery of the trails was immensely exciting . . . it was clear that we had before us unique evidence, of an unimpeachable nature, to establish that our hominid ancestors were fully bipedal a little before 3.5 million years ago"—the kind of thing anthropologists had argued over for many decades, with no real hope of proving or disproving their view.

MAKING HUMANS PALATABLE AGAIN

Louis wasn't the only Leakey interested in human odour. It also became the life's work of another one of his and Mary's sons—Colin, a leading plant scientist—though for different reasons. Colin Leakey spent decades attempting to breed a new kind of bean that makes us less flatulent. He first became interested in the subject when he saw that NASA were trying to work out how to send baked beans into space without stinking out the astronauts' capsules. NASA would later conclude that beans weren't ever going to be good space food, but Colin was already inspired and he continued to explore how you make beans cause less flatulence and be more digestible to people who suffered from conditions like Crohn's disease, which in turn would help them increase their consumption of plant protein. He also believed that a fart-free bean could help reduce the amount of meat being eaten globally.

Leakey even patented an invention called the "Flatometer," a device that slots into your rectum, with a tube coming out of it that connects to a balloon at the other end. He recommended tucking the balloon end into a shirt pocket.

Leakey dedicated decades to developing his beans, despite the non-stop ridicule, and his efforts were rewarded when he managed to breed numerous new varieties, including "Leakey's Stop beans," which can be bought in the UK via bean specialists Hodmedods, as well as "Prim" and "Proper," and which have become hugely beneficial in developing nations, helping to provide the elderly, children, and anyone pregnant with something that's guaranteed safe for them to eat. "My family were embarrassed, and I gained a certain amount of notoriety," he told the *Guardian*. "But I think people have stopped laughing now." And at least we humans might now be just a little more appetising to a passing predator.

CHAPTER 23
THE UNPREDICTABLE WORLD OF NOSTRADAMUS
THE THEORY OF PREDICTIONS

In 1988, the musician Nile Rodgers, co-founder of the band Chic, received an important phone call from a Hollywood director named John Landis. "I don't know who you are," said Landis, "but somebody told me that you're some kind of genius or something." Landis was calling to offer Rodgers the role as composer on his new film *Coming to America*, which was to star America's hottest new comedy actor at the time, Eddie Murphy. This was to be an exciting new project for Rodgers, who had never scored such a big-budget Hollywood film before. However, upon arriving at the studio for his first day of work, he was delivered some odd news. The film's entire production schedule was to be accelerated to breakneck speed. The reason: Eddie Murphy had recently come across a prediction by Nostradamus that maintained an earthquake would destroy California on one of the days he was supposed to be filming there. And so to ensure that Murphy wasn't there for when LA plunged into the Pacific, all of Murphy's scenes needed to be filmed ASAP so he could fly out before the great quake hit.* Rodgers suddenly found himself working 17-hour-long days in order to produce the music to match the daily footage being shot, while the rest of the production team were equally thrown into chaos.†

---

* Spoiler: It did not hit.

† The year *Coming to America* came out in cinemas, the actor Gary Busey would experience his own odd moment, which would eventually lead to an on-set debacle to rival Eddie Murphy's. After receiving emergency surgery for a head injury, during which he flatlined at one point, Busey claims that he visited heaven before returning to Earth again: "I was surrounded by angels. Balls of light floating all around me. And I felt trust, love, protection, and happiness like you cannot feel on Earth." He describes meeting three angels, who were represented as three balls of light, and that he himself at the time was just an inch wide and a foot long. "That is your soul, and your soul is housed in the column of your spine," he said. The orbs of light offered Busey the chance to stay in heaven, or return to Earth where he could continue his destiny. Fifteen years later the memory of his time in heaven would still have a strong hold over Busey. While on set filming a movie called *Quigley*, in which Busey plays the role of a man who dies but is reincarnated as a talking dog, Busey arrived to shoot a scene set in heaven, and was shocked by what he found. Unfortunately, the production had hired a set designer on the movie who had not been to heaven. Co-star Curtis Armstrong described the moment in an interview with the A.V. Club, saying that Busey started protesting against the design and refusing to play the scene saying, "It's nothing like this. I've been to heaven and it doesn't look like this. That sofa's all wrong. That mirror is ridiculous. They don't even have mirrors!" Things got even more heated when it turned out that, remarkably, another actor in the scene, who was playing an angel, had also briefly died and gone to heaven. According to Armstrong, the angel had his own take on what heaven looked like, and it didn't match up with Busey's. The chat over whose heaven was the correct one became so heated that the two men started to physically fight, forcing production to be shut down for the day.

Murphy learnt about the prediction from watching *The Man Who Saved Tomorrow*. The film was fronted by Orson Welles, who later disowned himself from the project following the number of embarrassingly incorrect predictions made in it, which included: Ted Kennedy being elected president in 1984 (he wasn't); World War III beginning by 1999 (it didn't); and an earthquake devastating San Francisco in May 1988 (didn't happen). The film showcased many of Nostradamus's predictions, my favourite being the claim made at the beginning of the film that in May 1791, when grave robbers dug up Nostradamus's body, they found a plaque around his neck on which the words "May 1791" were written, as a prediction for when someone would try to rob his grave.

I wonder what Nostradamus would have made of all the fuss he's caused in the 400-plus years since he died. Hollywood is not the only place where Nostradamus has caused headaches. In 1988 the Griffith Observatory in Los Angeles fielded months of phone calls, a dozen a day at least, from members of the public who were calling just to check if it was true that the city would be devastated by a huge earthquake following a planetary alignment. The calls became such a nuisance that the observatory's programme manager had to send out a company-wide memo properly debunking Nostradamus's claim, which could be read out by anyone manning the phones. The memo pointed out that even if the planets did align, the only effect of the resulting gravitational pull would be in the oceans—by 1/25th of a millimetre.

The idea of a devastating earthquake must have been troubling many Americans in the 1980s, as not only was it

Eddie Murphy as Prince Akeem in Coming to America.

being forewarned by a dead soothsayer from the sixteenth century, but it was the subject of a few popular-science books as well. One book, *The Jupiter Effect*, written by John Gribbin and Stephen Plagemann, predicted that a devastating earthquake would occur somewhere along the San Andreas Fault on March 10, 1982. Gribbin—some of whose subsequent hundred or so books have become classics of the pop-science genre, such as *In Search of Schrödinger's Cat*—has since distanced himself from this theory.

Predicting when an earthquake will hit is famously hard—and there have been many theories trying to work out how to do it. One method suggested included monitoring newspapers for missing cats. In the late 1900s, a Californian geologist named Jim Berkland claimed to have successfully predicated two earthquakes by tracking the number of ads for missing cats in newspapers. Berkland believed cats knew when a quake was on the way and would run away from home when one was imminent. Berkland said the number of "missing" ads would increase by up to 400 per cent in the lead up to one. One person who enjoyed success in predicting earthquakes was Raffaele Bendandi, an Italian self-proclaimed professional of "seismogenics" (a word he coined). Bendandi became famous in Italy after almost successfully predicting an earthquake would occur on January 4, 1924. He ended up being two days out. Despite this, Italian newspapers carried reports about him, and he started a life of infamy as the man who predicted earthquakes. According to the newspapers, he genuinely wasn't that bad at predicting them either, clocking up at least two other successful predictions. Mussolini, who was dictator at the time, was so impressed that he bestowed a knighthood on Bendandi. However, he also banned him from making any more public predictions as they had annoying consequences.

For example, on May 11, 2001, it was estimated that 20 per cent of Rome's population didn't go to work, with many even leaving town, because of a prediction Bendandi had made. The earthquake didn't hit, and, what's more peculiar, the prediction itself didn't even exist. But just like at the Griffith Observatory, Rome's Department of Civil Protection would set up phone lines to help reassure members of the public calling up to find out just when, exactly, the earthquake was going to strike.*

* * *

Nostradamus is often portrayed as a robed wizard sitting hunched over a parchment in a secluded room, furiously scribbling down the Earth's future events. Or at least, that's my impression of him. However, he was obviously a lot more three-dimensional than that in real life. For example, during much of his lifetime he was better known for his jam recipes. His book *EXCELLENT & USEFUL Treatise to all Needed who want Knowledge of Several Exquisite Recipes . . . Newly Composed by Master Michel de Nostredame, Doctor of Medicine in the city of Salon de Craux en Provence* was a big seller for him. It included instructions for dyeing your hair blond and recipes for marmalade, and gave directions on how to grind up sea-snail shells and cuttlefish bone to make toothpaste. He also used to run a shop, where he'd take bets on what sex an unborn baby would be.

Nostradamus gained national fame when he published the first of his books of premonitions. Nostradamus's *Prophecies* is a mixed bag, containing letters, notes, and predictions that stretch all the way to the 4000s, presented in no particular order. He became famous even within his lifetime for his incredible abilities. One story has it that while he was in Italy he gave way to some Franciscan monks who were walking

---

* A year later, six Italian seismologists would be jailed for failing to predict an earthquake that would end up killing 29 people.

Nostradamus.

towards him on the road. As they passed, he suddenly pros-
trated himself on the road and grabbed one of the monks'
habits. "I must yield myself and bow before his Holiness," he
told the stunned monks. The monk he had held was called
Brother Felice Peretti, who, many decades later, would become Pope Sixtus V.

For someone who has had 400 years to get something
right, you'd think that at least one prediction would have
come true. But none have. Even when he was alive he failed
to see what was just around the corner. One edition of
Nostradamus's *Prophecies*, published in 1558, carried a dedi-
cation to King Henry II, wishing him a happy life. Henry
died the following year. Interestingly, there's a theory that
Nostradamus didn't believe his own predictions, and that he
was just compiling existing predictions from multiple sources,

one of which was the wizard Merlin from Arthurian legend. Yet in spite of a jaw-droppingly low hit rate, our fascination with him has never waned. Whenever disasters occur, Nostradamus's name is once again invoked. For example, following the events of 9/11 many bookshops reported a surge in orders for his *Prophesies*.

★ ★ ★

So if he didn't get any of the predictions right, what precisely has he done for us? Well, the next time you apply insect repellent spray, say a quick thanks to Nostradamus as he hasn't had quite the acknowledgement he deserves for his part in this invention. Nostradamus was the first person to describe benzoic acid, which these days is used in the production of not only insect repellents, but also perfumes and dyes, and has been used to help preserve food, like jam, pickles, and other acidic foods. It's also a chemical that forms tiny clear crystals that look just like snowflakes. So thanks to Nostradamus we have snow globes.

And those aren't the only orbs that utilise the chemical. It is also used in benzoyl peroxide, which is often used to make acrylic. One thing acrylic is used for is making crystal-like globes. So next time you walk into a fortune teller's tent at a fairground, give thanks to Nostramaus, because the knock-off crystal ball being used by the soothsayer to predict your future, will most likely have been made using benzoic acid. I bet Nostradamus couldn't have predicted that.

CHAPTER 24

AN ARSE WRINKLE IN TIME

THE THEORY OF UNLIKELY ORACLES

Eddie Murphy isn't the only star to have had predictions to influence his career. Before reaching decisions about the movie projects he planned to take on, Sylvester Stallone would always consult his astrologist mother Jacqueline to see what the stars said. "In fact," wrote Jackie Stallone in her book *Starpower: An Astrological Guide to Super Success*, "his very first victory with *Rocky* happened because we jumped on a wicked Mercury Retrograde before it jumped on us!"*

Jackie Stallone was a formidable woman and I would have loved to have met her. Sadly, it was only by emailing her for the fifth time, asking her to take a look at photos of my bottom, that I learnt the news that she had passed away in late

---

* Sly Stallone is also a believer in reincarnation, and can remember four different past lives. In one life he was a boxer who was killed by a knockout punch; and in another he was a French Revolution soldier who was guillotined. He has also speculated that he may have once been a Guatemalan monkey.

Jacqueline Stallone, professional rumpologist.

2020. I'd somehow missed the announcement and as a result had been aimlessly emailing her over the last couple of years via her website contact form, in the hope that she might eventually pick up one of my letters.

Jacqueline was a unique astrologer; she didn't read palms but rather butt cheeks. "Rumpology," a word she coined, is, according to her own website, "The art of reading the lines, crevices, dimples, and folds of the buttocks to divine the individual's character and gain an understanding of what has occurred in the past and get a prediction of the future."

"The crack of your behind corresponds to the division of the two hemispheres of the brain," she once explained in an interview with *TV Guide Online*. "The buttocks represent areas of your personality. The central cleft meets the leg that divides the rump with the four quadrants that correspond to the four elements—air, fire, water, and earth." She claimed that rumpology was practised by the ancient Babylonians, Greeks, Romans, and Indians, although I've not yet come across any evidence to substantiate this.

The way rumpology works is that both butt cheeks perform different roles: the left cheek lets you look into your past, while the right cheek affords a peek at your future.

In order for Jackie to make her reading, she required you to send her a picture of your bottom. Her price was prohibitively high for a full reading, but fortunately she also offered a one-cheek-only service at just $300. For that money she promised:

- Your very own personal, condensed, no-frills report on the signs and markings on your bottom.
- A condensed one-year prediction of the direction your bottom is taking you, including your love life, career, and financial affairs.
- An 8.5 × 11-inch glossy colour print of your bottom.

Looking into the lives of others via asstrology wasn't the only way in which Jackie predicted the future. She could also see into the future via her psychic dogs. According to Jackie, her two Dobermans were able to tell future events by channelling them from the spirit realm and then telepathically beaming the messages to her. To be fair to her, they did pretty well.

Her predictions, via her dogs, were consistently correct about who would be voted in as president (the dogs predicted, for example, that George W. Bush would win the 2000 election by just a few hundred votes in Florida).

Unlike Nostradamus, Jackie decided never to predict anything with a doomsday quality to it. Seeding an end-of-days prediction into the world was unethical in her eyes and could possibly force a sense of destiny onto the person having the reading. One example of that happening was when John Wilkes Booth, Abraham Lincoln's murderer, had his palm read as a teenager. The fortune-teller told him that he was doomed to die young and would meet a bad end. According to his sister, Booth very much believed this would happen, often discussing it throughout his short life whenever he was feeling down.

I too have personally felt the helplessness that comes with a depressing palm-reading. A palm is criss-crossed by numerous lines, many of them indicating what your future will hold. They include a line each for: life expectancy, fate/career, heart, health, success, marriage, will, logic, and so on. I still remember, as a child in Hong Kong, someone looking at my palm and explaining to me what an absolute shitshow it was. All my lines were broken or short. For a while, my lack of life-life genuinely worried me, and I was convinced an early death awaited me.

Fortunately, I didn't continue to believe in such things, but perhaps some of you reading this book do. If that is the case, and you too have awful palm lines, I have good news for you. There's now something you can do about it.

For the last decade in Japan, people have been having their

palm lines physically altered by burning in some line extensions with a laser beam. This practice was first reported in 2011, when a surgeon wrote about a woman asking for her lines to be altered. The doctor, Takaaki Matsuoka, who had never heard of this kind of "surgery" before, discovered that these kinds of operations were being performed over in South Korea, and quickly learnt how to perform the procedure. Word spread, and requests for this kind of surgery started pouring in. As doctors are seldom experts in palmistry, the patient would often come in with the desired line traced on their palm with felt-tip or Biro, giving the doctor the straightforward task of simply lasering over the line.

According to an interview that Dr. Matsuoka gave to the *Daily Beast*, some positive results came out of this whole surprising business. One woman who had her marriage line extended (her older and deficient line indicated that her chance of marrying would peter out some time in her twenties) would later write to the doctor to tell him that she had got happily married not long after the operation. Other patients wrote in to say that they had won the lottery post-surgery.

Bizarrely, the Shonan Beauty Clinic, where Dr. Matsuoka works, no longer advertises the treatment because there was too much demand, and the emails I sent asking whether the practice continues remain, much like my bottom emails to Jackie Stallone, entirely unanswered. Which is just my luck.*

---

* Something I apparently ran out of in my early twenties, if my palms are anything to go by.

CHAPTER 25
A CREATIONIST ON THE MOON
THE THEORY OF THE APOLLO MOON LANDINGS

Did you know that Neil Armstrong's first step on the moon wasn't even his favourite footstep? You'd think there'd be no question as to where it ranked on his "My most exciting footsteps" Top Ten. But it wasn't No. 1. According to Thomas Friedman's book *From Beirut to Jerusalem*, occupying the pole position was a step he made in Jerusalem after he returned from his lunar mission. Armstrong was taking a walk with the Israeli archaeologist Meir Ben-Dov, when, as they reached the Huldah Gates, Armstrong asked if there was anywhere that Jesus would have stepped. "Yes," replied Ben-Dov. Given Jesus was Jewish, he'd have walked many times on the exact same steps Armstrong was now treading, as these specific steps, which dated back to biblical times, led to the Temple Mount, where Jesus would have prayed.

"I have to tell you," said Armstrong, "I am more excited stepping on these stones than I was stepping on the moon."

When I first read this fact, I found myself a bit shocked. I hadn't quite realised how religious the first man on the moon had been. But as it turns out, many of the Apollo astronauts were just the same.

And even if they weren't before they set off for the moon, it's entirely possible that the lunar experience might have converted them. Many people speculated that Alan Shepard, as the first American sent into orbit, would be struck by a profound divine revelation when seeing the Earth from space. As it happened, he didn't really have much chance to experience God, or anything at all, because NASA didn't give him a window—he only had a periscope. Much harder to have a divine awakening through a periscope, I imagine. On top of that, there was a lens on the periscope that Shepherd forgot to remove before use, so he basically saw the world through a moody black and white Instagram filter. We do know that Shepard did say a prayer as he was waiting to be launched into space. It's come to be known as "Shepard's Prayer," and it went like this: "Please, Lord, don't let me fuck up."

Buzz Aldrin, the second man to step on the lunar surface, was so religious that virtually the first thing he did, after he and Armstrong successfully touched down on the lunar surface, was to conduct the first ever communion on the moon. "During the first idle moment in the LM [lunar module] before eating our snack," he wrote in his autobiography, *Return to Earth*,

I reached into my personal preference kit and pulled out two small packages which had been specially prepared at my request. One contained a small amount of wine, the other a small wafer. With them and a small chalice from the kit, I took communion on the moon, reading to myself from a small card I carried on which I had written the portion of the Book of John used in the traditional communion ceremony.

When I met Buzz many years later, he said that it was a last-minute decision to take communion up there, and that he and his Catholic priest weren't able to find red wine in time for launch, so the blood of Christ was a nice white instead. Neil, meanwhile, despite his faith, opted not to take part, eating a ham-salad sandwich instead.

THE THEORIES OF THE FIRST STEP

Religious reasons apart, I can see why Armstrong's first moon steps weren't his favourite. For starters, in the lead-up to the moon mission, no one was quite sure what was going to happen once he placed his left foot on the ground. One theory had it that his foot would go up in flames. As Buzz wrote, "A modern scientist stated his theory that the lunar soil, roasted by the heat of the sun and the frigidity of space, was in such chemical imbalance that man's footsteps might trigger a monstrous fire."

Another worrying prediction was that the moon was so heavily covered in dust that it might swallow him up immediately. This was clearly on Armstrong's mind as he stood on the lunar module ladder, as Armstrong actually did a practice jump on the ladder to see if the lander would be thrust deep into the dusty surface. It wasn't. But one hell of a risky move, no? If he'd toppled the lunar lander he'd have taken Buzz along with him. At least if he'd disappeared into the moon on his own, Buzz could have tried to fish him out.

When Armstrong finally planted both feet on the moon, these two worries were shown to be unfounded as he neither burnt to a crisp nor sank through the surface. Buzz, meanwhile, was clearly relieved by the results of the "experiment," since when he made it to the bottom of the ladder, he immediately relaxed and, in front of the watching billions on TV, took a piss. "Neil might have been the first man to step on the moon," he wrote, "but I was the first to pee in his pants on the moon."* *The Guinness Book of World Records* subsequently acknowledged this accomplishment.

Another reason Armstrong didn't have a great time generally with his footsteps on the moon was due to the cables required to film his footsteps. "The one thing that gave us more trouble than we expected was the TV cable," Armstrong told his biographer James R. Hansen.

I kept getting my feet tangled up in it. It's a white cable and was easily observable for a while. But it soon picked up the black dust which blended it in with the terrain, and it seemed that I was forever getting my foot caught in it.

NASA didn't even really know the best way that the astronauts should walk on the moon. Again, there were many theories, and one NASA employee, Walter Kuehnegger (known to many as "Professor Moon"), took it upon himself to discover the answer, producing a five-volume report for NASA. His conclusion: hopping like a kangaroo would be the most efficient way to propel oneself across the moon's surface. "By performing a kangaroo-type leaping and jumping, you require the least amount of energy, and consume the least amount of oxygen," he told *Smithsonian Magazine*. Sadly, this didn't catch on.

---

* Interestingly, the first thing Edmund Hillary did when he got to the top of Mount Everest was have a pee. It's as if both men were marking their territory.

THE THEORY OF THE FIRST WORDS

Finally, the pressure to deliver some memorable opening words as he took his first step must have marred Armstrong's experience a touch too. There are many theories as to where Armstrong got his "That's one small step for [a] man, one giant leap for mankind" line from.

Some suggest it was written for him by a NASA PR team, others say that it was provided by the Presidential office. My favourite theory, though, has it that Armstrong took inspiration from J. R. R. Tolkien's *The Hobbit*. Armstrong, you see, was a massive Tolkien nerd. Just two years after landing on the moon, he bought a farm in Lebanon, Ohio, which he named Rivendell (the Elven town in Middle-earth where Elrond, among others, lived). And, according to his biographer, even his email address contained a reference to *The Lord of the Rings*.

In *The Hobbit* there's a scene where Bilbo Baggins turns himself invisible to jump over Gollum. The leap is described by Tolkien as "Not a great leap for a man, but a leap in the dark"; could this have been what inspired Armstrong's iconic line? Sadly, it looks as if it wasn't. When Hansen asked him if there was any truth to the rumour, Armstrong claimed that he hadn't read any Tolkien until after he got back from the moon.

THE THEORY OF THE SECOND WORDS

For many years there was a joke, presented as fact, that when Armstrong stood on the moon and uttered his iconic "one small step" line, he followed it up with the words, "Good luck, Mr. Gorsky." This story has been repeated many times, and even found its way into pop culture, most notably appearing in the opening sequence of the *Watchmen* film. The story goes that when he was a kid, Armstrong was playing baseball with his brother in their backyard when their ball landed just outside the bedroom window of their neighbours, the Gorskys. As Armstrong snuck over to pick up the baseball, he overheard Mrs. Gorsky yell, "Oral sex? You want oral sex? You'll get oral sex when the kid next door walks on the moon!"

The story is of course an urban legend, although it did make me wonder, when was the last time someone used the "They'll land a man on the moon before *that* happens" line? How close to the first moon landing might it have been? How many cultures, over how many thousands of years, have lobbed that line into their chat, while rolling their eyes at the same time? Did our oldest known civilisations plan space flight? Are there cuneiform tablets from the Babylonians and Sumerians conveying this sarcastic sentiment?*

---

* According to Irving Finkel, a curator at the British Museum, the ancient Babylonians did not record any interest in space flight. However, he told me, "They did conceive of maps drawn from a bird's-eye view, despite having never invented flight . . . The most interesting thing is that on the other side of the tablet containing the first bird's-eye map of the world, there's a qual-

Perhaps a variation of the line was used in sixteenth-century China, where the man who was possibly the world's first astronaut, Wan Hu, lived. According to the legend, Wan Hu attempted to fly into space by using nothing but a chair with 47 rockets attached to it. As he sat in the chair, waiting for take-off, the rockets were all lit, and according to the story, there then followed a big explosion, after which neither Wan Hu nor the chair were ever seen again.

Whether or not Wan Hu really existed is debated. However, his story has been officially recognised; he and his exploding chair are commemorated with a statue outside the Xichang Satellite Launch Centre, from where the first Chinese missions were launched.

Perhaps the line was said in the time of Dr. John Wilkins, the brother-in-law of Oliver Cromwell, who in the seventeenth century effectively came up with the first British plan to put a human on the moon. As well as being a well-respected clergyman, philosopher, author, and polymath who helped found the Royal Society, Wilkins wrote two books about the moon and worked out its distance from Earth to 99.9 per cent accuracy just using trigonometry. He also drew up plans to visit it by building his own space chariot.*

ifier which says who wrote it. Unfortunately, his name is broken, so we don't know it. But we can see his father's name, and he was called 'Birdie.'"

* Wilkins's theory was that the Earth would lose gravity above 20 miles up. He used the fact that clouds were able to hang in the air as his evidence. Food wouldn't be necessary for the trip, as eating would be impossible; the lack of gravity meant your food wouldn't be pulled through your body.

Wilkins's space chariot was designed to use clockwork gears, springs, and gunpowder. Wilkins said:

> *I do seriously, and upon good Grounds affirm it possible to make a Flying-Chariot; in which a Man may sit, and give such a Motion unto it, as shall convey him through the Air. And this perhaps might be made large enough to carry divers Men at the same time, together with Food for their Viaticum, and Commodities for Traffick.*

History doesn't record if he ever built the chariot, however.

Perhaps the last time the phrase was used was in 1964 when it was supposedly uttered when discussing the San Francisco Giants' new baseball recruit Gaylord Perry, who was a competent pitcher, but a terrible batsman. The story goes that journalist Tony Jupiter reported hearing the Giants manager Alvin Dark say, "A man would stand on the moon before he ever hit a home run."

The phrase is of course now extinct. It's use-by date having expired on July 20, 1969, when Armstrong took his first footsteps on the moon. One hour later, in a game against the Los Angeles Dodgers, Gaylord Perry hit his first home run.

If there was one place I never expected to find batshit thinking, it was the Apollo moon missions. To become an astronaut was to have what author Tom Wolfe called "the Right Stuff," which meant rational thinking, the ability to follow a meticulous series of procedures with very little need for improvisation. These missions were surely no place for spurious theories, supernatural occurrences, superstitions, and paranormal experiences.

TELEPATHY ON THE MOON

What's always surprised me about the precision operations that were the Apollo missions, with teams of people scrutinising every single nut and bolt, checking and rechecking every tiny detail, is how easy it was for astronauts to sneak contraband aboard. Indeed, many of the astronauts brought eccentric items with them to the moon with NASA remaining completely unaware. Alan Shepard snuck a makeshift golf club and golf ball on board, and hit what in theory is the longest golf shot ever.

Sometimes the astronauts themselves weren't even aware of what had been smuggled onto the spacecraft. When Alan Bean and Pete Conrad (Apollo 12) were on their lunar walk, they opened up a wrist-watch-like device, which contained a checklist for everything they needed to do. Each page was 3.5 inches square, laminated and bound like a book. While flipping through their checklist they each discovered that someone had included pictures of *Playboy* Playmates. Who was responsible for this? David Scott, who would go on to become the seventh man to stand on the moon. Liabilities, all of them.

So when Edgar Mitchell smuggled aboard a series of cards featuring mysterious symbols, it's possible that nobody batted an eyelid. If they'd known what the cards were for, however, they might just have been a little more concerned.

* * *

The Bahamas, late January 1971. Three guys, all called Ed, discussed an idea: how far could telepathic thought be communicated? Theoretically, could someone communicate a message from, say, the moon back to Earth? It was an interesting question. Fortunately one of the Eds, Edgar Mitchell (soon to become the sixth man to stand on the moon), was heading to the moon in a few days' time, and so they decided to try it out. At 200,000 miles from Earth, this was the furthest distance at which anyone had ever attempted telepathy.

The plan, as concocted by the three Eds (the other two being Mitchell's medical friends Edward Boyle and Edward Maxey), involved Mitchell sneaking some homemade Zener cards on board, displaying a square, a star, a circle, a cross, and a wavy line.*

The plan was for Mitchell to concentrate on a symbol and a random number, while back on Earth the two other Eds would attempt to visualise what he had selected. Mitchell carried out the experiment four times during rest breaks—on

---

* Zener cards were devised in the 1930s by Karl Zener for experiments conducted by J. B. Rhine, a parapsychologist. After training as a botanist, Rhine had been turned on to the world of the paranormal after attending a lecture by Arthur Conan Doyle, who presented what he claimed was evidence that contact with the dead had been made. Rhine became interested in the world of mediums, but quickly discovered much of it to be fraudulent, even exposing one, Mina Crandon, whom he discovered was creating the illusion of the presence of spirits by kicking a megaphone with her foot to create a booming noise. His attack on Crandon was not well received by the paranormal community. In an article written for a Boston newspaper Conan Doyle called him a "monumental ass."

the way to the moon and on the way back, but actually never while standing on it. Each experiment involved Mitchell taking out the Zener symbols and cards that showed random numbers, pairing them up, and concentrating on each pair for 15 seconds. Once he returned to Earth the three Eds examined the results and discovered that it had a success rate of under 10 per cent. Mitchell considered this "statistically significant."*

Though it would later transpire that, due to a delay in launch, the two Eds on Earth logged the choices of his telepathic messages 40 minutes before Edgar Mitchell actually made them.

A CREATIONIST ON THE MOON

Apollo 15 launched on July 26, 1971, and was NASA's first science-heavy mission to the moon. You'd have thought, therefore, that when NASA were conducting the interviews to find their astronauts they'd have tried to land some quite down-the-line men of science. So I ask, how did they end up sending a creationist to the moon?

A large part of Apollo 15's mission was geological—scientists were trying to work out how the moon was able to maintain its precise orbit. To do this they studied moon rock.

The rocks that Armstrong had brought back, as well as

---

* In a later account, Mitchell said there were no cards at all, he just used his mind, and claimed the experiments had a 25.5 per cent success rate.

Apollo 15 astronaut, James Irwin.

those brought back by the following two missions, were all dense basalt rock. This was a problem. It didn't make sense that the moon was made up entirely of this kind of rock—it would be too heavy for the moon to stay in a precise orbit. There must be lighter rocks on the moon, the experts said. And so it was that astronauts James Irwin and fellow moon-walker David Scott were tasked with finding a different kind of rock—a whiter, lighter rock. While exploring the mountains of the moon, Scott called out to Irwin, "Jim, do you see what I see? I think we've found what we came for." What they found was exactly what the scientists had hoped for: pure, white rock. It was rock that had been spat out from the moon's interior to form its mountains. It was "the most important scientific discovery of our mission."

For NASA it was a great discovery, because it proved their hypothesis that there were lighter materials on the moon. It was to become known as the Genesis rock. For Irwin, however, it was to lead to an even greater discovery. Once back on Earth, Irwin would learn that the Genesis rock was as old as the Earth. As he wrote in his book *More Than Earthlings*, "It confirmed the fact that the Earth and moon were created at the same time, giving scientific proof of the creation story of Genesis."

Irwin had quite the religious experience while up on the moon. When certain problems occurred on the lunar surface, he didn't ask NASA to fix them. Instead he consulted God.

I never asked Houston because I knew there would be a delay. I didn't have time for Houston to get an answer to me; I needed an immediate answer. I could see several logical ways to go about solving these mechanical problems, but I wanted to know the best way. I prayed, and immediately I knew the answer. I am not talking about some vague sense of direction. There was this supernatural sensation of His presence. If I needed Him I could call on Him, call on His power.

Irwin retired from NASA in 1972 and founded the High Flight Foundation, whose mission was to spread the word of God. "Jesus walking on the Earth is more important than man walking on the moon," wrote Irwin.

A few years later, while lecturing in New Mexico in 1976, Irwin met a man called Eryl Cummings. Cummings was an explorer, and he told Irwin about his expeditions to find Noah's Ark, which he'd attempted to locate 16 times already. Irwin was hooked and decided to tag along.* The missions to Mount Ararat carried a sense of destiny for Irwin, and he truly thought he might be the person to find the Ark. He wrote in his book *More Than an Ark on Ararat*:

> *because I had been part of the Apollo mission which discovered the "Genesis" rock on the moon, I truly felt that God would allow me to find something even more significant from the Book of Genesis on the earth.*

Although I'm not religious, I often find myself jealous of those who do believe, and reading Irwin's account of his adventure in his memoir really captures his awe for his Creator. When he spots a rainbow while climbing Mount Ararat, Irwin writes:

> *It arched right over us! What more Noah-like sign did we need? There was something particularly eerie about seeing a rainbow right where the first rainbow had been seen. We felt we had been blessed—surely we would find the Ark!†*

---

* Before looking for the Ark, Irwin, along with Cummings, would search for the Ark of the Covenant in the caves of Mount Nebo in Jordan.

† As reported in the Bible, Noah sees the first ever rainbow.

Just like Neil Armstrong, who was tremendously excited to have walked in exactly the same place, and on exactly the same stone, as Jesus himself had once walked, Irwin conveys a similar sentiment:

> *One of the most intriguing aspects of climbing Mount Ararat is that at any moment we might be walking where everyone's childhood hero, Noah, walked as he led his water-weary family down the mountain.*

The trip was not simply wall-to-wall religious elation, however. At one point, as he paused to kneel down and don his crampons, Irwin was struck from behind by a falling rock, knocking him down the mountain. He needed to be rescued, having sprained his neck and lost five teeth.

THE MISSION THAT CONFIRMED SUPERSTITION

For me, the Apollo 13 mission is the greatest adventure story ever told. If you recall, it was the only Apollo mission that failed to land its astronauts on the moon after their craft suffered an explosion just two days into the mission, leaving its crew stranded in space with a broken ship and virtually no way to get back home.

Many remarked that perhaps superstition was to blame for Apollo 13's bad luck. It was Apollo *13*, after all. Not only that, lift-off was at 13:13 p.m. And one of its crew, Jack Swigert, was the 13th astronaut in the Apollo programme. It was Swigert who clicked the switch that led to the explosion on board. Swigert flicked the switch two days after launch, on April 13.

AN UNEXPECTED HERO

One of the untold stories from the day Apollo 13 suffered the explosion concerns the man who initially helped to save the three astronauts' lives and the remarkable coincidence that helped him to do it.

Immediately after the explosion occurred, Apollo 13 started losing all water, oxygen, and electricity. Everything went wrong. Curiously, one man was already working out how to fix these exact problems: electrical engineer Arturo Campos knew precisely how to deal with the problem of three astronauts stranded in space in a broken spaceship, because, as it happened, a few hours before the explosion on Apollo 13 he was in the cinema watching a film about three astronauts stranded in space in a broken spaceship.

Marooned is a science-fiction film starring Gregory Peck and Gene Hackman, about the crew of a spaceship who are rapidly running out of oxygen following an explosion, with ground control desperately trying to get them safely back home. The film was released on November 10, 1969, just five months before Apollo 13 launched.

According to NASA engineer Jerry Woodfill, on the very day that the Apollo 13 incident occurred, a number of NASA employees went to watch the film at a local cinema. Among them was Campos, who served as the electrical power systems manager for the lunar lander.

In order to save the astronauts in the film, ground control

had to solve the problem of battery depletion, requiring specific instructions on how to charge the batteries. As Campos left the cinema he wondered what he would do if Apollo 13 suffered the same problem. Little did he know that he had unwittingly given himself a head start and was already working on the exact same problem he was going to need to solve in just a few hours' time.

Campos went to bed thinking about the problem, and was woken only a few hours later when his phone rang and he was ordered back into NASA immediately. As he raced into NASA's headquarters, he played the line "charge the batteries" from the film over and over in his head. It prompted him to remember a method he had figured out that would charge near-empty batteries using jump leads between the command module and the lunar module.

NASA engineer, Arturo Campos.

As Campos went about writing out the procedure, he had Woodfill and the other engineers go through the schematics to try to locate a wire that connected the two battery packs. They managed to find one, the theory was put into practice, and fortunately the charge worked. They managed to recharge the command module's batteries, contributing to the mammoth team effort that brought the crew safely back home.

The fact that they did make it home was nothing short of remarkable. It's an impossible survival story. So implausible, in fact, that when director Ron Howard made the story into the film *Apollo 13*, with Tom Hanks, a test screening had one person complain that the ending was unbelievable. "Terrible!" wrote the reviewer. "More Hollywood bullshit!!" finally adding: "They would never survive!!!"

CHAPTER 26
FOOTPRINTS OF THE CHARLATANS
THE THEORY OF UNEXPECTED HEROES

Charlatans fascinate me. Though mostly incredibly dangerous characters, the unintended consequences of their actions
sometimes lead to great things, for which they are often never
given credit. Don't get me wrong, though, few things give me
greater pleasure than seeing a charlatan exposed, like the
English occultist and High Priest of Wicca Alex Sanders
(1926–88), the self-styled "King of the Witches" no less, and
also known as Verbius. Sanders was exposed for conning his
followers when he took members of the press to Alderley
Edge in Cheshire to raise a man from the dead using an ancient summoning. The successful stunt propelled Sanders to
fame. However, years later, his ex-wife revealed that, not only
did he not resurrect the man, but the summoning itself was
just a Swiss roll recipe read backwards. I do sometimes wonder where we'd be without them though.

Take Tuesday Lobsang Rampa (1910–81), who has been
called the greatest hoaxer that the field of Tibetan studies

has ever known. Apparently the son of an aristocrat who worked for the Dalai Lama's government, Rampa was recognised as an incarnated Tibetan abbot and medical lama. He grew up in Lhasa, where he was looked after by Old Tzu, a seven-foot-tall retired monk policeman, and he later authored many bestselling books including *The Third Eye*, which sold half a million copies, and *Living with the Lama*, which was dictated to him by his cat, Mrs. Fifi Greywhiskers.

"Everything Dr. Rampa wrote is 100 per cent true," says his website to this day. However, Heinrich Harrer, the legendary Austrian mountaineer, former Waffen-SS soldier, ice-rink builder to the Dalai Lama, and author of *Seven Years in Tibet*, didn't agree and took it upon himself to out Rampa as a fraudster. His findings were shocking. Harrer discovered that Rampa had never been to Tibet, didn't speak any Tibetan, and was actually a plumber from Plympton, Devon, whose real name was Cyril Henry Hoskin.

Rather than admitting to conning the public, Rampa wrote another book to explain himself titled *The Rampa Story*, in which he admitted that, yes, he used to be Cyril Hoskin, but he stopped being Hoskin after falling out of a tree as he was trying to photograph an owl. While he lay on the ground, the spirit of a monk sidled up to him and offered to switch bodies. Hoskins then assumed the soul of the monk.

Interestingly, despite all of this conning, Rampa was an incredibly influential figure. American Tibetanologist Donald S. Lopez Jr. discovered, when mentioning Rampa's bestselling books to his contemporaries, that several cited Rampa as being the person who introduced them to and got them obsessed with the subject of Tibet. Despite being a total fraud, he was thanked for his work by many, including the Dalai Lama.

Then there was Grey Owl (1888–1938), a Native American conservationist who first came to global fame with the publication of his 1931 memoir *The Men of the Last Frontier*, which attracted rave reviews and made him an international star. It tells the story of his life, from his birth in Rio Grande to a New Mexico Apache Indian mother and Scottish father, both of whom were performers for Buffalo Bill's Wild West Show (Grey Owl would later serve as a knife-thrower in this same show), to his studies under Ojibwa chief Ne-Ganikabo, and his attempts at conservation, most notably in trying to conserve beavers. The book comes with a foreword that explains that it was written in many camps where Grey Owl was based, and that the manuscript was not an easy read to begin with. Not because of the nature of the subject, but because it was typed up by a French-Canadian "who knew little English."

Grey Owl originally was a fur trapper; however, after killing a mother beaver one day, he discovered her two young kittens and decided to adopt them. It was to be a transformative experience, which led him to pursue a life of campaigning for the preservation of all wildlife. He even set up a beaver sanctuary in Manitoba's Riding Mountain National Park.

The book was a huge success and led to Grey Owl touring the world, from America to the UK, where he met the Royal Family at Buckingham Palace, to spread the word of conservation. The non-stop lecture tours (which at one point in-

Grey Owl.

cluded 138 talks in three months) took a toll on him, and he became physically exhausted to the point where, on returning to his home, a cabin on Lake Ajawaan in Saskatchewan, he became ill, fell into a coma, and died a few days later.

Not long after his death, it was revealed that Grey Owl wasn't in fact Native American at all, but a former timber company clerk from Hastings in the UK called Archibald Stansfeld Belaney. Having moved to Canada aged 18, he created a false narrative of his life when he started writing. His parents were not, nor was he, ever part of the Wild Bill shows; he was in fact raised by two spinster aunts, having not ever really known his parents. To pass himself off as Native American, he was said to have applied henna on his skin to change his complexion, and dyed his hair black. As soon as this revelation came out, it caused huge problems both for his publishers (who either had to pulp his book or republish it with his real name) and the world of conservation, as having a charlatan as a poster figure for the movement set the cause back. However, his impact on the world remains great.

In the 1930s, a ten-year-old boy sat with his brother in a hall in Leicester as Grey Owl stood on stage, wowing a crowd with his tales of Native American life, and his message of conservation. The boy's older brother would many years later write:

> *It had been a defining moment for both of us, an event which managed perfectly to combine the disparate passions which were to absorb us for the rest of our lives . . . [My brother] was bowled over by the man's determination to save the beaver, by his profound knowledge of the flora and fauna of the Canadian wilderness and by his warnings of ecological disaster should the delicate balance between them be destroyed. The idea that mankind was endangering nature by recklessly despoiling and plundering its riches was unheard of at the time, but it is one that has remained part of [my brother's] own credo to this day.*

After the event the boys went to shake the hand of Grey Owl, and had him sign a book. They then fought over who got to keep possession of it. Despite being the younger brother by three years, David Attenborough managed to win the book off his brother Richard, and still keeps it treasured in his library to this day.

"He was a major figure, one of the first of his kind," David would tell Richard some 50 years later. "But, sadly, his death in 1938, and the revelations that followed, plus the outbreak of war, meant that all his warnings were ignored. The great tragedy is that if people had acted on what he was saying, the whole ecological movement would have been advanced by at least 30 years."

As we arrive at the end of this book, I find myself asking the question—what would life be like without all the "weirdos" in it? Would Attenborough have ever become such a great conservationist if it weren't for Grey Owl? Would Ringo Starr have ever become the great drummer he is, had his exorcist granny not turned him temporarily right-handed? And would Jane Goodall have ever found her calling, if not for the eccentric decisions of Louis Leakey? I could go on, but all you need to do is flick through the previous 300 or so pages of this book to remind yourself of more.

Attenborough, Starr, and Goodall would no doubt have soared regardless. Those moments didn't make them—they were just part of the journey. But I guess we'll never truly know.

Whether we like it or not, many of these alternative thinkers have shaped the world we live in today. Sometimes it's for the better, and many times it's for the worse. Mostly, it's a strange mixture of the two, as was the case with the life of Grey Owl. Proof, I suppose, that you can't always take the good without the bad—you can't have the Theory of Everything without the Theory of Everything Else.

Conclusion
WE CAN BE WEIRDOS

I know you're not supposed to have a favourite pandemic fact, but I'm afraid I do. Here it is: in January 2020, when Wuhan in China became the first city in the world to be thrown into lockdown thanks to a rampaging deadly virus, one of the few Brits who found themselves suddenly stranded in the city was a Mr. Bean impersonator.

It's funny how life works out, isn't it? For many this would have been the worst moment of their lives. For Nigel Dixon, Bean impersonator, it was as if this were the moment towards which his life had been always driving him.

Dixon was in Wuhan on a sightseeing trip, visiting friends at the time the pandemic broke out, and, not having been told that there were planes ferrying foreigners out of the city, he became stuck there. By the time he learnt of another chance to fly out, however, he'd already decided to stay, worried that he might harm others by passing on the disease should he have already caught it.

Dixon had been working as a professional Mr. Bean look-alike since he was 30 years old, playing the hapless character at birthday parties and corporate events. He wanted more, though, and had been travelling to the city of Wuhan, a major media city, for years in the hope that the Chinese people's love for Mr. Bean might give him his own lucky break. But it had never quite happened.

Now, holed up in a poky Wuhan apartment, stuck inside thanks to the government-imposed lockdown, Dixon started making videos for various Chinese online platforms as a character called Mr. Pea (who, let's be fair, dresses like Mr. Bean, speaks like Mr. Bean and has a Teddy, exactly like Mr. Bean, and so should really be called Mr. Bean).

A terrified nation took notice, and very quickly Dixon's Mr. Pea started amassing huge numbers of views, with a reported 450 million on his Weibo account, as well as six million people following his profile on Douyin, the state-run version of TikTok, turning Nigel Dixon's character into a household name.

Life is strange, and you never quite know how it's going to play out nor where your big adventure may take place. Nigel Dixon is an example of what can happen when you find yourself not in the right place at the right time, but in the *wrong* place at the right time. Most people live their lives trying to manufacture the next move and putting themselves in the right place at the right time. But that's too safe, too predictable. Life is more exciting than that—put yourself in the wrong place at the right time, and magical things can happen. And you don't have to go far to find the evidence; this book is full of people who found themselves in the wrong place at the right time.

⋆   ⋆   ⋆

I hope you have enjoyed this little voyage into the world of the weird. I hope it has done wonders for your Rough Corner, and has inspired you to go out and sprinkle a little bit of batshit into your life. Why not give it a go? Start talking to your house plants; spend a day guiding your movements with synchronicity; have your butt cheeks read by a rumpologist; go get infected with pubic lice (responsibly); start learning to speak Dolphinese; turn your child into a unique musician by performing exorcisms on them; try to get to the bottom of your "soft rock'; or maybe you could even try to realise a grand unified theory of shower curtains.

But just remember, as I said at the start, none of these theories are to be believed in, and indulging in them too much can turn into an unwanted addiction. One person I spoke to during the course of writing this book, the brilliant writer and performer Daisy Campbell, spent so much time guiding her life by synchronicity that she ended up developing a bad case of pronoia. (Pronoia is the opposite of Paranoia. It's the sneaking suspicion that everyone in the Universe is out to help you.)

However, I should add that while I encourage you not to believe in any of the theories in this book, I also want to warn against their being discarded or, worse, wiped from history.

When I think about the idea of losing these ideas, I think of the story of what happened in 1258, when the water of the Tigris River was said to have turned black.

Hulagu Khan (brother of Kublai) and his Mongol army had invaded Baghdad, and among the many places they ransacked was the House of Wisdom, a library known to be the intellectual centre of the Arab world. The Mongols stripped the library of all of its books, tossing thousands and thousands of them into the waters of the Tigris. There was said to have been so many books thrown in that they eventually stacked up all the way from the bed of the Tigris to its surface, allowing men on horses to ride across them from one side to the other. Then, slowly, the ink of 500 years of accumulated knowledge, theories, stories, remedies, histories, jokes, culture, recipes, *everything* slowly smudged into nothingness on the pages that held them, and mixed into the river to colour the water.

It's heart-breaking to think what we lost in those pages. How much information perished that day. Thank God for the University of Rejected Sciences.

Everyone has a theory, but I've not yet told you mine. So perhaps let's have it now—one more theory for the road. And just like all the theories in this book, I can't fully prove it.* My theory is that I've discovered when the biggest-ever simultaneous laugh took place on Earth. It happened exactly ten years ago (as I write these words) on July 27, 2012, and happened at the Olympic opening ceremony in London.

I still remember the moment—it was part of director Danny Boyle's brilliantly put-together extravaganza highlighting the achievements of the British, from the NHS and the

* Yet.

suffragettes to our innovations in the Industrial Revolution and the invention of the World Wide Web. The moment happened just after conductor Simon Rattle took to the stage, and the London Symphony Orchestra began its performance of Vangelis's theme tune to the film *Chariots of Fire*.

With an estimated global audience of between 700 million and 1 billion people watching and streaming the show live, we saw the cameras pan from the orchestra to a finger pounding a single key on a keyboard—DUN DUN DUN DUN DUN DUN, the same note, over and over. Then, with the camera slowly moving upward, we eventually saw the face behind the finger: Mr. Bean. A huge burst of laughter erupted through the stadium, as well as at the party in east London where I was watching the event on TV. I remember thinking, *This is being shown right now in the US, India, Africa, China, Australia, all around the world, and everywhere people will know exactly whose face this is.*

This moment stayed with me, because so often we're a planet of parts. We're all so different from each other with our ideas, our beliefs and theories, our cultures, and it's so very hard to remind each other that we are all in fact from the same single species. But sometimes, very occasionally, we do get a small glimpse that it doesn't need to be that way.

I really hope an alien spaceship was passing the Earth right at that second when the camera landed on Mr. Bean's face, because if it had been, it would have heard the best of us—an entire planet laughing together as one.

That's my theory at least, and I'm sticking to it.

NOTES AND SOURCES

A comprehensive list of notes and sources, including extra materials, expanded theories, corrections, newsletters, and more, can be found at www.theoryofeverythingelse.co.uk.

BIBLIOGRAPHY

Aldrin, Buzz and Wayne Warga, *Return to Earth*, Open Road Media, 2015.

Ballard, Robert, *The Discovery of the Titanic*, Grand Central Pub, 1987.

Beatles, The, *Anthology*, Cassell/Weidenfeld & Nicolson, 2001.

Beerbohm, Max, *Enoch Soames: A Memory of the Eighteen-Nineties*, Prabhat Prakashan, 2017.

Belaney, Archibald Stansfeld, *The Men of the Last Frontier*, Andesite Press, 2015.

Bird, Christopher and Peter Tomkins, *The Secret Life of Plants*, Harper Perennial, 1989.

Braun, Wernher von, *The Mars Project*, University of Illinois Press, 1962.

Brown, Rosemary, *Unfinished Symphonies: Voices from the Beyond*, Souvenir Press, 1971.

Clarke, Arthur C., *Greetings, Carbon-Based Bipeds!*, Voyager, 2000.

Clemente C. and D. Lindsley (eds), *Brain Function, Volume 5: Aggression and Defense Neural Mechanisms and Social Patterns*, University of California Press, 1967.

Crick, Francis, *Life Itself*, Futura, 1982.

Dick, Philip K., *The Exegesis of Philip K. Dick*, Gollancz, 2012.

Djokovic, Novak, *Serve to Win: The 14-Day Gluten-free Plan for Physical and Mental Excellence*, Corgi, 2014.

Downing, Barry, *The Bible and Flying Saucers*, J. B. Lippincott, 1968.

Drake, Frank, *Is Anyone Out There?*, Pocket Books, 1997.

Eade, Philip, *Young Prince Philip: His Turbulent Early Life*, HarperPress, 2012.

Finkel, Irving, *The Ark Before Noah*, Hodder and Stoughton, 2014.

Friedman, Thomas, *From Beirut to Jerusalem: One Man's Middle Eastern Odyssey*, HarperCollins 1998.

Fuller, John G., *The Ghost Flight of 401*, Corgi Books, 1979.

Gagliano, Monica, *Thus Spoke the Plant*, North Atlantic Books, 2018.

Gamow, George, *Thirty Years That Shook Physics: The Story of Quantum Theory*, Dover, 1985.

Gardner, Martin, *The Wreck of the Titanic Foretold?*, Prometheus Books, 1981.

Geiger, John, *The Third Man Factor*, Canongate, 2010.

Gollner, Adam Leith, *The Book of Immortality*, Scribner, 2013.

Good, Timothy, *Above Top Secret*, William Morrow, 1988.

Good, Timothy, *Alien Contact*, William Morrow, 1993.

Grimm, Jack and William Hoffman, *Beyond Reach*, Beaufort Books, 1982.

Hansen, James R., *First Man: The Life of Neil Armstrong*, Simon & Schuster, 2018.

Holzer, Hans, *The Psychic World of Plants*, Pyramid Books, 1975.

Hunt, David, *Girt Nation*, Black Inc., 2021.

Irwin, James B., *More than Earthlings*, HarperCollins, 1984.

———, *To Rule the Night: The Discovery Voyage of Astronaut Jim Irwin*, A. J. Holman, 1973.

Irwin, James B. and Monte Unger, *More than an Ark on Ararat: Spiritual Lessons Learned While Searching for Noah's Ark*, Baptist Sunday School Board, 1985.

Lavery, Jimmy, *The Secret Life of Siegfried and Roy: How the Tiger Kings Tamed Las Vegas*, Phoenix Books, 2008.

Levine, Joshua, *On a Wing and a Prayer*, Collins, 2008.

Lilly, John C., *Man and Dolphin: Adventures of a New Scientific Frontier*, Pyramid Books, 1969.

Lilly, John C., *The Mind of the Dolphin*, Doubleday, 1967.

Lockwood, Ingersoll, *Baron Trump's Marvelous Underground Journey*.

Lockwood, Ingersoll, *Travels and Adventures of Little Baron Trump and His Wonderful Dog Bulger*.

Lockwood, Ingersoll, *1900; Or, The Last President*.

Lovell, Jim and Jeffrey Kluger, *Apollo 13*, Coronet, 1995.

Michanowsky, George, *The One and True Star*, Barnes & Noble, 1979.

Miles, Barry, *Paul McCartney: Many Years from Now*, Vintage, 1998.

Miller, Arthur I., *Deciphering the Cosmic Number: The Strange Friendship of Wolfgang Pauli and Carl Jung*, W. W. Norton, 2009.

Mullis, Kary, *Dancing Naked in the Mind Field*, Pantheon Books, 1998.

Parr, Jerry, *In the Secret Service: The True Story of the Man Who Saved President Reagan's Life*, Tyndale House, 2013.

Poundstone, William, *Carl Sagan: A Life in Science*, Henry Holt, 1999.

Presley, Reg, *Wild Things They Don't Tell You*, Metro Books, 2002.

Rampa, Tuesday Lobsang, *The Third Eye*, Ballantine Books, 1986.

Randi, James, *The Mask of Nostradamus: The Prophecies of the World's Most Famous Seer*, Prometheus, 1993.

Rhys, Leona Benkt, *Primal Skin*, Black Lace, 2000.

Robb, Graham, *Victor Hugo*, Picador, 1998.

Rodgers, Nile, *Le Freak: An Upside Down Story of Family, Disco and Destiny*, Little, Brown, 2011.

Rosen, Robert, *Nowhere Man: The Final Days of John Lennon*, Soft Skull Press, 2000.

Stallone, Jacqueline, *Starpower*, Penguin, 1989.

Stone, Robert B., *The Secret Life of Your Cells*, Schiffer, 1997.

Whitley, Stieber, *Communion*, Walker & Collier, 2022.

Winkowski, Mary Ann, *Beyond Delicious: The Ghost Whisperer's Cookbook: More than 100 Recipes from the Dearly Departed*, Clerisy Press, 2011.

ACKNOWLEDGEMENTS

Writing this book has been a very rewarding experience. Firstly, because it meant I could finally justify to my wife why I've spent all these years "wasting" all our money on books with titles like *Who Built the Moon?* and secondly, because it has helped to open up conversations with people I know and love about the strange things they believe in. And I want to thank them all.

To start with, though, I must thank all the authors, journalists, documentary makers, and comic book artists whose works I have read to find the theories in this book. It would be nothing but blank pages without them.

Huge thanks go to my family: Mum, Dad, Chyna, Bluey (you four shaped this weirdo; thank you for always being there), and to Charbel, Georgia, Sofia, Alessandra, Colleen, Andrew, Martha, Isaac, Rosie, Martyn Sr., Martyn Jr., Charly, Christopher, Kit (welcome to the world, buddy), Liam, Pisey, Grandma, Grandpa, Popsy, Tammy, Hugh,

ACKNOWLEDGEMENTS

Dean, Bettina, Ash, Lucas, and all the Austrian Schreiber team.

Big thanks go to Carol, Will, Annabel, David, Lola, Ayla, Rob and Grace, Fo and Jonathan, who looked after me so well during the writing of this book.

To my gurus: John Lloyd, Rich Turner, and Rhys Darby—thanks, you three, for all the mind-expanding conversations over the last few decades. I couldn't have asked for better mentors.

To the ghosts of Ken Campbell (who coined the term "the Rough Corner" to refer to a Japanese gardening method), Robert Anton Wilson, and Spike Milligan.

To Andy, Anna, and James, who have taught me so much over the last nine years (including how to write)—it's been a wild ride with Fish, and I can't wait for all the adventures to come.

To Alex Bell, for always being there with that big brain of his. Big thanks also go to my *QI* family: Sarah Lloyd, Liz Townsend, and all the elves.

The brilliant team at HarperCollins—my incredible editor Joel Simons (if I had a spirit animal, it would be Joel), Sarah Hammond (honorary Avalonian), Hattie Evans, Ellie Game, Jamie Williams, Ajda Vucicevic, Adam Humphrey, Orlando Mowbray, Jessica Jackson, and Ameena Ghori-Khan. Thanks to the copyeditors Neil and Mark too.

Huge thanks to Sam Minton, whose illustrations make these stories sing.

None of this could have happened without Ben Dunn—this book simply wouldn't be here without him. Thanks so much, Ben. And to John Noel for taking a chance on me all those years go, and never giving up, and Nik Linnen for this next exciting chapter.

For their comments during the writing of this book, I want to say thanks to: Marc Abrahams, Jason Hazeley, Ken Plume, Jack Fogg, Louis Theroux, Jamie Morton, Alice Levine, Emma Moss, Ash Gardner, Jacqui Ellulgulug, David Bramwell, Daisy Campbell, John Higgs, Craig Glenday, Irving Finkel, Colonel John Blashford Snell, Sarah Darwin, Dan Neeson, Xander Milne, Joel Hill, Alex Edelman, Richard Curtis (for writing the joke that landed the greatest-ever laugh on Planet Earth), Darren Chadwick-Hussein, Chris Lochery, Joshua Levine, Mitchell Brooks, Georgie, Lise, Tom Tom, Milla, Henry, Tracey, Josh, Kara, KP, JP, Hugh, Benjamin, Meg, Jared, Alfie, Gwen, Chris, Arlo, Amy, my teachers at Steiner, and all of my friends in Avalon.

They say that writing a book is a very lonely experience. That's not true. Not when you have an elite force of Schitheads who are there day and night to chat, brainstorm, and go fact hunting with. This book could not have been written without Emma Govan, Mark Vent (the hero who fact-checked this whole book. You rock, Mark!), Shona MacLean, Paul Plowman, Tamsin Wilson, Ed Walwyn, Rigmor Hanken, Ingrid O. Rongen, Jody Pearce, Micah Bell, Emily Rich, Katrine Lisbygd Nielsen, Deirdre Jernigan, Kicki Wikström, Laura Wooton, Brianna Scanlan, and Daniela Herz.

The final bits of this book were written as I sat in the passenger seat of a car, while driving around the banks of Loch Ness, alongside my pal Leon "Buttons" Kirkbeck. Leon, you're a hero, and your contribution to the final leg of this book was invaluable.

The biggest thanks of all must go to Fenella, the love of my life—thank you for everything. And to my three beautiful boys, Wilf, Ted, and Kit. I can't wait to see what beautiful oddballs you turn into as the years roll by.

Finally, to you, the reader. Thanks for picking up this book, and may the wrinkles on your arse cheeks promise you happiness and great adventures ahead.

PICTURE CREDITS

PICTURE CREDITS

Page 179: Henry Groskinsky/The LIFE Picture Collection/ Shutterstock

Page 201: ZUMA Press, Inc./Alamy Stock Photo

Page 209: National Museum of the USAF

Page 211: Courtesy Savannah/Hilton Head International Airport

Page 231: Henry McGee/MediaPunch/Alamy Stock Photo

Page 250: Robert Gilhooly/Alamy Stock Photo

Page 263: akg-images/Erich Lessing

Page 267: GL Archive/Alamy Stock Photo

Page 270: GL Archive/Alamy Stock Photo

Page 283: Imperial War Museum/Ref CH7738

Page 294: Denver Post via Getty Images

Page 301: Paramount/Kobal/Shutterstock

Page 304: History and Art Collection/Alamy Stock Photo

Page 307: Ron Galella, Ltd./Ron Galella Collection via Getty Images

Page 323: HUM Images/Universal Images Group via Getty Images

Page 328: NASA/Courtesy of Campos Family

Page 333: © Hulton-Deutsch Collection/CORBIS/Corbis via Getty Images